FLAUBERT

in the **Ruins** *of* **Paris**

FLAUBERT
in the Ruins *of* Paris

The Story of a Friendship, a Novel, and a Terrible Year

PETER BROOKS

BASIC BOOKS
NEW YORK

Books published by Basic Books are available at special discounts for bulk purchases
in the United States by corporations, institutions, and other organizations. For more
information, please contact the Special Markets Department at Perseus Books, 2300
Chestnut Street, Suite 200, Philadelphia, PA 19103, or call (800) 810-4145, ext.
5000, or e-mail special.markets@perseusbooks.com.

DESIGNED BY LINDA MARK

Library of Congress Cataloging-in-Publication Data
Names: Brooks, Peter, 1938– author.
Title: Flaubert in the ruins of Paris : the story of a friendship, a novel, and
  a terrible year / Peter Brooks.
Description: 1 | New York : Basic Books, [2017] | Includes bibliographical
  references and index.
Identifiers: LCCN 2016042026 (print) | LCCN 2016059619 (ebook) |
  ISBN9780465096022 (hardback) | ISBN 9780465096077 (ebook)
Subjects: LCSH: Flaubert, Gustave, 1821–1880. | Novelists, French—19th
  Century—Biography. | Literature and society—France—Paris—History—
  19th century. | Paris (France) —Intellectual life—19th century. | Flaubert, Gustave,
  1821–1880. L'Education sentimentale. | Sand, George, 1804–1876. |
  BISAC: HISTORY / Europe / France. | BIOGRAPHY &
AUTOBIOGRAPHY / Literary. | HISTORY / Europe / General.
Classification: LCC PQ2247 .B683 2017 (print) | LCC PQ2247 (ebook) | DDC
  843/.8 [B]—dc23
LC record available at https://lccn.loc.gov/2016042026

10 9 8 7 6 5 4 3 2 1

For Michael Holquist
greatest of friends, from whom I learned so much

In memoriam

Contents

Figures

Figures follow page 122.

Timeline

1821 December 12: Gustave Flaubert is born in Rouen (Normandy).

1848 February 22–24: Revolution: the government interdiction of a political banquet leads to demonstrations, troops fire on the crowd ("Massacre of the Boulevard des Capucines"); King Louis Philippe abdicates in favor of his grandson and flees, and republicans prevail.

February 24: Flaubert and Maxime Du Camp witness the sacking of the Tuileries Palace.

February 25: Proclamation of the Second Republic, with poet Alphonse de Lamartine as chief executive

June 22–25: "June Days": the *ateliers nationaux* are disbanded; a workers' revolt is harshly suppressed by the government.

December 10: Louis-Napoléon Bonaparte is elected president of the Republic.

1849 October 29: Flaubert and Du Camp leave for their trip to Egypt and the Near East.

1851   June 16: Flaubert returns to Croisset.

        December 2: Coup d'état of Louis-Napoléon Bonaparte

1852   December 2: Louis-Napoléon becomes Emperor Napoléon III, marking the start of the Second Empire.

1856   October 1: The serial publication of *Madame Bovary* begins in *La Revue de Paris*.

1857   January 31–February 7: Flaubert and his publishers go on trial for *Madame Bovary*.

        April: Book publication of *Madame Bovary*

1862   Publication of *Salammbô*

1864   September 1: Flaubert begins writing *Sentimental Education*.

1866   February 12: George Sand attends Restaurant Magny dinner, and her close friendship with Flaubert begins.

1869   November 17: Publication of *Sentimental Education*

        December: Flaubert spends Christmas with George Sand at Nohant.

1870   July 19: France declares war on Prussia.

        September 2: French are defeated at Sedan; Emperor Napoléon III becomes a prisoner of the Prussians.

        September 4: Declaration of Third Republic in Paris

        September 19: Siege of Paris begins.

        December: Prussians occupy Rouen and take over Flaubert's house in Croisset.

1871   January 28: Capitulation of Paris, negotiation of peace terms

        February 12: The new Assembly meets at Bordeaux, with Adolphe Thiers as chief executive.

        March 18: Thiers's attempt to seize the National Guard cannon on Montmartre triggers the revolt of Paris; the government flees to Versailles.

        March 28: Proclamation of the Commune de Paris

April 1: Flaubert returns home to Croisset.

May 10: Treaty of Frankfurt ends the Franco-Prussian War.

May 21–28: The "Bloody Week": The French Army from Versailles invades Paris and destroys the Commune. Some 20,000 Parisians are killed.

June 5: Flaubert is in Paris.

June 6: Flaubert visits the ruins with Maxime Du Camp.

1872   April 6: Death of Flaubert's mother

August: Flaubert starts his research for *Bouvard and Pécuchet*.

1873   October: Comte de Chambord renounces attempts to ascend the throne.

May 24: The fall of Thiers; the election of Marshal Mac-Mahon as president of the Republic

1874   February: Publication of Victor Hugo's *Ninety-Three*

April: Publication of Flaubert's *The Temptation of Saint Anthony*

1875   January 30: The Wallon Amendment assures the continuation of the Republic.

July: Ernest Commanville's lumberyard fails, setting Flaubert's financial crisis into motion.

1876   June 8: Death of George Sand

1877   April: Publication of *Three Tales*

May 16: Mac-Mahon attempts to abrogate the parliamentary government; subsequent elections lead to a republican majority.

September 8: Flaubert joins the funeral procession for Thiers.

1878   January 19: Flaubert dines with Léon Gambetta.

1879   January 30: Mac-Mahon resigns.

1880   May 8: Death of Flaubert

Introduction

⤜ *The Terrible Year, Two Writers, and a Novel* ⤛

THIS IS THE STORY OF WHAT THE FRENCH STILL CALL THE Terrible Year, as lived by two great writers who were devoted friends, Gustave Flaubert and George Sand, and of Flaubert's novel that he thought should have kept his compatriots from the catastrophe they were enduring. It was a year of almost unimaginable suffering, defeat, humiliation, hatred, and fratricidal conflict, a year when war and surrender were followed by siege, cold, hunger, then class warfare on a scale never seen before, a national bloodletting that left France traumatized on the threshold of its most enduring experiment with republican government, even as it seemed poised to retreat into monarchy. Out of the ruins left by the Terrible Year and its paroxysm in the Bloody Week of May 1871 modern France emerged.

Flaubert and Sand wrote incessantly to one another as impassioned witnesses to the unfolding of events. They were separated in space, Flaubert in his Norman home, Sand in hers in the Berry, both following the war and its aftermath with all the information they could garner. Though they began seemingly at opposite ends of the political spectrum—Sand a dedicated socialist and reformer, Flaubert a believer in rule by the elite—they would eventually converge in their beliefs. Flaubert would travel the greater distance, eventually avowing himself, to his own bemusement, a republican. They observed, they evaluated, they judged. And they weighed why Flaubert's novel *Sentimental Education* (*L'Education sentimentale*), published late in 1869, on the threshold of the Terrible Year, had gone largely misunderstood and unheeded. Surely, Flaubert believed, it was prophetic of what had come to pass.

To give the barest historical sketch of events: Second Empire France under Napoleon III—who became emperor a year after his coup d'état on December 2, 1851, killed off the fragile republic born of revolution in 1848—seemed immensely wealthy and powerful. Paris was the undisputed capital of Europe. But the Empire came to an abrupt and unexpected end in the Franco-Prussian War that began in July 1870. The war was totally unnecessary, the result of diplomatic blunders and the deliberate provocation of German chancellor Otto von Bismarck, who thought that war with France would strengthen his hand in unifying the German states under Prussian hegemony. French confidence in its army and its vaunted new *chassepot* bolt-action breech-loading rifle was unbounded but misplaced: appallingly commanded and outmaneuvered, the French quickly suffered loss after loss on the battlefield. Whole army corps were made prisoner. And on September 2, so was the emperor himself. His fall quickly led to revolution in Paris and, on September 4, the declaration of a new republic.

But the war was not at all over. The Prussian Army advanced rapidly to Paris, captured outlying forts built to defend the city, and put it under a siege that would last through a long, frigid winter. The Government of National Defense struggled to maintain the war effort and to keep the capital alive. Paris ran out of fuel and food. Trees were chopped down, the Bois de Boulogne razed. Eating became a greater problem with each passing day: the animals in the Paris Zoo were sacrificed, including the beloved elephants Castor and Pollux. They went largely to the tables of the rich. Butchers, having exhausted dogs and cats, began selling rats. Ersatz food was the rule, including coffee ground from acorns. Besides, the Prussians began bombarding the city, making life dangerous as well as precarious. By the end of January 1871, the government had reached an armistice with the Prussians, with the stipulation that a new Assembly would be elected and empowered to make a final peace treaty. Paris finally began to see supplies arrive from the countryside. But national elections led to an ultra-conservative Assembly, with the old political pro Adolphe Thiers as chief executive, and then to a peace treaty in February that surrendered Alsace and most of Lorraine to the Germans, levied reparations of 5 billion francs on France, and stipulated a Prussian victory parade down the Champs-Elysées on March 1.

The people of Paris and the National Guard—a kind of citizens' militia whose loyalty to the official government was not secure—became increasingly restive. The terms of the treaty signed at Versailles appeared to be a betrayal of the heroic Parisian resistance. When the new government in March decided to terminate the moratorium on rent payments and commercial loan repayments—and sale of items left at pawnshops—that the wartime government had decreed, there was also a sense of class betrayal. The trigger point was reached on March 18, when Thiers decided he needed to disarm the National Guard by taking away its cannon, many of which had been purchased by public subscription and were affectionately given names ("Victor Hugo," for one). During the night of the 17th and into the morning of the 18th, troops climbed up the Butte Montmartre to the cannon park. They secured the cannon—but horses and limbers to haul them away were slow in arriving. A crowd gathered, largely women at first, to prevent the taking of the cannon. Finally General Claude Lecomte ordered his troops to fire on the crowd. They did not. He ordered again, and again—but his troops began to put their guns butt upward and to desert to the crowd. Lecomte was seized, and later in the day, along with another general, Jacques-Léon Clément Thomas, who happened upon the scene, shot. Thiers and his ministers fled Paris to the safety of Versailles, where the Assembly now sat, which would henceforth be the seat of the official government. In Paris, meanwhile, the Commune took power.

It has never been easy to define the Commune, since it was an ad-hoc creation, born in the midst of crisis, that comprised a disparate cast of leaders of very different political commitments. It marked an attempt at local government taking independent control of the capital and running it as a kind of workers' democracy, though without a single coherent ideology: there were various strains of utopian and pragmatic socialism and anarchism, old Jacobins and new visionaries, as well as more straightforward utilitarian concerns among those chosen to govern. They represented largely the petit bourgeois and artisan classes. During its brief existence, the Commune instituted some remarkable social reforms, including the separation of church and state, the secularization of schooling, and the legal equality of women, while trying to manage defense of the city, which, after the siege by the Prussians, was increasingly threatened by the Versailles government.

The existence of the Commune became more and more precarious. Its military attempts to break out from the city and attack the enemy in Versailles failed miserably. Eventually, Thiers directed the invasion of Paris by the French Army, unleashing the most savage and destructive class warfare Western Europe has ever known. French Army troops, or the Versaillais, as they were known, their ranks bolstered by prisoners of war released by Bismarck to counter the proletarian insurgency, fought their way through Paris and leveled the Communard barricades with a vindictive force that is difficult to fathom. A number of the generals had experience fighting in the French colonies of North Africa and treated the Communards as if they were "natives." Indeed, they were made to seem like they were of another race, degenerate, alcohol fueled, vicious. By the end of the Bloody Week in May, probably some 20,000 Communards had been killed, either in the fighting or in the summary executions carried out by the Versaillais. Much of central Paris was set on fire, first by bombardment, then by the retreating Communards, who sought to put a wall of flame between themselves and the attackers. Paris, when the fighting stopped, presented a grim spectacle of ruin as inhabitants and visitors—including Flaubert—came to view the devastated city.

The Terrible Year found exceptional observers and narrators in Flaubert and George Sand (the self-created name of Aurore Dupin), the woman who was not Flaubert's lover but his closest confidante. The two had spent the Christmas holidays together in 1869 and looked forward to a prosperous 1870. They had vowed to say all to one another, without restraint, and their letters record their absolute devotion and candor. Neither was in Paris: Sand was in her beautiful home in Nohant, south of the Loire River in the Berry, Flaubert in the house in Croisset, on the River Seine just outside the Norman city of Rouen, that his surgeon father had bought and that he shared with his aged mother. But both followed events in the theaters of war, and then in Paris, with acute attention. They found themselves more deeply patriotic in spirit than they imagined they could be—Flaubert even briefly became lieutenant in a local National Guard unit. They were made heartsick by war, defeat, and siege. Sand was a long-standing socialist who had played a public role in the Second Republic born of the Revolution of 1848. Flaubert was an anti-democrat who believed in the rule of a mandarin caste of the enlightened who understood the laws of science. In November 1869 he had published *Sentimental Education*, a novel claiming to be the history of his own generation, including its experience of the Revolution of 1848 and its aftermath. Neither approved of the Commune, but both hated the reactionaries even more and deplored the actions of the "turd-shaped" Thiers. Their correspondence throughout the Terrible Year offers a rich choral commentary on war, politics, insurrection, violence, ruin, and the ineradicable stupidity of their contemporaries.

Flaubert came to Paris just as soon as the fighting stopped and he could get a train down from Rouen. He toured the still smoking ruins of central Paris, where the seat of government and many public buildings had gone up in flames during the final agony of the Commune. Viewing the ruins, he commented to his friend Maxime Du Camp that if only his contemporaries had understood *Sentimental Education*, this—the devastating denouement of the Terrible Year—never could have happened. His remark claims an exceptional role for the novel in the writing and understanding of history: the novel as truer to grasping the meaning of historical action than what usually passes as history. *Sentimental Education* gives a picture of the previous revolution, in 1848, but he convinced himself that it should have been read as prophetic of the ruins he stood among. What did he mean, and how did the Terrible Year as a whole come to be portrayed and understood as the political and cultural crucible of modern France?

The story I have to tell bears witness to the Terrible Year and its bloody climax through the eyes of Flaubert and Sand. As they emerged from its horrors, they confronted an aftermath of warring commemorations of the event, including the improbable building of the Basilique du Sacré-Coeur (Basilica of the Sacred Heart) on the heights of Montmartre, where the National Guard's cannon park stood, in "expiation" of the sins of secular France during the Terrible Year, and Victor Hugo's novel *Ninety-Three* (*Quatrevingt-treize*), an attempt to reconcile the contending forces of the nation that reaches back to the year of the Terror during the first French Revolution to dramatize the clash of ideologies and persons that continued throughout the nineteenth century. Most of all, this story weighs Flaubert's claim to have written the history of his generation—a claim as well to a kind of right of historiography that makes the novel the best access to history. It's not only the history of the Terrible Year that interests me but also the contests about remembering and representing it and the relation of writing to event. The novelization of history, as you might call it, took on various forms, with far-reaching results.

What follows will first briefly trace Flaubert's career prior to the Terrible Year, from the time that his first novel, *Madame Bovary*, was published through his meeting with Sand and his experience as a lionized writer under the Second Empire, and then move into the Terrible Year itself as witnessed by the two writers. I will then ask what Flaubert meant when he said that an understanding of *Sentimental Education* would have saved his contemporaries from the folly and misery of the war and the Commune and its repression, as well as how that prescient novel fits with other attempts to claim the history of the Terrible Year in books, statues, and monuments. Along the way come the photographs of what Flaubert saw in early June 1871, as the ruins of Paris called forth a remarkable response in the maturing art of photography. I will talk about the continuing evolution of Flaubert's political views and his last writings, including a story he wrote for Sand that she didn't live to read. Finally, I will say a word about how the novel, including Flaubert's contribution, becomes the key to the understanding of modern history.

I wish, then, to tell a story that includes the catastrophic events experienced by Flaubert and Sand, and the fight over their meaning afterward, and as well a story about Flaubert, Sand, politics, and the novel. When Flaubert claims the force of his novel as predictive of events that unfolded shortly after its publication, he summons us to think about how the novel as genre can shape our understanding of events. *Sentimental Education* is, among other things, a meditation on the role of human agency in the making of history, and it touches on all the political ideologies and commitments of his time. Above all, it seems to be a reflection on the capacity of human action to inflect event. What can we who live in the midst of unfolding history do about it? How do we even go about cutting through the fog of event and the cacophony of competing voices to understand it?

Flaubert has most often been thought of as a dropout from public affairs who largely embodies conservative bourgeois political ideology despite a lifetime spent skewering the bourgeoisie. Some of his most clear-sighted critics have argued otherwise. In particular, Edmund Wilson, in his essay "Flaubert's Politics" in *The Triple Thinkers* (first published in 1938, then revised in 1948), sees Flaubert as a judicious figure who understands better than most the political stakes of his time and of the future. Contrasting Flaubert to some other writers of his time, Wilson concluded that "really Flaubert owed his superiority to . . . his contemporaries . . . to the seriousness of his concerns with the large question of human destiny." Much more recently, the biography of Flaubert by the French historian Michel Winock argues in its turn that Flaubert's political views evolved greatly in response to the Terrible Year, making this mandarin who expressed contempt for the plebes eventually turn into a republican. That is an important line in my story: how Flaubert the social and political conservative became a republican who feared the threatened restoration of a monarchy in France (it nearly did happen), and who came to understand that the

French could live together without slaughtering one another only in a republic. Undoubtedly Sand helped him in this political conversion: if, like him, she deplored the Commune, it was because she saw the Commune as being opposed to the legitimate republican government, however much the latter deserved censure. She remained always faithful to a generous dream of humanitarian reconciliation, with class warfare submerged in a new harmony that would offer the best to human aspiration.

Flaubert's political evolution is closely tied to his writing, but not in any simple way. *Sentimental Education* offers a version of political and social event with which he will continue to dialogue: his very last, unfinished novel, *Bouvard et Pécuchet (Bouvard and Pécuchet)* published only after his death, returns to the Revolution of 1848 that stands at the center of *Sentimental Education* and gives quite a different version of it. His scenarios for an unfinished novel on the era of the Second Empire, *Sous Napoléon III* (Under Napoleon III), also seem to take an unexpected political stance. The novel for Flaubert is an instrument of testing and discovery. Like history itself, it is never static. The incapacity to move, to change one's mind, and to entertain new possibilities is what the bourgeois are all about, and by the time of Flaubert's last work, he is seeking new ways around the bourgeoisie, using the language that its members think they own in order to unseat them.

Flaubert and Sand were not so much participants in the events of the Terrible Year as impassioned observers and commentators, writers who believed in the power of the word to explain, clarify, critique. They saw that the fate of their nation, perhaps even the future of humanity, was at stake, and that by the same token their own writing was tied to politics in ways they had not foreseen. Their anguished reactions to unfolding events returned again and again to the place that should be given to intelligence and analysis within politics and national culture. If one had to submit to historical events beyond one's control, there was nonetheless the need to recount them and try to understand them. Writing, if exact and honest, could change lives, maybe inflect the course of history. But it needed readers of intelligence and good faith, and where were they to be found?

So most of all I offer a book about politics and the novel. Not politics in any trivial sense, but rather the making of enormously important historical events. And not the novel as a simple mirror of political events or political ideologies, but something much more complex. The novel is in dialogue with political event, attempting to incorporate it, understand it, tell its meaning. The novel itself becomes part of history, read by—so often misunderstood by—one's contemporaries. It participates in a struggle to say who shall write the history of contemporary France. And beyond that, it is part of a longer history, a period that starts with the first French Revolution and the struggle to say to whom France belongs. That's what the historiography of modern France that is so important in Flaubert's time is ultimately about, and so is Flaubert's fictional writing. This novelist who is so often seen as a detached aesthete—and often wants to see himself that way—becomes a political participant through his work.

So "politics and the novel" here is not a concept that will yield a simple meaning. I look on it as an invitation, to myself and to the reader, to take seriously Flaubert's astonishing claim that an understanding of the novel that he published in November 1869 would, if properly understood, have prevented the events of 1870 and 1871. How can a novel teach a nation to avoid war, civil war, and self-immolation?

chapter one

From Emma Bovary to the Terrible Year

MADAME BOVARY WAS THE WORK OF A MAN IN HIS MID-thirties who up until then had published absolutely nothing. It brought him instant fame and opened before him the doors of Parisian literary life. The novel was published in 1856 as installments in the *Revue de Paris*, where his friend Maxime Du Camp held an editorial position—with passages censored, to Flaubert's total disgust. It would appear in two volumes in the spring of 1857, but before that, in January 1857, Flaubert faced the indignity of indictment and a trial for outrage to public morality. That trial became a legendary confrontation between a prurient-minded state censor and an eloquent defender of authorial freedom contending for the right to purvey moral lessons through the most brutal demonstrations of bad behavior and its consequences. Neither the imperial prosecutor, Ernest Pinard, nor the defense counsel, Jules Sénard, supported the artist's freedom to write as he chose or to defend his choices on purely aesthetic grounds. The arguments were all about morality. Pinard tended to cite passage after passage from *Madame Bovary* to illustrate its patent offensiveness to good bourgeois morality: its seeming claim that Emma Bovary is made more beautiful by adultery, that her turn to religious devotion is another barely disguised episode of sensuality, and perhaps most offensive of all, the author's apparent assertion that in adultery Emma discovers "all the platitudes of marriage." In sum, the novel was a manual of sinning for bored wives. Sénard, after establishing Flaubert's impeccable bourgeois origins and social standing, tried to demonstrate that vice is suitably punished throughout the novel. The court, in acquitting Flaubert, gave him a sermon about what is permissible in the novel. Total realism, said the judges, would be revolting and immoral.

So a classic was born under a dubious cloud of excessive "realism," a term Flaubert detested, though he had to grow used to the idea that he was the author of the most famous of all realist novels. And of course it profited from the publicity of prosecution. Flaubert turned with relief to his next project, a novel set in ancient Carthage, *Salammbô*. As critics have always noted, this was a novel written very much from the library, and from the painstaking research Flaubert undertook to make real a forgotten world of antiquity. It involved as well a trip to North Africa to contemplate the scant ruins of Carthage and study the sights and colors of contemporary Tunisia, on its way to becoming a French colony. Published in 1862, *Salammbô* sold decently, but with only modest critical success. Flaubert jousted successfully with critics: when the archaeologist Wilhelm Froehner called into question the authenticity of his reconstruction of Carthage, and the critic C. A. Sainte-Beuve doubted its novelistic effect, the novelist at least could cite his sources *in extenso*. The novel has had its admirers; in some ways it's a remarkable epic reconstruction of a lost world, and certainly it's the most operatic of Flaubert's creations. (It would later be adapted as an opera.) Its sonorous prose at times seems matched to a proto-western, here with battles of elephants and colossal destruction, and a somewhat perverse sexual underplot. To many readers it appears at once spectacular and inert, like a cinematic epic that moves at too stately a pace.

As he began work on his most ambitious novel, *Sentimental Education*, Flaubert, born in 1821, was in his early forties. He was tall, overtopping most of his friends, and fair, very much a Norman, and referred to by some of his acquaintances as a Viking. But his athletic figure was somewhat undermined by his health: early in life, he had had seizures that may or may not have been epilepsy; then he had syphilis as a young man, which was treated with mercury, as was the custom of the time, and suffered the loss of hair and teeth. Still, he was an imposing figure. Born into upper bourgeois affluence, he had never faced the question of working (or even writing) for a living—and he wouldn't until, near the end of his life, he chose to bail the husband of his adored niece Caroline Commanville out of bankruptcy. Flaubert's father, a famous doctor and the head of the hospital in Rouen, in Normandy, had sent him to Paris to study law (his elder brother Achille would directly inherit the paternal mantle and become a surgeon), but after abandoning that path, and after a trip in his late twenties with Maxime Du Camp to the Near East (which sometimes reads as a journey from one brothel to another), Flaubert settled in the commodious house that his father had bought in Croisset, on the banks of the River Seine just outside of Rouen. He lived there with his mother (his father died in 1846) as a self-declared monk in the service of art.

Much has been made of his hermit-like life; some of his friends urged him to circulate more and to marry. To analyze his choice of solitude—which he also repeatedly lamented—may not be profitable: he said himself that he had no idea why he chose such a monastic life; it's just the way things happened. He evidently loved the security of his nest in Croisset. His seizures, which became infrequent as the years passed, authenticated opting out of any profession other than letters. For many years he lived with his aged mother, and on her death he surmised that she was the person he had loved best in his life. His monasticism did not mean celibacy. There were a number of affairs, including the long and stormy liaison with Louise Colet, a woman of letters, ten years older than he; briefer relationships with actresses Béatrix Person and Suzanne Lagier; and, in the world of Second Empire courtesans, with such as Jeanne de Tourbey and Apollonie Sabatier, *La Présidente* beloved of Charles Baudelaire. Following the success of *Madame Bovary*, he took a pied-à-terre in Paris, where for weeks during the winter he pursued his social life with the cultural elite (he was at home to them regularly on Sunday afternoons) and carried forward his erotic adventures. And then there was the woman who was possibly the tenderest of his loves, Juliet Herbert, who came to Croisset first as English governess to his niece Caroline, the daughter of his beloved sister, also Caroline, who had always shared his literary and artistic interests, but who died in the aftermath of childbirth, not long after their father's death. Juliet undertook an English translation of *Madame Bovary* (never published, and lost) at the author's side, and kept trysts with him almost until his death. But it is clear that Flaubert held most of his women at a distance, writing dozens of letters about why they could not live together or even meet frequently. His greater investment seems to have been in friendship: many testified to his warmth and loyalty. With those he knew, he was open, frank, funny, and vulnerable. And, as George Sand would repeatedly tell him, for all his misanthropic ranting he was a deeply good person.

Flaubert was dedicated to the vocation that he often felt as torture, and Croisset remained his preferred residence, retreat, and workplace. As soon as *Salammbô* was published, he turned to his next project. This endeavor would return him to the real and contemporary world. Not, this time, the provincial Norman towns—Tostes, Yonville-l'Abbaye—where Emma suffers her imprisoned existence, but largely the Paris he knew as a youth. As he put it early on in a process of composition that was going to take him nearly seven years, he wanted to write "the moral history of the men of my generation." He corrected himself to say that "sentimental" would be more accurate than "moral." The word *moral* that he used at first embraces in French more than its English equivalent: it means as well the psychological, the ethos of existence, one might say. The *sentimentale* of the final title of the book is hard to duplicate in English. *L'éducation sentimentale* means "an education in the sentiments," an education in the things they don't teach in schools: in love, and in friendship, betrayal, and so forth.

The novel was to take a very ordinary hero from young manhood—we first see Frédéric Moreau on a riverboat taking him back home to Nogent for summer vacation between a visit to his rich uncle in Le Havre and the start of his law studies in Paris—through to maturity, with a brief glimpse at old age. And in the process, this novel, which begins very precisely on

November 15, 1840 (the date is included in the first line of the book), will take in the experience of Frédéric and his generation of the Revolution of 1848—the great year of European revolutions (and of the *Communist Manifesto*). In France those events led first to a republic, with the poet Alphonse de Lamartine as its chief executive, and to a number of very progressive reforms, but then also to a revolt by unemployed and starving workers, who were brutally suppressed in the June Days of that year, and then to the first presidential election by universal (male) suffrage, which saw the victory of Louis-Napoléon Bonaparte—followed by his coup d'état against the parliamentary regime in December 1851, and, a year later, his coronation as Emperor Napoleon III.

The Second Empire that spanned most of Flaubert's most productive writing years, from the composition of *Madame Bovary* through the publication of *Sentimental Education*, was a time of industrial expansion, capitalist investment, and the creation of great wealth for the upper bourgeoisie, but it also saw the making of an industrial proletariat and an urban underclass. It was under Napoleon III that Paris as we still know it largely emerged, from a vast urban renewal undertaken by the emperor's lieutenant, the Baron Haussmann, who, as *préfet* of the Department of the Seine, had nearly unlimited powers to remake the city and its infrastructure. Much has been written both for and against Haussmann's transformations, carried out high-handedly and with much financial and political corruption. Certainly he opened up a city that was in many of its quarters still medieval, impacted, and unsanitary. He made it possible to move in Paris, and across Paris, in the process creating the conditions for the great department stores, such as Le Bon Marché and Printemps, that drew shoppers from all over the city and sent delivery vans seemingly everywhere. As a result of his work, you could circulate in Paris, and you could see it in a way that captured the attention of painters (and photographers), who made of 1860s and 1870s Paris one of the great moments in the history of art. The railroad network was growing fast, making it easy for Edouard Manet, Claude Monet, Gustave Caillebotte, Pierre-Auguste Renoir, and others to work in the suburbs along the Seine. Paris was becoming the city of light, *la ville lumière*, and indeed, electric light would soon show up in paintings, giving them a new frosty illumination. It was the time when *la vie parisienne* was becoming a magnet throughout Europe, bringing—as in Jacques Offenbach's operetta entitled *La Vie parisienne*—the affluent from all over the world to enjoy its pleasures. It was a sexualized city as well, as Henri de Toulouse-Lautrec and Edgar Degas suggest in their differing ways, one coded as both feminine and welcoming (if you had the means, and if you weren't among those exploited for the pleasure of others). The new Paris also displaced its working class to the peripheral quarters.

The greatest self-representation of the Second Empire may have come in 1867, with the Exposition Universelle, which from April to October attracted some 6 million visitors, including a large sampling of royalty from around the globe. A vast oval building, glass and cast iron, was constructed in record time on the Champ de Mars, first leveled of its hill. Around it stood the various national pavilions in some simulacrum of their native styles. At its heart was the Hall of Work, providing a history of technology from the Neanderthal forward. In the Hall of Industry, designed by the young engineer Gustave Eiffel, were steam engines, turbines, the new elevator with a safety brake invented by Charles and Norton Otis—every imaginable machine to make life comfortable, it seemed. At night the Hall of Industry shimmered like a monstrous jewel. Flaubert visited it three times, once with the Princess Mathilde. It was thanks to her also that he was present at the grandest ball of the season, held in honor of the Russian emperor, Alexander II, on June 10 at the Tuileries Palace, which he had last visited in February 1848, when the revolutionary populace was sacking it. Now the garden paths were illuminated by lines of porcelain lanterns that glowed like "big, brilliant pearls." The women passed through rows of potted orange trees in dresses with long trains, fully décolleté. It all was gorgeous and artificial, "colossal" and "crazed," he told Sand on June 12. "The fountains change color every minute—from time to time a ray of electric light races across the ground." It was a great magnificence, and a fragile one, as the year 1870 would prove. The Empire erected so lavishly, seemingly so well-supported by industrial wealth and commerce, including the contributions of the French colonies, would collapse in an instant.

Flaubert had little use for the Second Empire, which he accurately saw as run by corrupt, rapacious, and philistine entrepreneurs and speculators, but he accepted it as the imposition of order on a fractious nation. He claimed to detest despotism and all dogmatism and to be a "ferocious liberal"—which meant rejecting authoritarian socialism as well. But he generally prospered under the Empire. In particular, he became a prized member of the salon of the Princess Mathilde. She was cousin to Emperor Napoleon III—and once, when they were younger, proposed to be his wife—and with his ascension to grandeur, she became the quasi-official center of literary and artistic cultural life from her palace on the rue de Courcelles and her country house in Saint-Gratien, a few kilometers outside of Paris. Mathilde, on best of terms with the emperor, was by now the estranged wife of an immensely rich Russian, Count Anatoly Demidov, and mistress to Emile de Nieuwerkerke, director of fine arts for the Empire. She was also an amateur painter and would-be intellectual who had formed a close friendship with the dominant literary critic and journalist of the day, Charles Augustin Sainte-Beuve, who prepared a curriculum of study for her. He came to dominate her Wednesday evening gatherings, which included much literary and artistic talent, such as the sculptor Jean-Baptiste Carpeaux; composers Charles Gounod and Camille Saint-Saens; the architect Eugène Viollet-le-Duc; and writers Maxime Du Camp, Prosper Mérimée, Alexandre Dumas (père), and Edmond and Jules de Goncourt. Another one of the regulars was the Prince Jérôme Napoléon, known as Plon-Plon, a declared progressive who was often at odds with the conservative Empress Eugénie and who became a good friend to Flaubert. Mathilde, who was both imperious (a bit of a spoiled child, Flaubert would later call her) and marginally bohemian, reveled in the attention of her clan, and in return she saw to it that they received appropriate awards: Flaubert would receive his own red ribbon of the Legion of Honor in 1866, demonstrating that his reputation had recovered from the trial for immorality just nine years earlier.

Flaubert responded to Mathilde's attentions—his letters to her can seem to us today a bit too toadying—and appears to have reached her inner circle. He was invited to at least one of the series of grand long weekends at the Château de Compiègne, where the emperor and Empress Eugénie entertained. Especially elegant was the *fête de l'Impératrice*, which Flaubert attended. It included a dress ball with charades and card games; a shoot the next day followed by a theatrical performance; on the third day an excursion to the nearby Château de Pierrefonds—a medieval castle that had recently been restored in somewhat Disney World–style by Viollet-le-Duc—then riding to the hounds. And so on. Flaubert's reaction is mainly recorded in a letter written from room 85 on the second floor of the Château de Compiègne to his friend Jules Duplan with precise orders to go to the florist Madame Prévost in Paris and order a bouquet of white camellias ("I insist that it be ultra-chic") to be delivered on Monday morning, so that he could present it to the Empress that evening.

This was heady stuff for the provincial bourgeois Flaubert—and yet he maintained his independence. When he was well into his work on *Sentimental Education*, he refused some of Mathilde's blandishments. His devotion to writing mattered above all. And according to Du Camp, once when someone in the circle around the Empress spoke disparagingly of Victor Hugo—now a political exile on the isle of Guernsey, who had criticized the emperor in *Napoléon le Petit* (Napoleon the Little) and the poems of *Les Châtiments* (Punishments)—Flaubert called his polemical political poems "magnificent" and offered to recite them from memory. That, of course, would have created a scandal. The more he studied the political history of his time, as preparation for his novel, the more he came to pass judgment on the men of the Empire who had snuffed out the fledgling republic and instituted a regime of hollow grandeur and gangland political manipulation.

Here one would like to be able to describe the novel Flaubert later planned to write about this time of his life, *Sous Napoléon III*, but it exists only in fragmentary outline, in notes written between 1874 and 1880. It appears to have been structured around three couples, at least one of them with explicitly political concerns. The notes depict the Second Empire, accurately, as a time of pleasures and fundamental corruption. The political figure among the principal actors is someone who refuses to swear allegiance to the Empire after the coup d'état, and ends up as a member of the Commune insurgency in 1871, while also in love with a conservative Catholic woman. All of this suggests a tantalizingly political Flaubert, but the sketchy notes do not allow us to say much more.

Another center of Flaubert's Parisian life during the Empire was the ritual Monday dinner at the Restaurant Magny, a tradition launched by Sainte-Beuve that brought together, among others, the Goncourt brothers, Jules and Edmond, who wrote their novels collaboratively; historian and philosopher Ernest Renan; historian and literary critic Hippolyte Taine; and poet and apostle of "art for art's sake" Théophile Gautier. Speech was free, often polemical, with shouting matches about the worth of various writers past and present, tales of sexual experience, and much drinking. (Years later, Edmond de Goncourt, estimating the degrees of dirty-mindedness among his companions, concluded that Flaubert was only a "pretend swine," in fact a sentimentalist.)

Among the others who joined the dinner there was, on February 28, 1863, Ivan Turgenev, with whom Flaubert immediately bonded. He sent Flaubert three of his books the next day, and Flaubert responded two weeks later with great enthusiasm. The two would become fast friends and readers for one another's work until the end, though always lamenting that they saw each other so little. Turgenev lived in Paris in a famous ménage à trois with the singer and actress Pauline Viardot, the love of his life, and Pauline's husband; he made visits every year to his estates in Russia, from which he was officially a political exile ever since publishing *The Huntsman's Diary*, one of the books he sent to Flaubert, and also frequent visits to the baths at Baden-Baden for his gout. Flaubert's time in Paris was always limited, and so he was ever summoning Turgenev to join him in Croisset (which did happen on occasion). Turgenev's fictional representations of life seem to give a larger place to tenderness, even to spirituality, than Flaubert's, and it is interesting to note that Flaubert responded to them with complete admiration. It was on February 12, 1866, that George Sand attended her first Magny dinner, where she met Flaubert—not quite for the first time, but the earlier crossings of their paths had been brief—to become, along with Turgenev, the other truly lifelong friend and absolute confidante. The attraction was immediate. If she was no longer considered

beautiful, Sand still had much allure. Flaubert, though balding and suffering from all sorts of ailments, was a tall, impressive, handsome man—the
Viking still, who liked to swim in the Seine. Sand would visit Croisset
twice in the summer and fall of 1866. She and Flaubert found a way to
become the fastest of friends without becoming lovers.

She was seventeen years his senior, and the famous veteran of well-
publicized loves with Jules Sandeau, Alfred de Musset, Frédéric Chopin,
and others, but by the time she met Flaubert she had declared herself no
longer to be a woman, in fact thinking it would be better henceforth to live
as a man. But she also lived, when at home in Nohant—in the Berry, south
of the Loire Valley—very much as mother and grandmother, presiding
over a clan that centered on her son Maurice and his family, and all the creative entertainments they managed in their country house, including the
famous puppet theater created by Maurice, for which they all wrote scripts
and made costumes. The friendship between Sand and Flaubert is in itself a curious phenomenon that would deserve deeper analysis, could one
provide it. He didn't really admire her writing—it was too prolix and sentimental for his taste, though he claimed in a letter of 1866 to have reread
her *Consuelo*, and declared himself charmed by it (she expressed surprise
at this). She remained, in his view, too much affected by the Romantic
generation from which Flaubert sought to escape: the Romantics, he believed, inculcated an unsatisfiable longing and falsified reality. Nor did he
really share her feminist commitments—his own relations with his lovers
show him as passably blind to the needs of his partner—or her politics.
He found her socialism tedious, though he respected her allegiance to the
Revolution of 1848 in its first democratic and liberal phase, and understood her loyalty to the inveterate revolutionary Armand Barbès—who
spent most of his life in prison or in political exile. With Barbès, in fact,
thanks to Sand's mediation, he entered into correspondence regarding the
horrible treatment of political prisoners following the suppression of the
workers' uprising in June 1848. It's not clear that Sand really admired Flaubert's writing that much, either. She did write a warmly favorable review
of *Salammbô*, in which she recognized the beauty of the author's spending

years in deep study of a difficult subject, and Flaubert responded warmly to her praise, asking her to send him her portrait. She would also react against the negative press for *Sentimental Education* with a kind review of her own. But his writing always seemed too cool and impersonal to her. She wanted to see more of his soul in his writing, an idea to which he reacted with horror. The writer, as he had long ago declared, must in his work be like God in his creation, present everywhere but nowhere visible.

What, then, did draw these two together—to the extent that Flaubert would announce that she was the only person to whom he could confide everything, and she would describe their exchanges as lovers' caresses? I think it has something to do with their investment of eros in their correspondence and dialogue, without any thought that it might be of the flesh. Flaubert, despite his many friendships, was a lonely man, and Sand, for all her large and complex family to manage, had exhausted passionate sexual relationships with men and needed something else. Their correspondence (often recognized to be one of the greatest preserved for us) gives a sense of the intimacy of lovers who know they can't be together, or perhaps of siblings bound by an unspoken eros. *Chère Maître* (Dear Master), he addresses her, attaching a feminine adjective to the masculine noun that one traditionally used to indicate homage to an intellectual or artistic mentor. To Sand, he is *Cher Vieux* (Dear Old Friend), *Cher Ami de mon coeur* (Dear friend of my heart), then *Cher vieux troubadour* (Dear old troubadour). Flaubert often signs himself as "Troubadour," singer of tales and of love from afar, though he at times takes on the pose of the "Reverend Father Cruchard, Jesuit priest and confessor." There are many playful poses in the correspondence: Flaubert enjoyed mimicry and parody, and she was a good audience for it. He always addressed her as *vous*, whereas she treated him to the intimate *tu*. That can be explained by their difference in age, though it could perhaps also signal some protocol on his part to keep their intimacy formal, as it were.

As Flaubert moved more and more intensely into the composition of *Sentimental Education*, his letters to a number of correspondents became calls for research assistance. It is striking how obsessed he was with detail and accuracy. *Madame Bovary*, too, is a novel of detail: we know Emma and her world through the accumulation of small facts and things singled out for attention. We never get an overall view of Emma or her beauty: we are told of her polished fingernails and velvety eyelashes, her fashionable foot and boots, and her petticoats, as if she were the object of the fetishist's gaze. Flaubert's imagination is relentlessly visual and specific. For *Sentimental Education*, the details had to be accurate not only as to place but as to time—they needed historical precision and verifiability. As was the case for all his novels, he consulted a number of sources, including newspapers from 1848, memoirs, and histories, one of them the famous *Histoire de la Révolution de 1848* (History of the Revolution of 1848), signed "Daniel Stern," penname of the Countess Marie d'Agoult, who had fled her aristocratic milieu for a long liaison with Franz Liszt. He also referred to the indispensable Du Camp's *Souvenirs de l'année 1848* (Memories of the year 1848). His trips to Paris became itineraries of visits to sites for the novel: Nogent, the Valley of Montmorency, funeral homes, Père Lachaise Cemetery, boutiques of religious wares, a birthing clinic for unwed mothers. He learned about techniques for making and glazing pottery and visited a factory near Paris for one of his episodes. He went to a public auction for another. He made many notes. In addition to his own recollections of a time he had lived through, for this novel he especially called upon friends for their knowledge of the historically apt detail.

The examples accumulate. When composing the scene of the duel between Frédéric Moreau, the novel's protagonist, and the Baron de Cisy, he wrote in 1867 to Paul de Saint-Victor asking in what part of the Bois de Boulogne such encounters took place in 1847—it had to be near enough to a road for the duelists to see a carriage arrive (Jacques Arnoux will be in it), to interrupt them. In 1868, he was working on the moment where the *cocotte* Rosanette, on an escapade to Fontainebleau with Frédéric, becomes confessional about her childhood and her sale as an adolescent, by her mother, to a gross old man. Rosanette comes from Lyon, the center of silk weaving, and Flaubert demanded of Jules Duplan information on the life of the silk weavers, the *canuts*, among the most exploited and alienated of the urban working classes:

I need details about the homes of such people.

1. Describe for me, in a few lines, the living quarters of Lyon workers.
2. The *canuts* (as I believe the silk weavers are called) work in very low-ceilinged rooms, don't they?
3. In their own houses?
4. Do their children work too?

I find the following in my notes: the weaver working at a Jacquemard loom is continually struck in the stomach by the shaft of the roller on which the cloth is being wound as it is completed.

5. Is it the roller itself that strikes him? Make this sentence clearer.

In short, I want to write a four-line description of a working-class domestic scene, to contrast with another interior that comes later—the luxurious establishment in which our heroine is deflowered.

No wonder the composition of the novel took so many years: if a four-line description requires this kind of background documentation, progress can't be rapid. Details need to be backed up by evidence that will be left on the cutting-room floor.

Another striking instance came a few days later: Flaubert had written a scene where Frédéric returns from Fontainebleau to Paris by train to visit the bedside of his friend Dussardier, who has been wounded during the insurrection of June, only to discover in a guidebook that in 1848 there was no train link between Fontainebleau and Paris. The train line from Paris at that time reached only as far as Corbeil—but how then did you get from Fontainebleau to Corbeil? He threw this and a number of other questions at Duplan—leaving a blank in his text, to be filled in when the needed information arrived. Then there was the problem of Frédéric's movements once he had reached Paris: on October 27, Flaubert wrote to Ernest Feydeau (writer, father of the playwright Georges Feydeau) asking him where the headquarters of the National Guard stood in 1848, and whether on the night of June 25 it was the National Guard or the army infantry that was occupying the Left Bank. Again, he left a blank in the text to be filled in when the necessary information arrived. Maxime Du Camp provided an account of his own experiences in Paris during the June Days, including a number of striking details that would make their way directly into the novel.

One gets the impression of a kind of *pointilliste* technique, in anticipation of Georges Seurat. Even though Flaubert knew perfectly well where his novel was headed, and what its overall plot was going to be, the details accumulating along the way were of such importance that a number of blanks needed to be left for later filling-in. We will see Flaubert during the Terrible Year complaining to George Sand about his contemporaries' lack of devotion to "science," that is, to the scientific study of society, government, economics, and history. In order to write the moral history of his generation, Flaubert convinced himself of the need for a quasi-scientific attention to realist detail. Literature must not argue or teach but expose. He had to get things absolutely right in a kind of mania for the precise and perceptible detail. This technique is striking throughout *Sentimental Education*, sometimes to the point of seeming to slow the action to a very deliberate pace, sometimes also producing a kind of hallucinatory visual effect. Flaubert indeed had an interesting exchange of letters on hallucinations in 1866 with Hippolyte Taine, who was composing his book *De l'Intelligence (On Intelligence)*: Flaubert found hallucinations "as true as the objective reality of things." When describing a room, "I *see* all the furniture (including the stains on it)," he wrote. Frédéric will often experience crucial moments of both experience and reality as hallucinatory, as hyperreal. It's as if Flaubert's attempt to deal with the things of the real world led him beyond realism, even beyond impressionism, to the elements of a nearly surreal re-creation of sights and sensations.

The Revolution of 1848 and its aftermath were from the outset conceived to be what this novel, which began on September 15, 1840, was working toward. Flaubert had himself been eyewitness to the start of that revolution as a young man: in company with his close friends Maxime

Du Camp and Louis Bouilhet, he had seen the first bodies, victims of the fusillade of the Boulevard des Capucines, wheeled through Paris on a cart during the night of February 23, and then, with Du Camp, the sacking of the Tuileries Palace. Back in Croisset to finish the first version of *La Tentation de Saint-Antoine* (*The Temptation of Saint Anthony*, pronounced a failure by his friends), he had watched the sequel from afar. (The unfolding of the revolution in the provinces gets an account in the later unfinished novel *Bouvard and Pécuchet*.) He was again in Paris at the moment of Louis-Napoléon Bonaparte's coup d'état in December 1851. Between revolution and reaction, he was off on his grand trip to Egypt and the Middle East with Du Camp. The coming of a new empire, on the first anniversary of the coup d'état, seemed to him, so far as we can judge, an inevitable outcome. Though he had attended one of the prerevolutionary reform banquets in Rouen, and he admired Victor Hugo, who had gone into exile following the coup d'état of 1851 and had become the symbol of resistance to the Empire, he was not (yet) a republican. He became the intermediary in delivering correspondence from Hugo (code-named "the crocodile") on the isle of Guernsey to a host of recipients via the poet Louise Colet, Flaubert's mistress in the 1840s and early 1850s: to evade political censorship at the border, Hugo sent his letters in a packet to Mrs. Jane Farmer, former tutor to Flaubert's sister Caroline, in England, who then sent them on to Flaubert. Flaubert took out whatever was addressed to him and sent the rest on to Louise, who extracted her own letter before distributing the others to their addressees. Return letters made the same journey. The hand of Second Empire censorship was heavy indeed. Flaubert did not hesitate to be in private opposition.

The Revolution of 1848 in the novel furnishes the dramatic moment of climax, pathos, and reversal, a great historical cataclysm. Frédéric and most of the other characters will prove inadequate to this moment, a moment at which history itself, paradoxically, seems to stumble and fail. Writing these chapters entailed gathering the oral testimony of witnesses such as Sand, Duplan, Ernest Feydeau, Du Camp, and Maurice Schlesinger, in addition to vast reading: not only histories and memoirs but also the works of the socialists, utopians, and other political thinkers whose ideas were influential before and during the revolution. "I have just swallowed Lammenais, Saint-Simon, and Fourier, and I am now going over all of Proudhon," Flaubert wrote to Edma Roger des Genettes, sometime mistress of his friend Louis Bouilhet, and one of Flaubert's favorite correspondents, not long after he had begun work on the novel. He found in all of those authors a "hatred of liberty, of the French Revolution, of philosophy." There was a strange current of religiosity in the socialist thinkers—Henri de Saint-Simon's real master was the arch-reactionary monarchist and Catholic Joseph de Maistre, and Pierre-Joseph Proudhon and Louis Blanc owed much to the liberal Catholicism of Félicité Lammenais. They didn't succeed in 1848 because people instinctively understood that at the core of all social utopias lay "tyranny, anti-nature, the death of the soul." To George Sand four years later Flaubert wrote, "All the Christianity I find in Socialism appalls me!"

Sand became alarmed when he told her his novel would not please "the patriots," by which he meant those who had engaged themselves in the revolution. He then assured her that the "Reactionaries" would be even less well treated, "since they seem to me more criminal." He would have occasion to repeat this judgment more than once as the events of 1870–1871 unfolded. The socialists and radicals of 1848 made the mistake of thinking they could enroll humankind in a system—they were at heart religious believers—and to them Flaubert opposed the critical spirit of Voltaire and of the first, liberal stage of the French Revolution. He was viscerally a libertarian, opposed to Jacobin as well as imperial authoritarianism. But whatever the errors and misguided beliefs of those forming the whole spectrum of republicanism and socialism that came to the fore in 1848, there was no excuse for the reaction that followed, which was monstrous, repressive, and inhuman. As a line in *Sentimental Education* summing up the reaction following the workers' revolt of the June Days has it, "intelligent men were made idiots for their whole life." That was the real crime of the history of his time for Flaubert—the victory of idiocy over intelligence. There was plenty more of that to come.

He and Sand found a point of common political ground in their disgust at Adolphe Thiers, whose long political career continued, with interruptions, throughout their lifetimes. Thiers had been in and out of government under Louis Philippe in the 1830s, had incurred the wrath of labor and the Left in his savage repression of the revolt of the Lyon silk workers, had emerged as a leader of conservative republicans under the Empire, and would return to power in 1871 as the chief executive of the provisional government charged with making peace with the Prussians. A short, pugnacious man (Marx called him a "monstrous gnome"), he then put down the Paris Commune with spectacular bloodshed and went on to lead the fledgling Third Republic. He had also written a popular history of the French Revolution. Flaubert decided to work Thiers's book in defense of property rights, *De la propriété* (*The Rights of Property*), into his account of the reaction to the June Days in his novel, where he sees property becoming the ultimate bourgeois idol and fetish. It was a speech of Thiers's against Italian unification that set him off in a letter to Sand in December 1867: "Can one find a more triumphant imbecile, a more abject pustule, a more turdlike bourgeois! No! nothing can give you the idea of the vomiting that this old diplomatic melon inspires in me, rounding off his stupidity on the dungheap of the Bourgeoisie! Is it possible to treat with such naïve and inept nonchalance philosophy, religion, peoples, freedom, the past and the present, history and natural history, everything! And more! He strikes me as eternal like Mediocrity itself! He crushes me."

Sand rose to the challenge, replying, "Finally! Someone who thinks like me in the matter of this political boor. It could only have been you, friend of my heart. *Turdlike* is the sublime word to characterize this kind of *shitshape* growth." She goes on to say that she has friends who admire all politicians in the opposition, for whom Thiers, this "clown without an idea," is a God. She encourages Flaubert to "dissect" him in his novel, although she fears he will be gone and forgotten by the time the novel is published. "Such men leave nothing after them," she wrote. She and Flaubert were to learn how wrong this prediction was.

On the last day of 1868, Flaubert wrote to Madame Aupick, mother of the poet Charles Baudelaire, who had died the year before, thanking her for sending him the new edition of *Les Fleurs du mal* (*The Flowers of Evil*). This edition had been augmented by several poems not published in the first edition of 1857, though it still lacked those that had sent Baudelaire before the criminal court, with less happy results than in Flaubert's case: Baudelaire was found guilty and fined, and six of his poems were banned. Flaubert had always appreciated Baudelaire's poetry, and as well the warm review of *Madame Bovary* the poet had written. Then, on January 1, 1869, Flaubert and Sand each wrote to the other with wishes for the New Year. Flaubert's letter was the longer one. He responded to Sand's doubts about the wisdom of his cloistered life, saying he could not accommodate both the Muse and Woman: "One has to choose. My choice was made long ago. There remains the question of the senses. Mine have always been my servants. Even in the days of my greenest youth I did with them exactly as I pleased. I am now almost fifty, and their ardor is the least of my worries. This regimen is not very merry, I agree. There are moments of emptiness, of hideous boredom. But these grow rarer as one grows older. To be truthful, *living* strikes me as a trade I wasn't cut out for! And yet!"

Flaubert's senses as his servants would bear commentary. It's true that he avoided any lasting commitments to women. His major relationship, with Louise Colet (to which we owe his exceptional letters during the composition of *Madame Bovary*), always left her demanding more, and despite his declarations of passion he was always postponing their meetings. Later on, he arranged erotic rendezvous of one sort or another, especially when in Paris, to make up for his monastic life; he also seems to have masturbated frequently while working at his books. But his comment on the difficulty of living might need even more reflection: if he wasn't cut out for living, then how could he create novelistic life? That's in fact an engaging problem that his correspondence with Sand will explore further.

Flaubert succeeded in finishing his novel by early May 1869. But 1869 turned out to be a year of grief. It brought the death of Louis Bouilhet, his oldest friend, in July, and then that of Sainte-Beuve in October. The heart and soul of Princess Mathilde's circle, Sainte-Beuve had recently had a falling-out with her: when *Le Moniteur Universel*, the newspaper that conveyed governmental views, wanted to censor an article that contained an unfavorable reference to the bishop of Montpellier, the critic had taken his pen to the opposition paper, *Le Temps*, infuriating Mathilde, who had obtained for him a seat as senator, with an annual stipend of 30,000 francs. That, according to Mathilde, should have bought his services outright. Flaubert tried to serve as mediator, but he found both parties to blame. He was especially shocked when Sainte-Beuve, to protest his good faith, expressed praise for Napoleon III. That, despite Flaubert's acceptance at the imperial court, was too much. He never wavered in holding a view of Napoleon III similar to Karl Marx's.

Flaubert had benefited from a favorable review of *Madame Bovary* by this major tastemaker of the Second Empire, but he did not really approve of Sainte-Beuve's kind of literary criticism, which focused on the personalities and biographies of authors. He thought Saint-Beuve neglected pure criticism—neglected "the *unconscious* poetics"—"la poétique *insciente*"— that brought a work of art into being, its composition, its style, its author's point of view. While Sand believed that literary criticism was reaching its dead end, Flaubert believed it was just beginning. He felt as he grew older that he'd like to be a literary critic himself, to teach a true discrimination of excellence, a view of art from the point of view of the artist. Yet Sainte-Beuve, who had reigned as "official" literary critic for half a century, was nonetheless a man of great erudition with a complete devotion to literature. "Another gone," Flaubert wrote to Maxime Du Camp. "The little band diminishes! One by one the rare castaways of the raft of the *Méduse* disappear. With whom can one talk of literature now? He loved it. And although he wasn't precisely a friend, his death grieves me profoundly."

On May 6, after a final marathon of writing that lasted from 8 a.m. Saturday until 5 a.m. Sunday, Flaubert announced that *Sentimental Education* was finished. But Bouilhet had been supposed to serve as the first reader of the manuscript, the one who would offer helpful suggestions for final edits, the man who had always been Flaubert's spiritual coauthor, and he was no more. Flaubert accepted Maxime Du Camp's offer to take Bouilhet's place—he was especially concerned that his book be punctiliously correct on points of grammar and usage. Flaubert's relation to the French language is idiosyncratic; it has been suggested that he suffered from early dyslexia, which may or may not be true, but one does sense something labored and strenuous in his writing, a conquest of the beauty for which it is reputed. Du Camp had 251 stylistic, grammatical, and syntactical comments. Flaubert accepted about two-thirds of them, rejecting the others because he claimed to find authoritative examples in the Littré dictionary. In any event, Du Camp claimed in his *Souvenirs littéraires* (*Literary Recollections*), Flaubert always insisted on a freedom to reject the dictates of the grammarians, who, he said, did not know how to write. All the greatest writers allowed themselves to break the rules in a good cause.

In the run-up to publication of the novel, Flaubert read three hundred pages of it to George Sand when she was in Paris (for the production of her play *L'Autre* [The other]), and then, over five afternoons, in sessions of four hours each, apparently the whole of the novel to Princess Mathilde. That scene is hard to imagine, given the slow unfolding of the novel, and its willed avoidance of anything approaching theatrical drama. And, especially, its very grim portrayal of Louis-Napoléon's coup d'état on December 2, 1851: a moment recorded in the novel as a scene of terror, betrayal, and horror. If he read the novel without cuts to Mathilde—and one cannot imagine him doing otherwise, since any omission always seemed to him the complete disfiguration of a work of art—we can only assume that she loved him enough to let the politics of the novel pass without comment.

Sentimental Education was published on November 17, 1869, the same day, Flaubert remarked, as the opening of the Suez Canal. It might be worth recalling that the inauguration of the Suez Canal was followed a year and a half later by its companion in magnificence, the Cairo Opera House, and that the opera commissioned for the occasion was Giuseppe Verdi's *Aida*. *Aida*'s imperial grandeur represents the taste of Napoleon III's Second Empire far better than the deflationary narrative of *Sentimental Education*. The opera house that Napoleon III was building—the so-called Palais Garnier, from its architect, Charles Garnier—was under way but unfinished at the time the Second Empire collapsed in war and insurrection. It reflects much of the same taste for opulence—though without Verdi's message of liberation for the oppressed.

After publication came the reviews. They were generally baffled or savage, or both. Flaubert in a letter to Sand on December 3 gave a rundown of the results. He had been absolutely panned by the late-Romantic and flamboyant Catholic critic and novelist Jules-Amédée Barbey d'Aurevilly in *Le Constitutionnel* ("Since he has absolutely no ideas on anything and since he is only able to describe, his technique, to get up two volumes totaling a thousand pages like these, is very simple. He tacks and attaches pictures to other pictures.") and the veteran critic Francisque Sarcey in *Le Gaulois* ("It's not boredom that one experiences in reading M. Flaubert's new novel; it's some sort of withering of the soul, which goes so far as nausea; the hero of it isn't hateful; he is repugnant."). He was also panned in *Le Figaro* and *Paris*. Everyone found the ending of the novel, where Frédéric and his friend Deslauriers recall a youthful visit to a brothel, cynical: Sarcey went so far as to make a comparison to the Marquis de Sade. Flaubert in his letter to Sand reported also that the bourgeois of Rouen were furious because of his grim portrayal of the treatment of the imprisoned insurrectionists of June 1848: "They think that 'you shouldn't be allowed to publish things like that' (literal quotation), that I am joining the reds, that I am guilty of reigniting revolutionary passions, etc. etc.!" It is interesting to see Flaubert, on the threshold of the Terrible Year, accused of left-wing sympathies; in some manner, it seems prophetic.

Flaubert did find three favorable reviews, in *Le Pays*, *L'Opinion Nationale*, and *La Tribune*. This last was by a young journalist and novelist just beginning to make a name for himself (Flaubert hadn't yet met him), Emile Zola. Zola's praise for the novel was intense—one senses that it held lessons for him as he embarked upon his multivolume "Natural and Social History" of a family under the Second Empire, the *Rougon-Macquart*. "I don't care in the least," Flaubert declared of the negative reviews, "but it does surprise me that there is so much hatred and dishonesty." And he closed his letter: "None of this destroys my composure. But I keep asking myself: Why publish?" Despite his disdain for public opinion, newspapers, and the popular critics of his time, he was hurting. Sand sensed this right away, and offered to speak out. Flaubert responded that if she cared to take on that role, she would oblige him. By two in the morning on December 9, she was able to write to Flaubert: "Mon camarade, it's done." She asked his advice on where to submit it. He replied by telegram, and she sent it to Emile de Girardin, editor of *La Liberté*, where it appeared on December 22, the day before Flaubert arrived at Nohant for Christmas. In the meantime, he could not find the words to thank her enough. He wrote, "What a good woman you are, and what a fine man!"

Sand's review made an effort to lead readers to see Flaubert's impassive portrait of his age, his refusal to enter an explicit authorial judgment, as providing a critical mirror. What does the novel prove? she rhetorically asks its author. "Don't say anything. I know it, I see it. It has proved that this social condition has reached the point of disintegration [*décomposition*] and that it must be changed very radically. It proves it so well that no one would believe you if you said the contrary!" It's not certain that Flaubert intended the reading of his novel to be focused so exclusively through politics: the disintegration of life may have yet deeper causes in human nature than Sand's analysis implies. But Sand surely was right about the fundamental political engagement of the novel, not only from her perspective but from ours: the experience of Frédéric's generation proved, among many other things, the need to change the world.

At the same time that she offered her public defense of *Sentimental Education*, Sand wrote to Flaubert that he should not be surprised by the reception given to the novel. "You seem astonished by the ill will. You are too naïve. You don't know how original your book is, and how much it must rub people the wrong way by its force. You think you are writing things that will pass through like a letter in the mail, sure!" And Sand was certainly right that in *Sentimental Education*, far more than in *Madame Bovary*, Flaubert had created an enigma of a novel, one so radically new—so implicitly critical of the novelistic tradition—that it would take generations for readers to come round to it, and to understand it. And that people would not necessarily ever love it in the manner that *Madame Bovary* is loved. It remains a book that challenges more than it pleases.

Around their collaboration in the launch and defense of the novel, a plan formed between Sand and Flaubert: that he would come down to Nohant for Christmas, along with her good friend Edmond Plauchut, journalist, republican, and devoted admirer. They left Paris on the 9 a.m. train on December 23 and were at Sand's house by 6:30 in the afternoon.

After dinner, Flaubert told stories—he was, by many accounts, a great raconteur whose oral tales unfolded without the agony of his writing. They stayed up talking until one in the morning. On December 24, it snowed and rained all day. Sand descended for lunch at 11 o'clock (she wrote every morning). Flaubert gave presents to the little girls, Sand's granddaughters, who were enchanted with them. After dinner, there were marionettes, a tombola (like bingo), and the trimming of the Christmas tree. The children went to bed at nine, and the adults prepared for a midnight supper. "Flaubert enjoys himself like a child," Sand wrote in her diary. "Splendid Christmas Eve. I go upstairs at 3 o'clock." On Christmas Day, after lunch, Flaubert read aloud the *féerie* he had long been working on, *Le Château des coeurs* (*The Castle of Hearts*)—a *féerie* being something like a pantomime with music, spectacular effects, and supernatural happenings. It took over three hours. "Delightful, but not destined for success," Sand judged in her diary. Flaubert kept them all laughing until late at night with his tales and mimicry.

The next day was cold and sunny, and Flaubert joined the others for a walk to the farm. In the afternoon, Sand's son Maurice and one of her great-nephews (there were many children around in Nohant) staged a marionette show. "Flaubert splits his sides laughing," Sand wrote. They went to bed at two in the morning. Then, on the afternoon of December 27—a day of steady snow—after Lolo (Sand's adored granddaughter Aurore) danced all her dances, "Flaubert puts on woman's clothes and dances the cachucha with Plauchut. It's grotesque, we all laugh like lunatics." On Tuesday morning he was off. He wrote on Thursday to say that the trip back had gone well despite the intense cold. The worst of it was in Paris, riding through messy streets in an unheated cab. He spoke of how touched he was by the hospitality of Nohant. "What fine and loveable people you all are."

Flaubert wrote again on the morning of January 3, 1870, to wish Sand a good new year. He thanked her again for the Christmas cheer she had brought him. "Those were the best moments of the year 1869, which was not gentle to me!" They both hoped for a better year in 1870. That decidedly was not to be.

chapter two

The Terrible Year

WITH THE COMING OF THE NEW YEAR, FLAUBERT WROTE HIS note of warm thanks to George Sand for the Christmas visit to Nohant, expressing the hope that 1870 would be far better than an 1869 saddened by deaths of friends and the incomprehension that greeted *Sentimental Education*. But now public affairs, history itself, was going to dictate otherwise. In July 1870, France went to war with Prussia. If the origins of many wars seem trivial, those of the Franco-Prussian War were ridiculous, artificial, trumped up for the occasion. Emperor Napoleon III wanted to prevent Leopold, a prince from the Hohenzollern family who was related to the king of Prussia, from succeeding to the vacant Spanish throne, sensing that France would in that eventuality be surrounded by Germans. The Germans retreated on Leopold, but France pressed for guarantees that there would be no further attempts to occupy the Spanish throne. The German chancellor, Otto von Bismarck, though, in fact wanted war with France as a needed part of his plan for the unification and consolidation of Germany, and manipulated public opinion—in part through a doctored telegram that made it seem as if the king of Prussia had insulted the French ambassador. A reluctant Emperor Napoleon III was pushed into war by his commanding spouse, the Empress Eugénie, who saw war as a counter to the rising force of liberal opposition to his autocratic rule, a chauvinistic National Assembly, and a bellicose populace. And there was an unfounded confidence in the French Army and its new breech-loading, bolt-action *chassepot* rifle. The French declared war on July 19. In fact, their armies were unprepared, their railways inadequate for moving vast numbers of troops, and their generals incompetent. The campaign ended swiftly, with French armies surrounded in the east of France, the emperor himself made prisoner, and the Prussian armies advancing with little interference right to the gates of Paris. The Empire fell, and the Third French Republic was proclaimed on September 4.

Then began the protracted agony: the siege of Paris by the Prussians, resulting in famine and misery during the cold, hard winter of 1870–1871. Those who couldn't escape from Paris suffered, the poor far more than the rich. Long lines formed at the bakers and the grocers and the butchers. Soon, for most of the population, all that could be found was ersatz bread, made from straw, rice, and other unidentified ingredients, and at the butcher shops, horses, cats, dogs, and then, finally, rats. Of some 100,000 horses in Paris at the start of the siege, only a third remained at the end. An estimated 25,000 cats were eaten, and *salami de rat* was standard fare. The wealthy dined for a time off the animals from the zoo in the Jardin des Plantes: one by one, antelope, camel, and then, finally, Castor and Pollux, the elephants dear to the heart of Parisians, were shot. The Bois de Boulogne was shorn of its trees for fuel and stakes to repel invasion. The City of Light went black at night for want of gas for the streetlamps. Death from disease and malnutrition was on the rise. Then, in January, the Prussians, frustrated by French resistance, did what most thought was unthinkable: they began bombarding Paris from their positions encircling the city. The whistling of shells became part of everyday reality. The western part of the city suffered large zones of destruction. Finally came armistice on terms humiliating to France, including a parade of Prussians down the Champs-

Elysées, the loss of the eastern provinces of Alsace and Lorraine, and the payment of an indemnity of 5 billion francs. Food returned to Paris. But there followed the revolt of Paris, which proclaimed itself an independent Commune that would refuse the terms of the armistice and fight on. The official government fled to Versailles. Then came a new siege of Paris by French troops, bombardment anew, and finally, invasion of the city by the French Army (many of them liberated from Prussian prisoner-of-war camps for the purpose), and the bloodiest civil war France has ever known.

By the end of *la semaine sanglante*, the Bloody Week, on May 28, 1871, some 20,000 Parisians had been gunned down, many in summary executions, and thousands of others marched off to Versailles for trial—resulting in execution or deportation to New Caledonia. Central Paris was a scorched ruin, many of its buildings—especially governmental headquarters such as the Hôtel de Ville and the Treasury, and the royal and imperial palace of the Tuileries—torched by the retreating Communards or destroyed in cannonades. The Cartoucherie Rapp, where munitions were stored, went up in a gigantic fireworks display. The Grenier d'Abondance, where grain was stored against famine, and also petrol, burned with a heat like the sun. Photography, then about half a century old, was put to immediate use recording the impressive devastation. Illustrated guidebooks to the ruins were rushed into print and circulated throughout the country. Flaubert, who spent the war mainly in Rouen, visited Paris immediately after the fall of the Commune, in the first days of June. He went to the library for research, but he also toured the ruins with his friend Maxime Du Camp. That's when he told Du Camp that if only his compatriots had read and understood his novel of a few months earlier, *Sentimental Education*, "none of this would have happened"—a reaction that will bear thinking about.

Let us pick up Flaubert's story where we left it, early in the year 1870, in the months following his visit to George Sand in Nohant, before the coming of war and disaster. Following the failure of *Sentimental Education*, Flaubert had promptly begun work on another book, or rather, on another version of a book he'd been composing for decades, on the temptation of St. Anthony. He mainly stayed in his apartment near the Parc Monceau and worked in Paris libraries during those winter months, reading esoteric works on obscure religious heresies, the history of Christian dogma, Plotinus, a Coptic manuscript, and other erudite stuff that many a reader would find weighed down rather than enlivened *The Temptation of Saint Anthony*. George Sand was in Paris also, to supervise rehearsals of her play *L'Autre*—Flaubert missed the premiere because he was at the deathbed of an old friend, Jules Duplan. This, too, was a cold winter, a rehearsal for the next year's glacial winter of the siege, and both Flaubert and Sand suffered through bouts of the flu. She returned to Nohant, inviting Flaubert to join her—but he replied that he didn't need the countryside so much as he needed to work.

Back he went to the Bibliothèque Impériale (better known by its later name, the Bibliothèque Nationale). He took it upon himself, though, to straighten out a misunderstanding between the Empress Eugénie and Sand: the Empress thought she had been satirized as an adventuress in one of Sand's short stories, and Flaubert, as a valued friend of the Princess Mathilde, was able to make peace. Flaubert, as I've noted, like Sand, had no use for the Second Empire, which he thought was ruled by unscrupulous entrepreneurs and political pirates, but he was something of a celebrity and moved with ease in social circles when he chose to do so. In May, he was back in Croisset with his aged mother, where life was comfortable, he could bathe in the Seine, and his study was a place of refuge—or artistic martyrdom. Sand had visited Flaubert, his mother, and his niece Caroline—who came close to being a daughter for Flaubert—late in August 1866, and she noted the beauty and ease of the Flaubert homestead and its gardens: his "citadel," she called it.

"Your old Troubadour," Flaubert most often signed letters to the friend he regularly addressed as "*Chère Maître*," the salutation of a disciple to a master, put into the feminine gender. Sand, now aged sixty-six, was some seventeen years Flaubert's senior, and he used *vous* to her while she addressed him with the intimate *tu*. His letters in the spring of 1870 were largely a litany of gloom—another death, that of his friend Jules de Goncourt, who had fallen into imbecility from the final stages of syphilis, in June, survived by his brother and collaborator, Edmond; outrage at his publisher Michel Lévy's condescension (with the requisite anti-Semitic remarks); continued mourning for Bouilhet, which he invested into writing a preface to his works. Sand, on her side, was saddened by the death of Armand Barbès, the noble romantic revolutionary who had finished his life in exile at The Hague. "Let us love one another till the end," she told Flaubert in a letter on June 27, where she noted how death was winnowing the circle of their friends. Flaubert replied by lamenting the parade of deaths in the past year, affirming that it was now only Sand and their mutual friend Ivan Turgenev to whom he could open his heart.

Then came war, on July 19. In his first recorded reaction, Flaubert wrote, in a letter to Sand on July 22:

> I am nauseated, *distressed* by the stupidity of my compatriots. The irredeemable barbarity of Humanity fills me with a black sadness. This enthusiasm that has no idea behind it makes me want to croak so I don't have to witness it.
>
> The good Frenchman wants to fight 1. because he is jealous of Prussia, 2. because the natural state of man is savagery, 3. because war contains in itself a mystical element that sweeps the crowd off its feet.
>
> Have we gone back to wars between races? I fear so. The frightful butchery that is in preparation doesn't even have a pretext.—It's the wish to fight, just in order to fight.
>
> I weep over bridges destroyed, tunnels collapsed, all this human labor lost, in sum so radical a *negation*. . . .
>
> Hobbes was right: *Homo homini lupus!*

War was to him the utter negation of civilization, of everything he lived for. At the outbreak of this first in a series of more and more murderous and insane contests of French and Germans, he was among the more prescient about the consequences. Sand agreed with him: "I find this war infamous. . . . Men are vain and ferocious beasts," she wrote back on July 26. Crops in the Berry were dying from extreme heat, but everyone liked the war. Flaubert in reply on August 3 expressed his dark pessimism about humanity: "Boast about Progress, enlightenment and the good sense of the masses, and the gentleness of the French people. I can assure you that here one would be beaten to death for preaching Peace."

For Sand, mother and grandmother as well as liberated woman, novelist, and public conscience, the human cost of war became the theme of her letters, as of her private journal, in August, as news of French defeats began to reach the provinces. "We see only poor peasants weeping over their sons leaving for the army." (The affluent could buy a substitute for military service.) "Will this horrible experience finally prove to the world that war should be abolished or else civilization will perish?" And, a week later: "This human butchery shreds my poor heart to pieces." Yet, more optimistic than Flaubert, she hoped that principles for future government would emerge from the crisis. Flaubert meanwhile made a quick trip to Paris (concerning the publication of Bouilhet's posthumous work), where he found his fellow men stupid, cowardly, and ignorant, perhaps meriting the punishment meted out to them (but the punishment so far was little indeed compared to what was to come). At loose ends back in Croisset, he volunteered as a medical assistant at the Hôtel-Dieu, the Rouen hospital headed by his brother, Achille. And he told Sand, on August 17, that he had his rifle ready—if Paris came under siege, he would go fight.

Meanwhile, relatives from Nogent, in the Champagne region, had fled the combat zone to take refuge with him (they were fourteen under the roof at Croisset). Four hundred wounded were shipped to Rouen from the theater of war. The destitute multiplied. Flaubert became patriotic and bellicose—and, like so many of his compatriots, self-deceptive. He wanted to believe that the war was not yet lost, that other divisions of the French Army would arrive to drive out the Prussians, who were beginning to approach Rouen. He began fulminating. The war, he claimed, was only act one. Afterward, France would enter "la Sociale"—that is, socialism—which in its turn would be followed by a long and vigorous reaction. He was on target with this prediction. Then he went on to complain: "That's what Universal Suffrage has led us to, that new God which I find as stupid as the old!" Napoleon III had initially ascended to power as the first French president elected by universal (male) suffrage during the short-lived Second Republic, following the Revolution of 1848—then brought off his coup d'état that ended the republic. So Flaubert's rant was not entirely unjustified: it seemed that popular democracy, as a long tradition of political thought maintained, eventually led to tyranny.

Sand's studied reply to Flaubert's tirade became so long and detailed that she decided to publish it as an open letter, a "letter to a friend," in the newspaper *Le Temps* on September 5. By that time, with the emperor the captive of the Prussians, the Assembly on September 4 had declared the Second Empire dead and proclaimed a new republic. To this new republic, Sand, an active partisan of the socially enlightened republic of 1848, responded with a paean of hope:

> Greetings to you, Republic! You are in good hands, and a great people will march under your banner following a bloody expiation. The task is hard: but if you were to fall, you will always rise again!
>
> The rights of man are imperishable!

This is a Sandean voice that Flaubert could never accept, though that never altered their fast friendship. In retrospect, Sand's optimism and enthusiasm sound both pathetic and true. The republic was hardly in good hands, and the "great people" would behave in ways of extreme barbarism at crucial moments. The republic would be sorely tested, and almost succumb, in civil strife and the attempt to restore monarchy. Yet in the long run it would survive, as the regime that, in the famous words of Adolphe Thiers, who became head of the provisional government and eventually signed an armistice with the Prussians, "divides us least." That was something of a comedown from Sand's rhetoric, but she was right that the republic alone could move France out of its murderous political and social divisions.

Flaubert was not convinced. "You distress me, with your enthusiasm for the Republic!" he responded on September 10. He continued: "Note that I defend this poor Republic. But I don't believe in it." He found that the present state of affairs came from a refusal to *"see the truth,"* from "the love of fakery and jokery"—ideas that will be repeated many times over the next months, and are indeed at the heart of Flaubert's beliefs: the cant and blindness of his fellows are means of keeping truth at bay, and truth, exposure of the underside of human illusions, is the only prophylactic that can help. His prophecies became a bit wild: "We will become a Poland, then a Spain. Then it will be the turn of Prussia, which will be swallowed by Russia." He described himself as destroyed.

But with despair came what Flaubert himself felt as an unexpected upsurge of patriotism. He joined the National Guard, and since he came from a notable family in Rouen, was elected lieutenant. He began drilling his squadron, began, too, taking a course in military strategy. There exists a drawing of the uniformed Flaubert: the image is wonderfully incongruous. Yet large numbers of middle-class men were joining the Guard—which, in a radicalized Paris, would eventually play an enormous role in the Commune—and Flaubert, as the somewhat dropout member of a distinguished family, was always much aware of civic responsibility. And also, despite his gloomy prophecies about the war and its outcomes, his sentiments were becoming more and more patriotic, chauvinistic, and even militaristic. He even bought a revolver. The tough Prussian terms for an armistice were pushing his compatriots to fight to the death. He wrote to his niece Caroline Commanville (her husband had sent her to England for safety) on September 27:

> Today I begin night patrols.—I just gave "my men" a paternal speech, in which I announced that I would thrust my sword in the breadbasket of the first who retreated, while asking them in turn to shoot me if they saw me turn tail and run. Your old windbag of an uncle rose to an epic tone!
>
> What a droll thing our brains, and especially mine! Would you believe that now I feel practically gay! I've begun working again, and regained my appetite!

And to Sand the next day he declared that he felt himself a "Savage." Alluding to a legend that there might be American Indian blood in his mother's side of the family—two members had settled in Newfoundland in 1696—he claimed: "The blood of my ancestors the Natchez or the Hurons boils in my literary man's veins, and seriously, stupidly, animally *I want to fight."* He was in fact somewhat puzzled at his own ferocity, since he sensed that whatever the outcome of the conflict, a new world would emerge that would hold no place for him. He added in a PS: "Here we have *all* decided to march on Paris if Hegel's compatriots lay siege to it." He advised Sand to rouse her Berrichons. The identification of Prussians with Hegel touches on a source of his stupefaction and anger at the war: Prussia, to him, as to many of his contemporaries, represented culture both philosophical and literary, largely German Idealism and Goethe.

A letter to his close friend Maxime Du Camp the next day was full of hope and assurance about the French armies, and he mentioned that he had bought himself a soldier's knapsack. But his militaristic fanfaronades don't quite pass the test of his critical thinking. He went on, to Du Camp: "What saddens me is the immense stupidity that will fall upon us, afterwards! All kindness, as Montaigne would have said, is lost for a long duration. Children will be raised in hatred of the Prussian. Militarism and the most abject positivism, that's our lot from now on." He echoed the views of his politically reactionary interlocutor on an issue they could agree upon, the falsity of the Second Empire: "You are right! We are paying for the long lie that we have been living in, for everything was fake: fake army, fake politics, fake literature, fake credit and even fake whores.—Telling the truth, that was being immoral!" (Shades of the trial of *Madame Bovary* for immorality.) And then to Caroline on October 5: "Whatever happens, the world to which I belonged has run its course. The Latins are finished! Now it's the turn of the Saxons, who will be devoured by the Slavs. And so on. Within five or six years, we'll have the consolation of seeing Europe in flames. It will be at our knees, pleading with us to unite against Prussia." Another crazy, but in its way accurate, prophecy.

For many weeks, Flaubert, like most of his compatriots, swung between hope and despair. Marshal Achille Bazaine was still in the field with a large corps, but by October 27 he had surrendered, with 140,000 troops, at Metz—in the view of many because he held no loyalty to the fledgling republic, and indeed carried on his own negotiations with Prussia. Then, an Army of the Loire had been constituted, and it seemed to promise a new surge against the Prussians. But there was never any news of its engaging the enemy. And in fact, after Bazaine's surrender, the Prussian divisions that had been tied up besieging Metz in eastern France raced toward the Loire to neutralize that threat. Even with frustrating delays in the transmission of accurate news from the front, the extent of the debacle of the French armies was becoming clear. The Prussians meanwhile had encircled Paris, neutralizing many of the forts built to defend the city, and on September 19 began the siege that would last into January.

"There's never been, in the history of France, anything grander or more tragic.—The siege of Paris! That word alone makes one dizzy, and it will furnish the dreams of future generations," Flaubert wrote to Caroline on October 13. Paris was cut off from the rest of France: pigeon post and hot air balloons became the principal means of communication over the German lines. The Germans in turn soon had anti-balloon artillery in place, and started importing falcons to bring down the pigeons. Léon Gambetta, the energetic minister of the interior, made a daring escape from the city by balloon on October 7 to try to rally the government and rebuild an army, first at Tours, in the Loire Valley, and then further southwest, in Bordeaux.

And now the Prussians were reported to be only twelve leagues from Rouen. "And we are without orders, no command, no discipline. Nothing, nothing," Flaubert wrote to Sand on October 11. "I have as distraction patrols and exercises of the National Guard." Sand, in reply three days later from the town of La Châtre—she and her family had left Nohant because of an outbreak of contagious disease there—stood firm in her refusal to despair: "Let's not despair of France, she is undergoing an expiation of her insanity, she will be reborn, whatever happens." "Expiation," because the Second Empire of Napoleon III was seen as a time of excess, corruption, and immorality—by Sand on the Left of the political spectrum, but even more strongly by the political Right, for whom expiation would take on the mantle of religious orthodoxy. France was in a crisis of political ideology as well as political event. Flaubert never accepted the expiatory consolation: misfortune doesn't purify; on the contrary, it makes people "egotistical, and nasty, and stupid," he told Caroline in December. "The present is abominable. And the future savage," he said in a letter of October 17 to Ernest Feydeau.

By October 23, Flaubert, along with his second lieutenant and his captain, had resigned his command in the National Guard. His intention was to force the mayor of Rouen to form a disciplinary council—since "we have no authority over our pitiful militia!" as he told Caroline on the 24th. The move did not produce the desired result, however. Rouen, full of the destitute who had been dislocated by the war, continued to wait without any real defense the arrival of the Prussians—who might number 20,000 or 80,000: reports varied. To Sand, a month later, Flaubert announced that he and his fellow Rouennais were still awaiting the arrival of the Prussians any day. He described himself as the saddest man in France, destroyed by: "1. The ferocity of men; 2. The conviction that we are going to enter a stupid era. We will be utilitarian, militarist, American, and Catholic. Very Catholic! You'll see! The Prussian war marks the end of the French Revolution, and destroys it." He saw the combat as one between north and south, Huns against Latins. "The Latin race is in its death throes. France will follow Spain and Italy. And *loutishness* begins." Flaubert's nearly untranslatable word here is *pignouflisme*, one he may have invented, from *pignouf*, apparently derived from the archaic verb *pigner*, to groan and complain, meaning essentially a rude, rustic, ill-mannered and stupid being. The reign of *pignouflisme*—alternatively, *muflisme*, an era of selfish brutishness—is a theme that would now recur obsessively as Flaubert looked to the future. By March, he was giving a succinct version of history: "*Paganisme, christianisme, muflisme.*" Characteristically, Flaubert zeroed in on language: language that masked reality, that needed deflation (including, implicitly, that of his correspondent). "The conventional phrases aren't lacking: 'France will rise again! We mustn't despair, it's a salutary punishment, we were really too immoral! Etc.' Oh the everlasting snark! No! one doesn't recover from such a blow!"

The last source of hope for a military rebound was the Army of the Loire, recruited from the provinces of France not under Prussian occupation. That came to bitter disappointment in the Battle of Loigny, in the Loire Valley, on December 2. In addition to the republican army, here descendants of the legendary anti-republican heroes from the Vendée, in the west of France—which had resisted the revolutionary government during the great Revolution—threw themselves into battle against the Prussians, some of them in uniforms of the Papal Zouaves. (They had gone to defend the pope, unsuccessfully, during the campaigns to unify Italy and secularize the old Papal States.) These forces unfurled, in a final gallant and misguided charge against the enemy, the banner of the Sacred Heart of Jesus, with the battle cry "Sacré Coeur de Jésus, sauvez la France." It didn't work. But the cult of the Sacred Heart would be back, as the expiatory emblem of the extreme Right following French defeat, and the martyrs of the Battle of Loigny would end up in gold mosaics over the altar of the Basilica of the Sacred Heart.

The Prussians had arrived, and the reality of occupation now fell upon Flaubert, who was forced to move from Croisset into Rouen with his seventy-seven-year-old mother in December to occupy the Commanvilles' apartment. The family house in Croisset became a billet for Prussian officers and their staff, forty of them eventually. He had buried the manuscript of *Saint Anthony* that he had been working on and locked his study—but the Prussian officers frequently demanded the key from Emile, the servant he had left in charge: his books were scattered throughout the bedrooms. (The Prussian officers amid Flaubert's library would deserve a short story, maybe by Anton Chekhov.) By the dawning of the new year, 1871, defeat had become part of daily reality. "*I had no idea* of what invasion was like," Flaubert wrote to Caroline on January 23. Furthermore, the winter was turning out to be bitterly cold. Ice in the Seine. Snow. With his mother failing, Flaubert took charge of doing accounts with the cook while listening to Prussian officers' sabers scraping on the frozen ground outside. "I live in sadness and abjection!" he wrote to Caroline on the 28th.

Things were of course worse in Paris: under siege since September, then subject to Prussian bombardment from the surrounding forts beginning on January 6, Parisians were running out of even the disgusting rations that had sustained them for the past weeks. The city was being denuded of its trees, which were needed for firewood during this freezing weather. The command of General Louis-Jules Trochu, governor of Paris, was feckless; the rare attempts he made to break the siege ended in disaster. He and others in the provisional government feared an insurgency of Paris radicals—there were some attempted uprisings—and seemed intent on proving that surrender to the Prussians was the only solution. The capitulation of Paris, when it finally came on January 28, seemed as inevitable as it was humiliating. The Prussians turned the screw of humiliation by demanding a triumphal parade down the Champs-Elysées, which would take place on March 1, as Parisians closed themselves indoors behind shuttered windows. Flaubert wrote to Princess Mathilde on March 4 that he could see in his mind's eye their bayonets flashing in the sunlight, and hear their "odious music" resonating under the Arc de Triomphe. Meanwhile, on January 18, King Wilhelm of Prussia had himself proclaimed German emperor in the Galerie des Glaces of the Palace of Versailles, from which the French kings once commanded the respect of all Europe.

Capitulation plunged Flaubert into "an indescribable state," as he told Caroline on February 1. "It's enough to hang oneself from rage!" he continued. "France is so low, so dishonored, so disgraced that I'd like to see her disappear completely. But I hope that civil war will kill off many for us. May I be among them! As preparation, we're going to vote for deputies. What a bitter irony! Of course I will abstain from voting. I no longer wear my cross of honor [the Legion of Honor].—For the word honor is no longer French.—And I consider myself so much no longer French that I will ask Turgenev (as soon as I am able to write to him) what's needed to become Russian." This was a manic and depressive reaction to defeat, to be sure, from someone who had always considered himself above politics, and contemptuous of his compatriots. At the same time that he stated his extreme reactions to national defeat, he studied the very emotions he was feeling: "Oh! What hatred! What hatred! It suffocates me! I who was born so tender, I have bile rising to my throat."

And to Sand on March 11, he asked why he should be so full of despair—more so than at all the other moments of loss in his life:

I never thought of myself as progressive or humanitarian, though. It doesn't matter, I had illusions! What barbarity! What a fall back! I am angry with my contemporaries for having given me the feelings of a brute from the 12th century! Bile *is stifling me*! These officers who

break mirrors in white gloves, who know Sanskrit and grab the champagne, who steal your watch and later send you their calling card, this
war for money, these civilized savages appall me more than Cannibals.
And everyone is going to imitate them, will become soldiers! Russia now
has four million of them. All Europe will wear a uniform. If we take
our revenge, it will be ultra-ferocious. And note that we're not going to
think about anything else but taking revenge on Germany! Whatever
our government, it won't be able to survive except by speculating on that
passion. Murder on the grand scale will be the goal of all our efforts, the
ideal of France!

A fair estimate of the decades to come, a twentieth century marked by
murderous revenge and counter-revenge between France and Germany.

Flaubert for a few weeks in February and March managed to escape
Rouen, heading north to Neuville, near Dieppe, to meet with Caroline and
her husband. Then he traveled to Brussels with Alexandre Dumas (fils) to
visit Princess Mathilde. After that, he went briefly to London, for one of
his amorous trysts with Juliet Herbert, the English governess who was his
lover during the rare time off that her position allowed her. When he did
get back home to Croisset, on April 1, he found the Prussian officers had
caused less damage than he feared—they had respected the study in which
Madame Bovary and *Sentimental Education* were composed—though he
objected to finding his books strewn about in various rooms. And the prudent bourgeois in Flaubert was appalled at the amount of firewood they
had burned—three or four hundred francs worth! He dug up the notes for
Saint Anthony that he had buried before departing.

In response to Flaubert's expressions of despair, Sand replied on March
17 with an affirmation of her belief in liberty as the only solution: only "liberty full and entire could save us from these disasters, and put us back in
the path of possible progress." Her letter was written on the eve of a fateful
date. In Paris, the political situation was swiftly polarizing. The National
Assembly in Bordeaux, now headed by veteran politician Adolphe Thiers,
made peace with the Prussians and voted to reassemble at Versailles late in
March, signaling by its choice of the former seat of monarchy an aversion

to and a fear of Paris. Paris had never accepted the onerous terms of the peace treaty, which included loss of Alsace and much of Lorraine and war reparations of 5 billion francs. The city began to come under the sway of its radicals, including the National Guard, which had become a political force, proposing to replace the French government with a confederation of municipalities. The "Fédérés," as the Guard was called, would play a large role as events unfolded. The National Assembly, elected following the armistice and heavily composed of rural conservatives who wished to restore a monarchy in France, voted on March 10 to end three wartime measures that had helped to alleviate the stressful conditions of Paris under siege, one suspending rents for housing, another payments due on promissory notes, and a third preventing the sale of items left at pawnshops, which functioned as a species of savings and loan offices for the Parisian poor. (The *London Times* claimed there were 1,500 pairs of scissors left in pawnshops by impoverished seamstresses.) These moves of a conservative bourgeoisie, for which rents and contracts were sacred, inevitably proved inflammatory in a city emerging from its most terrible winter. The spark of insurrection came when Thiers, returning from Bordeaux, decided not to treat with the radicals of the "Central Committee" elected by the National Guard, but instead sought to disarm the Guard. He ordered the cannon park atop Montmartre removed. There stood some 171 cannon, which the National Guard had placed on the heights of that highest point in Paris to defend the city. Many of the cannon had been bought by public subscription. They were sacred objects.

Before dawn on March 18, troops moved quietly up Montmartre to seize the cannon. There was a delay in removing them: horses and limbers, the gun carriages needed to drag the cannon, hadn't yet arrived. An early morning crowd began to gather, at first predominantly women who were out to buy the daily bread. They made an attempt to protect the cannon. The crowd grew denser, the troops were hemmed in. General Claude Lecomte, in command, ordered his troops to fire on the crowd—and they would not. He tried to order them again, and again, and again—only to have the crowd overwhelm and disarm the troops—many of whom turned their rifles butt in air and passed to the other side. Lecomte was

captured and later summarily executed, along with retired general Clément Thomas, who was well known for his role in putting down the 1848
workers' revolt. The mayor of Montmartre, Georges Clemenceau, who had
counseled Thiers against the operation, noted that it was a scene of blood-
lust. Thiers and other officials fled the city to Versailles, withdrew remaining loyalist troops from Paris, occupied the forts to the south and west
of the city, and made plans to subdue it from the outside. Paris was anew
under siege, this time by Frenchmen. By March 28, Paris had organized
itself as the Commune, raising the red flag over the Hôtel de Ville. Civil
war was close at hand.

A "sphinx so tantalising to the bourgeois mind," Karl Marx called the
Commune. Defining the Commune of 1871 still is a problem for historians. Its name reached back to the Paris Commune of 1792, during the radical phase of the great Revolution. It was resolutely urban in character (and
sought an alliance with other major cities, such as Lyon and Marseille) and
devoted to a number of long-wished-for reforms: the separation of church
and state (which included anticlerical persecution), the institution of universal education, including for women; the abolition of the death penalty
(the guillotine was dragged from the shed next to the Roquette prison,
where it habitually resided, and burned); a more frugal government (the
pay of officials was set at only 6,000 francs across the board); and, ideologically, a commitment not to state socialism of the Marxist variety so
much as classic anarchism as preached by Proudhon, who promoted the
notion that power should be in the hands of those who are concerned by
its exercise. Its flag was red, its partisans sometimes called "communists,"
but the Commune bore little resemblance to later exercises of state socialism. It did not abolish private property, except insofar as it expropri-
ated some clerical holdings, and it was resolutely local, making a claim on
power over and against the National Assembly, which was dominated by
benighted, priest-ridden rural France. Administration was to be decentral-
ized, lodged mainly in local governments: Paris was to be "the Washington
of France" rather than the all-controlling center. In its brief existence, the
Commune of 1871 was largely a government of artisans, skilled workers,
teachers, and the like—in part because much of the upper bourgeoisie had

left Paris, or gone into hiding within the city. What it might have been as a model of government, of course, was hampered by the situation in which it came to power: war, scarcity, the constant need to invent ways to make sure Paris had provisions, and to prepare for the invasion that seemed increasingly inevitable.

It was a time of much talk, continuous debate about how to move forward—some ninety newspapers vied for attention, though those that represented the Versailles government, such as *Le Figaro*, were banned. The beliefs and methods expressed ran the gamut from the totalitarian Jacobinism of Raoul Rigault, who took over the police department, to the pragmatism of François Jourde, who at once made peace with the Bank of France, and received a large loan and was given continued cooperation from its staff. The Commune elected a governing council on March 26, but authority was far from centralized, since the mayors of the *arrondissements* shared power, and "commissions" were charged with the administration of finance, supplies, the post office, social assistance, education, war, and so forth. Some of them worked extremely well, including a reorganized public medical system. But not the War Commission, which became an inextricable mess, exacerbated by rivalries between the Commune and the Central Committee of the National Guard. Toward the end, in frustration at the disorganized response to the military threat from Versailles, power was transferred to a five-person Committee of Public Safety, another echo from the extreme days of the great Revolution. This solution appealed to Jacobins and Blanquists (followers of Louis Auguste Blanqui), but it was opposed by the more liberal minority, including the painter Gustave Courbet and the journalist and novelist Jules Vallès. The committee governed more and more arbitrarily, with ever greater disregard for personal liberties: Rigault's police searched houses and people without warrant, and there were occasional arrests on suspicion of treason. Outside Paris, those who held power throughout Europe feared and loathed the Commune.

"The great social measure of the Commune was its own working existence," claimed Marx from London, in *The Civil War in France*, a pamphlet (written in English) containing his "Address of the General Council of the International Working Men's Association," and published as the events in

Paris were still unfolding. For Marx, the genius of the Commune was its ad-hoc invention of the proletarian state that theorists had been looking for. "Its true secret was this. It was essentially a working-class government, the product of the struggle of the producing against the appropriating class, the political form at last discovered under which to work out the economical emancipation of labour." That "political form at last discovered" was crucial for Marx—it showed the path from bourgeois hegemony to its overthrow and instant replacement. He wrote further: "The civilization and justice of the bourgeois order comes out in its lurid light whenever the slaves or drudges of that order rise against their masters. Then this civilization and justice stand forth as undisguised savagery and lawless revenge." This was of course not Flaubert's view. Yet there is some rapprochement of extremes here: Flaubert the bourgeoisphobe would also increasingly see the regime of "this civilization and justice" as savagery and lawless revenge. He would never take the side of the Communards, but would find them the less reprehensible combatant in the battle of slave and master.

Flaubert, on his way back from England on March 30, wrote to his friend Edma Roger des Genettes that "our brothers"—sarcastic reference to the Communards—were preventing him from coming to Paris. He noted that the future must lie with the workers' International, unless "a strong clerical and monarchical reaction sets in. Which is equally possible." And to Sand the next day: "The French Revolution must cease to be dogma and must return to Science, like the rest of human affairs." That is, it must be subject to reasoned analysis, not remain simply a mystique. In fact, the mystical formula "Republic" can't raise armies to defeat a million well-disciplined Prussians. He submitted a piece of astute political analysis, albeit in hindsight: it would have been more intelligent to "leave Badinguet [one of the nicknames for Napoleon III] on the throne *on purpose* so he could sign the peace treaty, then throw him in prison afterward." As for the emergent Commune, it was medieval (in its localism) and inept (property rent and contract were part of natural law). More to the point: "Many conservatives who, from a love of order, wanted to preserve the Republic will now regret the emperor. And in their hearts call for the Prussians. The people who took over the Hôtel de Ville have *displaced the object of hatred.* That's what I begrudge them. I think we have never been lower."

Once again—and this is something that has not always been understood about Flaubert's politics—his condemnation of the workers and their leaders as inept, scorning "natural law," was, in a further movement, trumped by his prevision of a reaction that would be worse. The Communards "displaced" the Prussians as the object of hatred and gave the conservatives license to kill. "We are hung up between the Society of Saint-Vincent-de-Paul and the International," Flaubert wrote. The International, though, was committing too many stupidities to last long, including "requisitions, suppressions of newspapers, executions without trial, etc." Even if the International were to carry the day against troops from Versailles, then the Prussians would come in to subdue Paris, and "order will reign in Warsaw," he said, citing the infamously callous phrase used after the brutal suppression of the 1830 uprising in Poland. A few weeks later, he wrote to Edma Roger des Genettes that socialism was missing a unique opportunity and would be dead for a long time to come. The scenario didn't unfold quite in the way Flaubert had predicted, but he was not far off: after Thiers signed the Treaty of Frankfurt as the final conclusion to the war on May 10, Bismarck ordered the liberation of French troops in prisoner-of-war camps, so that they could join the Versailles army and carry out the invasion of Paris. The proletariat in revolt was the universal enemy of those who ruled Europe.

No reply to Flaubert's letter of March 31 came from Sand. He wrote again on April 24, querying her silence. He added: "You know what's worst of all in this? *It's that one grows used to it,* yes! You come to accept it. You get used to doing without Paris, to not caring about her any more, almost to believing she doesn't exist." Unlike the bourgeois, he didn't see the Commune as a further outrage—after invasion, there are no greater misfortunes. And then he reached for an analogy that he had already used in *Sentimental Education* to characterize the aftermath of the Revolution of 1848, and the bloody suppression of the workers' uprising during the June Days of that year: "The Prussian war had the effect on me of a great upheaval of nature, one of those cataclysms that arrive every six thousand years, while the insurrection of Paris is, to my eyes, something very clear, and almost simple." And then: "I fear that the destruction of the Vendôme Column will broadcast the seed of a Third Empire!" Another Napoleon would come to power. That column in the Place Vendôme, encased in bronze from melted-down cannon of the Grand Army, had been erected to commemorate Napoleon I's victories. The Commune, including Gustave Courbet, who headed the new Federation of Artists, declared it a monument to imperial conquest (which it certainly was) and pulled it crashing to the ground on May 16 in a ceremony that, like the killing of the generals Lecomte and Clément Thomas, would come to haunt the Communards at the moment of reckoning.

Sand's reply to Flaubert's letter of April 24, dated April 28, was long and generous. In it she refused to accept the path of Flaubert's despair, despite her prostration at the turn of events. His anguish was met by her faith in humanity: "For me, the ignoble experiment that Paris is trying out or undergoing proves nothing against the laws of the eternal progression of men and things, and if I have a few mental principles, good or bad, that I've acquired, they have not been shaken or changed. Long ago I accepted patience the way one accepts the weather, the length of winter, old age, lack of success of all kinds. But I think that (sincere) partisans should change their formulas and come to see the emptiness of any *a priori* formula."

It may come as something of a surprise, given Sand's long-standing commitment to a humanitarian socialism, that she condemned the Commune as much as Flaubert did—as much as anybody, one might say, condemned it, since the entire French bourgeoisie, of whatever political persuasion, seems to have been pretty much united in the view that the Commune was a tragic error. One searches largely in vain across the spectrum of French middle-class opinion for any favorable report on the Commune from outside Paris, despite its clearly progressive legislation—on the laicization of education, on labor laws, on women's rights—that might in other contexts have brought approval from someone such as Sand. She had greeted the Second Republic of 1848 with enthusiasm, and played an important public role in it (though she refused to stand for election to the Assembly), and she had spoken out against its suppression of the workers' revolt in the June Days of that year. In particular, the unprecedented role played by women in the Commune ought to have elicited her sympathy: the Union des Femmes, created on April 11, 1871, enjoyed government backing, and proved influential in many domains. Some of the most famous names remembered from the time are those of Louise Michel, schoolteacher, leader, and historian of the Commune, and Elizabeth Dmitrieff, Marx's envoy to Paris; there were many others as well—women who were organizing production, running the ambulance services, and even manning the barricades and serving in the National Guard.

But the Commune appeared to Sand as the *enemy* of the Republic, an illicit insurrection against the elected government, however much she might sympathize with the egalitarian social goals that Communards espoused. Sand in fact dismissed the experiment of the Commune as an utter disaster:

> One feels sorry for a baby bird that fell from its nest, how can one not feel sorry for a mass of consciences fallen into the mud? We suffered less during siege by the Prussians. We loved Paris when it was unfortunate through no fault of its own. We feel even more sorry for it now since we can no longer love it. Those who never love pay themselves off by hating it mortally. What to say in response? Maybe nothing! The contempt of France is perhaps the necessary punishment for the notable cowardice with which Parisians accepted the insurrection and the adventurers who led it. It's the sequel to their acceptance of the adventurers of the Empire. Other crooks, same cowardice.

Once again, we hear the note of punishment, of retribution for the sins of the Second Empire, even in a liberal conscience such as Sand's. There seems to have been no way to come to terms with the convulsions of war, siege, defeat, and insurrection except as some form of Flaubert's natural cataclysm, or else the language of crime and punishment.

The Prussians had withdrawn from Rouen, and Flaubert now was comfortable again in his study in Croisset, back to work on *The Temptation of Saint Anthony* after unburying his notes. He replied to Sand on April 30 with a kind of world-annihilating bitterness: "'Thank God the Prussians are there!' is the universal cry of the bourgeois. I put in the same bag messieurs the workers, and let the whole of it be dumped into the river!" A pox on both sides, then. The Commune was at its death throes, "the last manifestation of the Middle Ages," one can hope. And he generalized: "I hate Democracy (such as it is understood in France at least) because it stands on 'the morality of the Scriptures' which is immorality itself, whatever they say: it is the exaltation of Pardon to the detriment of Justice, the negation of Law, in a word: the anti-social." Universal suffrage resulted in the "terrible farce" of the right-wing Assembly that would suppress the people. It would be time to get rid of political "principles" and to enter the realm of "Science," that is, the world rationally examined, without ideological blinders. That was the kind of thought he admired. The only reasonable government would be that by the caste of mandarins— the only "legitimate aristocracy." (Flaubert always considered himself a mandarin.) If more Parisians had known their history, we would never have had the war or the Commune. "The current folly is the result of too much stupidity. And this stupidity came from an excess of jokery. From too much lying we became idiots." One hears an echo in anticipation of W. B. Yeats's "Meditations in Time of Civil War," at a later moment of civil strife in another country. Yeats:

> We had fed the heart on fantasies
> The heart's grown brutal from the fare;
> More substance in our enmities
> Than in our love . . .

Flaubert, in his final flourish, echoing what he had already written to Du Camp: "Everything was fake; fake realism, fake army, fake credit, even fake whores. . . . And this falsity (which is perhaps a sequel of romanticism, the predominance of Passion over form and of inspiration over rule) applied especially in the realm of judgment. . . . One required art to be moral, and philosophy to be clear, and vice to be decent, and knowledge 'to be within reach of the people.'" He ended by apologizing for the length of his letter; but: "When I start calling out my contemporaries, there's no stopping."

The Commune, which emerged from war and siege by the Prussians, had from early in April been at war with the rest of France, represented by the Versailles government. Sorties against the Versailles-held forts outside Paris were disorganized and failed abjectly. Governing Paris under the threat of invasion was a matter of constant improvisation. How well it worked depended in part on one's political perspective. Life kept going: Paris was supplied with food (the Prussians in the forts to the east and north of the city didn't try to block supplies), members of the National Guard—in theory, every able-bodied male, and a number of women besides—subsisted on the thirty sous that were their daily pay. The Banque de France and the Commune established from the first a judicious truce, the bank allowing the Commune to call on revenues and loans as if it were the legitimate government, though more radical Communards wanted to seize the bank. It was a time when the Paris streets belonged to the people—*le temps des cerises*, cherry time, as the song by Jean-Baptiste Clément, which came to be associated with that springtime, declared it to be. It was perhaps more fatefully the time of the *Internationale*—though actual members of the International were a minority in the Commune—which was composed by the Communard Eugène Pottier while in hiding following the Bloody Week:

> *Debout, les damnés de la terre!*
> *Debout, les forçats de la faim! . . .*
> *C'est la lutte finale.*
> *Groupons-nous, et demain*
> *L'Internationale*
> *Sera le genre humain.*
> [Arise, the cursed of the earth!
> Arise, slave laborers of hunger! . . .
> It's the final struggle.

Keep together, and tomorrow
The International
Will be the human race.]

Though it was a time of illusions as well, of course, as the failed military sorties demonstrated. And it became ever more evident that it was just a matter of weeks, or even days, before a situation of siege and skirmish became one of invasion of the city by the France outside it.

On May 22—just as the actual invasion of Paris by the troops from Versailles got under way, though he didn't yet know this—Flaubert wrote to the Princess Mathilde of his fear of the coming reaction against the Commune: "Whatever name it covers itself in, this reaction will be anti-liberal. The fear of the Social will throw us into a conservative regime of a reinforced stupidity." He continued: "When I think of the gigantic stupidity of my country, I ask myself if she has been sufficiently punished." Note that at a moment when the Left saw punishment resulting from the excesses of the opulent Second Empire, and the Right saw punishment for the impious excesses of the republic, for Flaubert what needs the corrective lash is the excess of stupidity that led France into the war, then into the illusions of the Commune, and finally to reaction. Readers of *Sentimental Education* can begin to discern the application of that novel (really, of all Flaubert's writings) to the Terrible Year of 1870–1871: everything traces back to stupidity and the immense human capacity for self-deception. When Flaubert evokes "Science"—usually capitalized—as the answer, it is in the sense of knowledge, method, wisdom, and the precise measurement of reality. Though not a natural scientist, Flaubert, son and brother of physicians, wanted his own writing, so carefully worked and reworked in his novels, to take the exact measure of things, to offer an analytic study of social relations. Anything less was a lie, one of those falsities he enumerates. Bad style, especially the remnants of Romantic illusionism, is lying, and therefore to be censured.

It is in this same spirit that Flaubert wrote to Charles Lapierre on May 27, concerning an article attacking Victor Hugo's expression of sympathy for the Communards—and his poetic reputation, as well—which Lapierre, as editor, had published in *Le Nouvelliste de Rouen*, the most important local paper. In the interest of public order and the reestablishment of morality, wrote Flaubert, the first requirement is to write only about those things one can write about accurately. It is acceptable to criticize Hugo's political sympathies, but not his poetry. Here, Flaubert's desire to separate art from politics stands as an ethical gesture: nothing is to be gained by a confusion of realms. The first principle of all is clarity of thought and expression. Flaubert truly believed that without these, nothing else could be set right. It's not that he is disinterested in the realm of politics—far from it—but that he believes politics, like everything else, must start from "science," from a rigorous mental hygiene. Lapierre is guilty of unwittingly lending a helping hand to "the coming Reaction."

Meanwhile, in Paris, the nightmare was unfolding over what would forever be known as the "Bloody Week." It started when the government troops, the Versaillais, entered Paris through the western suburbs on the night of May 21. Already for weeks the Versaillais had kept up an intense bombardment of the western parts of the city. All efforts at mediation and compromise had come to nothing. The invasion of Paris by France—as represented by the Versailles government—had for some time appeared inevitable. The Communards in preparation had built barricades at strategic points throughout the city, prying up cobblestones, bringing out bedsteads, using whatever would serve. Some of them looked like formidable fortresses. The trouble was that a ruthless enemy could always outflank a barricade by smashing through the houses on either end of it, then attacking its defenders from the rear, or racing to an upper story to rain shot on those below.

The city was in fact poorly defended by a disorganized National Guard. The Versaillais, with 100,000 men, advanced methodically, in a pincer movement along the Right and Left banks. They were intent to redeem their losses in the war against Prussia. They showed no quarter. Destruction marched with them, and the retreating Communards began to set buildings ablaze in a vain attempt to arrest the progress of the army, as well as from vengeance, and perhaps at last in a gesture of self-immolation. The fires gave rise to the largely legendary figure of the *pétroleuses*, the savage and vengeful revolutionary women who spread fire throughout Paris, who somehow came to incarnate for the bourgeoisie the most fearful aspect of the revolutionary proletariat: underclass women on the rampage. Paris in flames: the holocaust (the word recurs often) of the city at the heart of French civilization was unforgettable to eyewitnesses, even to those who merely heard the reports. From balconies all over the city, you could see bursts of flames. Close up, the Tuileries Palace was illuminated as in an infernal festival. Communard Prosper-Olivier Lissagaray bore witness: "A blinding light rises in the night. The Tuileries are burning; the Legion of Honor, the Conseil d'Etat, the Cour des Comptes. Formidable detonations come from the palace of the kings whose walls collapse, whose vast arches fall in. Flames, sometimes lazy, sometimes sharp as darts, shoot from a hundred windows. The red water of the Seine reflects the monuments and doubles the fires." The sky was dark with smoke, everywhere, with the smell of burning petrol. "The burning of Paris makes a day like that of an eclipse," Edmond de Goncourt wrote in his journal on May 24.

Emile Zola's novel *La Débâcle* (*The Debacle*, the next-to-last of his *Rougon-Macquart* series, published in 1892) recounts the war and ends with the burning of Paris, witnessed jointly by Henriette, the good-hearted Frenchwoman who will work for a better future, and her cousin the Prussian officer Otto Gunther. "What have we done, in the name of the Lord, to be punished so?" exclaims Henriette. The Prussian officer's response: that the punishment has been brought by the "God of armies to chastise a perverse population. Paris was burning as punishment for its centuries of bad living, the long piling up of its crimes and debauches." And the dying Maurice—killed by his would-be brother-in-law in this fratricidal struggle—has a final vision of Paris in flames at sunrise on May 27: fire as purification, the necessary burning away of the "unhealthy" part of the nation. "But this bloodbath was necessary, and it had to be of French blood, the abominable holocaust, the living sacrifice, in the midst of purifying fire. Henceforth, Calvary had been ascended to the most terrifying of agonies, the crucified nation was expiating its faults and was going to be reborn." Granted, this is the vision of a feverish, dying man. Nonetheless, the rhetoric represents a common reaction, invoking sin, expiation, purifying fire, and burnt offerings. It's as if even someone moderately sympathetic to the political Left, such as Zola, could not, even with some years' retrospect, come to terms with the disaster other than in these primitive sacrificial terms. They are echoed more than a century later by the historian of French revolutions François Furet, who calls the Commune "the ultimate exorcism of a violence which had been an inseparable part of the French public life since the end of the eighteenth century. . . . In this Paris in flames, the French Revolution bade farewell to history."

The Communards retreated street by street, at the last into the working-class districts in the northeast of Paris. Intense final combats took place in and around Père Lachaise Cemetery, and the last major group of combatants taken by the Versaillais were lined up—batch after batch—and shot against the wall that became known as the *Mur des Fédérés* at the foot of the cemetery. Justice meted out at the end of the Bloody Week was that of swift, brutal retribution. The officers in charge decided on the spot who was an insurgent and who not, on the basis of "evidence" of having used a firearm or simply showing a dirty face, and the result was rarely being made prisoner: it was almost always summary execution. The sickening sounds of firing squads at work lasted well beyond the last Communard resistance. The Communards didn't help their cause by beginning, in the middle of that week—in response to executions of Communard leaders— to shoot hostages it held, many of them clergy, including the archbishop of Paris, Monsignor Georges Darboy. Never had France—rarely has any country—known such savage fratricidal strife.

Zola, strongly anti-Communard like the rest of the bourgeoisie, reported on the Bloody Week for the Marseille newspaper *Le Sémaphore* with some compassion for the defeated. When he managed to make his way through a city largely reconquered by the Versaillais, he reported in the edition of May 31: "I managed to cross Paris on foot. It is atrocious. . . . I want to speak only of the heaps of bodies that have been piled under the bridges. No, never will I forget the heart wrench I felt at that pile of bleeding human flesh, heaped haphazardly along the towpaths. Heads and limbs are entangled in horrible dislocations. From the pile emerge faces fixed in convulsion."

Zola was one of the first witnesses to enter Père Lachaise after the Commune's agony in the cemetery. In *Le Sémaphore* of June 2:

> All this part of the cemetery is trampled as if a savage hand-to-hand combat had taken place. Here and there, pools of blood, corpses that no one has bothered to pick up. I saw a seventeen-year-old boy stretched out on a white stone, arms crossed, like one of those rigid statues the Middle Ages laid out on its tombs. Farther on, one of the National Guard had fallen on the sharp points of an iron fence, was still impaled on it, folded in two, horrible, like a slab of beef hung out in a butcher's shop. Blood had splattered on the floral wreaths on the graves, and all along the marble tombstones were bloody fingerprints, as if some wretch, mortally stricken, had held on to their edges before falling.

And then the executions he could hear, often with machine guns, going on and on. It is to the point that many of the army generals who commanded the invasion of Paris and the suppression of the Communards had seen service in French colonial wars in Algeria and Mexico, and were used to meting out harsh treatment to "native populations" that didn't bow to French rule. During the Bloody Week, they treated the Paris populace like an other and inferior race, ready for slaughter without deference to the forms of justice. As Edmond de Goncourt concluded on May 31: "It is good. There has been neither conciliation nor compromise. The solution has been brutal. It's been pure force. . . . The solution has restored confidence to the army, which has learned in the blood of the Communards that it was still capable of fighting. Finally, the bloodletting has bled white; and bloodlettings like this, in killing the fighting part of the population, put off for a generation the next revolution. Our old society has twenty years of repose ahead of it." A chilling but honest estimate by an unapologetic reactionary.

Flaubert must have reached Paris just about as soon as it was possible to do so, when the trains began running again. He was certainly there by June 5: he wrote the next day to Ernest Renan, keeper of oriental manuscripts at the Bibliothèque Nationale, to solicit his help in finding a

Turkish manuscript that he hadn't been able to peruse the day before. But research for *Saint Anthony* didn't prevent his joining others who had spent the past months in chosen exile from Paris, or in hiding, as tourists in the burned-out city. It quickly sprang back to life as people came out of their hiding places and back from suburb and countryside: the boulevards were again filled with strollers, and prostitutes. He toured in company with Maxime Du Camp, who recorded his reactions. All this had been foretold—by Flaubert himself in his account of the earlier failed revolution, 1848, in *Sentimental Education*. If only his compatriots weren't so stupid. If only they knew how to read. Du Camp recounted, as he and Flaubert were together on the terrace of the Tuileries Palace, along the Seine:

> as we were looking at the blackened carcass of the Tuileries, of the Treasury, of the Palace of the Legion of Honor and I was exclaiming on it, he said to me: "If they had understood *L'Education Sentimentale*, none of this would have happened."

I think Flaubert meant what he said; we will need to come to terms with it.

Flaubert's first letter from Paris to the outside world came on June 8, to Caroline, on a day of rain and cold. "The air of Paris isn't at all unhealthy"—written evidently from a concern that the many, many hastily buried corpses would be contaminating the air—"But you will see some beautiful ruins. It is sinister and marvelous." Flaubert's finding of beauty in the sinister ruins was not unique to him. Edmond de Goncourt, visiting the ruins of the Hôtel de Ville on May 28, noted in his journal: "This ruin is a marvel of the picturesque, to be preserved, if we weren't condemned to the restorations of M. Viollet-le-Duc." Petrol on stone apparently produced striking effects of iridescence, rendering the stone as if transparent. One of the many guidebooks to the ruins—published hastily after the event, often illustrated with exceptional photographs recording the ruins—noted of the Ministry of Finances that it was only mediocre as a building, but had become "superb" as a ruin. "Fire is a worker of genius," the guidebook comments. Guidebooks, photographs, postcards, and paintings—such as Ernest Meissonier's rendering of the Tuileries as a kind of

Roman ruin—suggest some reaction beyond the political, beyond even a sense of tragedy: an appeal to the eternal majesty of the ruin. Paris was like Pompeii: a city that had become a ruin overnight, to be looked at with an awe that could—momentarily—stun political strife to silence.

Flaubert pushed his Paris visit on to Versailles, to be a spectator at part of the trial of the Communards—those not executed on the spot during the Bloody Week were marched off to Versailles, penned like animals, then tried in batches. He reported to his friend Agénor Bardoux on June 9: "The spectacle yesterday [the Communard trial] nauseated me! What beings! What poor monsters! But what flabbiness of the clowns judging them!" Again, an equal pox on both houses, though one senses greater outrage directed at the self-satisfied judges than at the benighted insurrectionists. To novelist and playwright Marie Régnier two days later (he had just returned to Croisset) he wrote: "I am *overcome*, less by the ruins of Paris than by the gigantic stupidity of its inhabitants. It's enough to despair of the human species."

Then on the same day, June 11, he wrote a long letter to Sand—never had he had a greater desire, a greater need, to see her than now. "I am back from Paris, and I don't know whom to talk to." Again, it's not the ruined buildings but the ruined minds that overwhelm him:

> I am overcome or rather nauseated!
>
> The odor of the corpses disgusts me less than the swamps of egotism exhaling from all mouths. The sight of the ruins is nothing next to the immense Parisian stupidity! With some very rare exceptions, *everyone* appeared ready for the madhouse.
>
> Half of the population wishes to strangle the other half, which reciprocates the feeling. You can read that clearly in the faces of the passers-by.
>
> And the Prussians no longer exist! People excuse them and *admire them*! "Reasonable" people want to become naturalized Germans.
>
> I assure you that it's enough to make one despair of the human species.

To blame: most of all, the rulers of the Second Empire. When history untangled the story of the burning of Paris, it would be Prussia and the "men of Badinguet" who would be found to blame. Once again, Marx seems apropos: "The bourgeoisie of the whole world, which looks complacently upon the wholesale massacre after the battle, is convulsed by horror at the desecration of brick and mortar!" Flaubert's condemnation of his compatriots' stupidity, their misplaced venom, finds an echo in the philosopher of bourgeois undoing.

We were so cheerful when we parted from one another eighteen months ago, Sand replied on June 14, and so many atrocities have taken place since. She called the Commune "infamous." She admitted to her discouragement, the flickering of her faith in humanity in the midst of such deep shadows. She had, she said, sown on her own personal volcanoes grass and flowers that were growing well—and had falsely concluded that everyone could become more enlightened, could correct or control themselves. "And now I awake from a dream to find a generation divided between cretinism and *delirium tremens*. Everything is possible now!" At the present moment, she continued, she could not keep her calm and balance. "I am as troubled as you, and I don't dare speak, or think, or write, so much do I fear to open the gaping wounds in all souls." As for her silence following his long letter of April 30, she admitted to having received it, but had to wait for the courage to respond. "I am devoured by indignation and poisoned by disgust."

To Edma Roger des Genettes, to Turgenev, to Ernest Feydeau, Flaubert's lamentations were repeated over the course of June: the ruins of Paris are impressive, worth visiting—but they are nothing compared to the stupidity of Parisians, which almost makes one want to admire the Commune. We'll have to resign ourselves to living between cretinism on the one hand and total madness on the other. "The madness, the stupidity, the *senility*, the mental abjection of the *most intelligent people in the universe* goes beyond all dreams," he wrote to Ernest Feydeau on June 29. One can't exactly call this a political position, but it makes sense as a moral reaction. Far worse than the misdeeds of the Commune, far worse than the burning of Paris, was the resulting idiocy of his countrymen. In *Sentimental Education*, summing up the suppression of the workers' revolt in June 1848 and the reaction that followed, Flaubert wrote, "Des gens d'esprit en restèrent idiots pour toute leur vie" (Intelligent people were made idiots by it for the rest of their life). Idiocy was the unpardonable sin, and politics had made idiocy endemic to a generation.

By now, there were no more Prussian helmets to be seen in Rouen. Sand wrote again on July 23, as calm began to settle over the land, and it seemed that the bourgeois republic might endure. "It will be stupid, as you predicted, I have no doubt. But after the inevitable reign of the grocers, it's necessary that life reach out and begin again on all fronts. The garbage of the Commune shows us dangers that hadn't been foreseen and which command a new political life for everyone: do things on one's own, and force the lovely proletarian created by the Empire to learn what is possible and what not. . . . If they go on the way they did, they will die of hunger. That's what they need to be made to understand, right away." This was a remarkably bleak assessment by Sand—she had come to sound like Flaubert. Note that she, like Flaubert, sees the urban proletariat as the creation of the Second Empire: its capitalist expansion, manufactures, luxury, vast inequalities in wealth. Marx would not disagree, though he would run the history further back in time. In some logic of the inevitable, the Empire brought the Commune into being.

Flaubert, responding from Paris on July 25, agreed that the bourgeois republic might be able to establish itself. "Its lack of elevation is perhaps a guarantee of solidity? It's the first time that we live under a government that has no principles. Perhaps the era of Positivism in politics is about to begin?" Pragmatism without idealism or illusion was what France needed. From this, he reaffirmed his plunge back into the past—from disgust with his contemporaries—and his return to work on *The Temptation of Saint Anthony*. And he pleaded with Sand for a visit to Croisset, following that by Turgenev in mid-August. He needed to return home and stay put because of his mother's failing condition (she in fact had less than a year to live). But he did manage to get out to Versailles in early August for another view of the military tribunal, still at work on the fate of the remaining Communards. He showed a strange fascination for what he found most abject. If he appeared to find the judges as repugnant as the judged, he did not denounce the proceedings in the manner of Zola, who had begun to make regular appeals for amnesty (this would not come until the next decade), and to report regularly on executions by the firing squad at the Satory military base. Each one, Zola wrote the following year, "brings a weight to all our consciences." Not all consciences, surely. Much of France was still in a mood for revenge.

On September 6, Flaubert wrote with approval, to Sand and to others, of an article Sand had published in *Le Temps* the previous day, where he thought that for the first time she spoke the truth about the Parisian working class: the need for it to rededicate itself to reality and to work, and to cease chasing the chimeras of revolution. He had acerbic yet somehow delighted remarks to make about one of the so-called *pétroleuses*, Mademoiselle Papavoine, alleged to have had sex with eighteen men on a barricade, and who did not deny the allegation. Flaubert found that better than the end of *Sentimental Education*, where the old friends Frédéric and Deslauriers remember their visit as timid teenagers to a brothel—an ending deemed far too cynical when the novel was published (especially since the two men describe the scene as the best time of their lives), but now eclipsed by reality. We find again a kind of fascination with a populace that infringes all bourgeois rules. In summary, Flaubert wrote: "Ah! How tired I am of the ignoble worker, the inept bourgeois, the stupid peasant, and the odious priest!" That about takes care of things.

Sand agreed with his nausea and indignation, but replied two days later that she could not hate the human race of "our poor dear country." Flaubert, responding to her letter of September 6, in which she sent portraits of granddaughters, by which Flaubert was appropriately charmed, and to a false newspaper report that she had been ill, turned to a diatribe against newspapers—"free and obligatory education" would turn everyone into readers of newspapers, he said, a school of degradation where one learns not to think—and against universal suffrage, which makes numbers win out over intelligence. Then he diagnosed Sand's problem: "Ah! Dear good master, if only you could hate! That's what you have lacked: Hatred." When Sand sat down to answer this letter, on September 15, her response grew to such a length that she decided to publish it as a "Letter to a Friend" in *Le Temps*, in which she continues to express, in the place of

Flaubert's hatred, both suffering and hope. In the personal letter she then sent her friend, she ended by returning to the children's portraits, which she knew would please him. "You are so good. . . . However much you are a mandarin, you aren't Chinese at all, and I love you with all my heart." The diagnosis of goodness, by someone to whom goodness meant so much as it did to Sand, is worth remembering amid Flaubert's disgust and cynicism. These are the emotions of a disillusioned idealist who was capable of great warmth and affection to those he trusted.

Flaubert was moved by Sand's article in *Le Temps*, but not persuaded. Writing to her on October 7, he again underlined the need for "justice": "Pardon, humanitarianism, sentiment, the ideal have played us falsely enough that we should try *Law* and *Science*." He agreed that class distinctions were outmoded. But he believed that the Poor hate the Rich, and that the Rich fear the Poor. "That will be true eternally. To preach love to one another is useless. The most pressing need is to teach the Rich, who are at bottom the strongest. Enlighten the bourgeois first! For he knows nothing, absolutely nothing. The whole democratic dream is to raise the proletarian to the same level of stupidity as the bourgeois.—The dream is partly fulfilled! They read the same newspapers and have the same passions." There lies the illusion of democracy, in Flaubert's analysis. What's needed is a legitimate aristocracy of educated talent. As for French education, a subject much debated in the wake of defeat, he noted that higher education allowed the Prussians to win the war, that secondary schooling produced the French bourgeois who had founded the republic of September 4, and that primary schooling produced the Commune. In a postscript, Sand's "old troubadour" complained gently that he appeared rather as an unlovable egotist (in his playful emphasis, "*HHégoïste*") in Sand's essay.

Sand perceived at once that she had wounded her dear friend, and responded first to the postscript when she wrote back on October 10. She was, she said, speaking only to a part of his views, which wasn't the whole of him, combating only a fragment of what he had written to her. "You are a troubadour after all, and if I had to write to you *publicly* your character would appear as what it is. But our real discussions should remain between us like caresses between lovers, even sweeter, since friendship has its mysteries also, without the storms of personality." She would like to find a synthesis of his truth of reason and hers of sentiment. But France wasn't with either: "She is with blindness, ignorance, and stupidity."

Flaubert's letter of October 12 waved off any sense of personal offense—no excuses needed, even your blows would be caresses to me. He then launched into one of his more ferocious commentaries on events: Princess Mathilde had returned to her château in Saint-Gratien, northeast of Paris, while the town was still occupied by the Prussians, a bad gesture that Sand had excused as "brave." Really, he said, the princess came back because she is a spoiled child, and as a result forced Flaubert to pass between two Prussian guards to make his way into her château, which made the blood rush to his face. She should have remained in exile until the Prussians decamped (they would not leave French soil entirely until the war reparations were paid). What's lacking at present, Flaubert returns to the charge, is a sense of Justice. This quickly modulates into a lack of appreciation for talent, and for the "intrinsic worth" of a book (attack here on the critics Sainte-Beuve and Taine, interested only in the author's personality or in literary history). Attacks, once again, on Romanticism for falsifying values, for being more interested in redemption than in justice. The stupidity, also, of the military tribunal in Versailles, which was handing out stiffer sentences to ignorant minor players than to the principal instigators (including Gustave Courbet, who was held responsible, though not necessarily justifiably, for the Vendôme Column destruction). The Communards were on the whole being sentenced to death or to deportation in New Caledonia. Flaubert believed these "bloody idiots" should instead all have been condemned to clean up the ruins of Paris, "with chains around their necks, like simple convicts." That's harsh and dismissive judgment, but a more lenient treatment than most were in fact receiving.

Flaubert's bile once again brought him a long, meditative reply from Sand (and she was moved to write another article for *Le Temps*, this one couched as a reply to a woman friend who shared many of Flaubert's ideas on rule by an elite). In her letter of October 25, she described her attempts as a child to work out the meaning of life, to understand the principles by which to lead it: love, self-sacrifice, a horror of egotism, and the ideal of justice. Human society must, like that of the ants and the bees, be built on mutual service, the concourse of all toward the same end. She had lived through revolutions—that of 1848 was particularly important to her—and seen the shallowness of their principal actors. Only Armand Barbès stood in her view as a true leader. She saw the same shallowness in writers and artists. Flaubert was the only person with whom she had really been able to exchange ideas, personal ones—not just shoptalk. She felt sorrow and sympathy for the class whose brutal existence could lead to the production of arsonists and murderers. "I feel sorry for humanity, I would wish it well because I don't want to detach myself from it; because it is me; because the evil that it does strikes me in the heart; because its shame makes me blush; because its crimes twist my guts; because I cannot understand paradise in heaven or on earth as for myself alone. You must understand me, you who are goodness from head to foot." Sand's plea for human sympathy and solidarity ends here with her once again recruiting Flaubert to the party of humanity: she certifies his own personal goodness, from head to toe.

Is this to make of Flaubert's vituperation of his contemporaries simply a fit of pique? I think it is rather to see Flaubert's solitary rage as strongly allied to her own idealism and communitarianism. In Sand's view, you cannot rail against humanity in such a manner without having had high expectations of a human capacity for goodness. And Flaubert's personal goodness—his friendship, his sympathy, his utter devotion to his mother and his niece, and to Sand herself, whatever their political divergences—bears witness to ideals that he is loath to articulate, that appear in his novels only in quick vignettes: Dr. Larivière in *Madame Bovary*, the dedicated physician (perhaps a tribute to his father) who is summoned too late to save Emma, or Catherine Leroux, the nearly deaf and dumb peasant who is given a medal for "half a century of servitude" on the same farm, or, later, Félicité of the tale "A Simple Heart," which he will write for Sand. The idealist who refuses to surrender her ideals in the face of savage inhumanity and stupidity and the ranting misanthrope are shown to be the recto and verso of the same text.

But this does not mean that Flaubert was to be calmed. He was back, in his letter of November 14, to declaring the "formidable and universal" reign of stupidity. To speak of the servile condition of the working class was unjust and incomplete: he had just read through the platforms of all the candidates in the local elections, sixty fine flowers of the bourgeoisie, to find them all asses. "Conclusion: we must enlighten the enlightened classes." He confessed that there were days when his anger choked him. "I would like to drown my contemporaries in the latrines. Or at least, rain down on their heads torrents of insults, cataracts of invectives. Why thus? I ask myself why." Yet one should add that during these weeks of agony over the affairs of the world, Flaubert was spending much of his time attempting to assure the posthumous glory of Louis Bouilhet: prefacing his works, negotiating with publishers, and overseeing the production of Bouilhet's play *Aïssé* at the Théâtre de l'Odéon in Paris (it would not be a success). And he was aiding Sand in a charity mission, to succor an elderly neighbor of Sand's left destitute by the war, by calling upon help from Princess Mathilde (who sent a check for one hundred francs but apparently forgot to register the envelope, with the result that the check was lost or stolen).

The year 1871, the completion of an *année terrible*, ended with Flaubert again invited to spend the Christmas holiday with Sand and her brood in Nohant, as he had done in 1869—with no suspicion that the world of politics would visit disaster on France in the year to come—but forced to decline because he was deep in rehearsals of *Aïssé*. (Sand claimed a few days later that at Nohant they called aloud his name three times at the stroke of midnight on Christmas Eve.) The play had its premiere on January 6 to a largely invited audience. By the second night, however, the theater was mostly empty. The reviews were hostile or stupid, and the management of the Odéon didn't push the play, instead moving on to a revival of Victor Hugo's *Ruy Blas*. Flaubert's posthumous devotion to Bouilhet loomed large again in this post–Terrible Year period: he was involved not only in the performance of *Aïssé* but in its publication as well, along with that of Bouilhet's *Dernières chansons* (Last songs), prefaced by Flaubert, and a public letter to the Municipal Council of Rouen, denouncing the

councilors for refusing to dedicate a space in the city for a fountain to
Bouilhet's memory, to be paid for by public subscription. The ghost of
Bouilhet brought no calm, but rather more occasions to rail at bourgeois
ineptitude. "At your age," Sand wrote on January 25, 1872, "I'd like to see
you less irritated, less taken up with the stupidity of others." But then she
added, as an afterthought, "Perhaps this chronic indignation is a need of
your makeup. As for me, it would kill me."

Sand preached calm and refused to visit Paris—her only regret was that
she couldn't be there when Flaubert read *Saint Anthony* to Turgenev—
because she didn't want to spend her time in disagreeable political arguments with friends. Yet she claimed, in the same letter, "It is impossible that
people won't grow tired of this sectarian spirit that results in their being
no longer French, no longer men, no longer themselves. One no longer
has a country, one belongs to a Church; one does what one disapproves of
so as not to break ranks with the sect. I can't argue with those I love and
I can't lie. I prefer to remain silent." Flaubert, on the other hand, offered
a defense of his refusal to be silent, his need to protest, which he claimed
had made him respected by the Rouen establishment, because in his ex-
postulation, "I provided figures (*sic*)!" Talking money made you respectable. Meanwhile, the reading to Turgenev went forward: 115 pages of *The
Temptation of Saint Anthony*, with "exquisite" critical comment from his
listener. To latter-day readers, including myself, who find *Saint Anthony*
hard to digest even when taken in small doses, this reading, of one literary
giant to another, takes on somewhat mythic proportions. How could they
do it? Both the speaking and the listening must have been epic.

Sand reported that she had read both Bouilhet's poems and Flaubert's
"splendid" preface—this would lead soon after to Flaubert's request that
she write a review of the volume for *Le Temps*—but she noted that Bouilhet died young from living too much in his mind. "I beg you, don't get so
absorbed in literature and erudition," she wrote to him on January 28. "Get
out, move about, have mistresses, or wives, as you wish, and during these
phases, don't work, because you don't want to burn the candle at both
ends, you need to change the end you're lighting." What was needed was
more *farniente*.

But Flaubert was busy in Paris—though needing to return to Croisset at Easter, to relieve Caroline of the care of his mother, which was becoming more and more difficult. He was reading the most arcane material for *Saint Anthony*, reading also Kant and Spinoza, making the acquaintance of Pauline Viardot, famed singer and Turgenev's longtime companion, and then—his big news—paying a visit to Victor Hugo, whom he found "charming . . . not at all the great man, not at all pontificating!" Hugo had become a pariah to many of the French because of his sympathy for the defeated Communards, some of whom had found refuge in his house in Brussels, his temporary place of voluntary exile—he was then forced to move on to Luxembourg. His collection of poems on the war and the Commune, *L'Année terrible* (The Terrible Year), was published in April 1872, and Flaubert apparently read it right away. He reported in May to Edma Roger des Genettes that he'd found much of beauty in it. "But I don't feel the need to reread it," he said. "It lacks *density*. But who cares. What a jaw he still has, that particular old lion. He knows how to hate, which is a virtue, one that my friend George Sand lacks—but what a pity that he hasn't a finer eye for the truth!" In person, he went on to say, he found Hugo exquisite—he'd seen him often, even dined with him—and not at all as he was portrayed in public.

It would be tempting here (but a temptation to be resisted) to quote line after line of *L'Année terrible*, if only because it seems an extraordinary way to recount the events of the Terrible Year—in thousands of *alexandrins*, rhyming verse that Hugo manages with an ease and suppleness beyond that of nearly any other French poet. In a kind of book of hours, divided into months, he moves from the disastrous French defeat at Sedan through to the final executions of the Bloody Week, not as a partisan but nonetheless with deep sympathy for the plight and fate of the people. One of the most celebrated pieces from the collection concerns a boy who has set fire to a library during the final days of the defense of Paris. A long sermon on the barbarity of this civilization-destroying act ends with the boy's monosyllabic reply: "Je ne sais pas lire" (I don't know how to read). The deaths of Communards along the Mur des Fédérés on the final day of combat are rendered as a liberation from decades of oppression rather than the just punishment that most of France wanted to see.

"This century is in the dock, and I am its witness" ("Ce siècle est à la barre et je suis son témoin"), Hugo writes at the outset of his poem. That's a remarkable stance for a poet, though for Hugo, it culminates many years of acting as a poetic social visionary sitting in judgment on political affairs. A deputy to the National Assembly during the short-lived Second Republic in 1848, he was exiled by Napoleon III's Second Empire—he spent most of those years on the island of Guernsey—and pilloried the emperor in *Napoléon le Petit* (Napoleon the Little) and the polemical poems of *Les Châtiments* (Punishments). His return from exile on day two of the new republic, September 5, 1870, was an event. He served again in the Assembly, then resigned in protest at the terms of the armistice. He had written his epic version of French history in *La Légende des siècles* (*The Legend of the Ages*). Still, to write contemporary history, almost journalism, as fragments of an epic and satirical poem is not so expected. Hugo's poem, despite his characteristic grandiosity and bombast, is a moving act of witnessing. More convincing—to Flaubert as well—was the novel that would come in 1874, *Ninety-Three* (*Quatrevingt-treize*). The book was named for the year of the Reign of Terror during the first French Revolution, and conceived as an effort to reconcile the warring camps of Hugo's compatriots: to bring into harmony Blues and Whites, republicans and royalists, in a sovereign rhetorical act of antitheses postulated and resolved. If Flaubert believed that his novel *Sentimental Education* could have, and should have, taught his compatriots a lesson that would have prevented the horrors of the Bloody Week, Hugo believed that writing itself could bring an end to conflict in a kind of performative speech act.

On March 5, Flaubert reported to Caroline that he would be dining later that week with Hugo, whom he found more and more charming. And on March 11, he reported to Sand that Hugo had talked of her "in exquisite terms" and sent her greetings. Later that month, a warm and grateful letter to the pretty widow Léonie Brainne suggests that he may have a new lover. But Parisian and other pleasures were eclipsed soon after his return to Croisset: his mother, who had come to Paris with Caroline, returned home with her son weaker than ever, and in the night of April 5 she died. Among several letters he wrote in the early hours is one dated 1 o'clock in the morning of April 6 to Sand: "Dear good master, My mother *just died!* I embrace you." She replied on the 9th with a characteristically sympathetic and touching letter about his loss and his mother's difficult final years: "What a bitter conquest of repose! And you are going to miss worrying about her, I'm aware. I know this sort of consternation that follows on the fight against death." As Flaubert would confess a few days later—and Sand seems to have known all along—his mother was the only woman he loved without reservation. A week later, Sand wrote again, suggesting that if he needed a voyage of distraction, she had a bit of money she'd just earned, and would happily give him. Flaubert did not accept, but he was deeply touched by her gesture.

His mother's will left the family house in Croisset to her granddaughter Caroline Commanville (daughter of the other Caroline, Flaubert's sister, who died after giving birth to her), with the proviso that during his lifetime Flaubert would always keep his rooms there, including his study. But he was not yet sure how much he would have to live on (this would become a graver problem over the next few years, with the bankruptcy of Commanville's lumberyard, Flaubert's sale of inherited farms to bail him out, and his decision to give up the Paris apartment in the rue Murillo for a more modest one in the rue Saint-Honoré). Private affairs, for the moment, came to eclipse public ones. It was hard to have to reorganize life at age fifty. A stunning letter from Turgenev, back in Russia, in June spoke to the problem of old age, and told of his finding a "powerful bath" in wandering through an old country garden, "all full of country smells, of strawberries, of birds, of rays of sunlight and shadows all sleeping, the one as much as the other.... You are immobilized in a sort of grave and immense sensation—also stupid—made in part of animal life and in part of God." Such peace and rejuvenation were closed to Flaubert, who was ever more irritable, his sense of hearing, in particular, seemingly exacerbated, so that he found almost everything other than his solitude at Croisset unbearable. But he was lonely as well, though he did acquire a greyhound, Julio (perhaps named after Juliet Herbert), to keep him company.

His letters were full of references to the "execrable business" that he was obliged to transact in settling his mother's estate, which kept him in

Croisset—though he escaped to Paris in June, just in time to catch Sand, who was making a visit there. She was not at all changed, Flaubert told Caroline. But to Sand he wrote on July 1 that their time together was inadequate: there was so much that they didn't get a chance to talk about. Sand replied on her birthday, July 5 (or rather, the date she long believed to be her birthday, which really was July 1): she was now sixty-eight, and in perfect health, bathing regularly in a stream cold as ice. Flaubert's vacation in the Pyrenees, in July and August, was not a success in calming his nerves. Later in the year, after Sand and Flaubert had commiserated together over the death of Théophile Gautier, old friend and fellow artist, she suggested that he should get married, since "being alone is hateful." In reply, Flaubert at first avoided the issue; he returned to Gautier, to suggest that he died from his disgust at modern life, from "modern carrion," in his own words. He would be recognized someday as a great poet—if ever the world came back to a concern with literature. When he came to Sand's marriage prescription, he called the idea "fantastic." "Why? *I have no idea.*" He offered various reasons, including his lack of a fortune, and probably came as close to the truth as he was able when he declared: "There is an ecclesiastical side of me that people don't know." In the absence of a belief in god or the republic, he could be a kind of (lapsed) monk in the service of art. He offered as guide a maxim from Epictetus: "Hide your life."

Flaubert's letters by this point exhaled such depression that Sand wrote to Turgenev, urging him to pay Flaubert a visit, to cheer him. Turgenev in turn wrote repeatedly to Flaubert that he wanted to come to Croisset but couldn't because of his recurring bouts of gout—Flaubert must come to him in Paris. (The gout was a real problem, but Turgenev was also very much under the thumb of Pauline Viardot, who dictated his comings and goings.) Why, he asked, was Flaubert so concerned with the people—"*la plèbe*"—which was not the dominant class? The popular playwrights Alexandre Dumas (fils), Victorien Sardou, Jacques Offenbach—they were not of the people, "nonetheless they smell very bad," he wrote. "The people smell too, but with the odor of Cambronne's word [that is, shit]; whereas the others stink of rot." What was really bothering Flaubert, in Turgenev's diagnosis, was not politics, but "the sadness of entering one's fifties." Sand had an admirable serenity, simplicity, interest in life, goodness. If for that (here he is taking up words Flaubert has used to describe Sand) one needed to be a bit of "a blesser, a democrat, even evangelical, my word!—let's accept those excrescences." One comes to understand why Turgenev was so prized a friend, to Flaubert, to Sand, as later to Henry James (whom he introduced to Flaubert on December 12, 1875, a visit memorable to the young American novelist but unrecorded by Flaubert).

But Flaubert was not about to give up his rage. His illness, he replied to Turgenev on November 13, was incurable. Not only his loss of friends to death but the "social condition" enraged him. "Public stupidity submerges me. Since 1870, I've become a patriot. In seeing my country croak, I realize that I loved it. Prussia can take down its rifles. We don't need anyone else to make us die. . . . I feel the sadness felt by Roman patricians of the IVth century. I feel rising from the earth an irremediable Barbarity." Beauty and things of the spirit were despised. "I have always tried to live in an ivory tower. But a floodtide of shit beats at its walls, to bring it down. It's not a matter of politics but of *the mental state* of France." He found a symptom in the circular issued by the minister of education, Jules Simon, on the reform of public education, in which the instructions on physical exercise were longer than those concerning French literature. Then we learn that he has undertaken a book—not *Saint Anthony*, which he finished in April, but a new project—one that would allow him to "spit his bile." This is a reference to *Bouvard and Pécuchet*, the "novel" (the word doesn't quite fit) about two copyists who set out to master vast domains of human knowledge from their reading—and make a botch of everything. Flaubert never finished this book, which in its second volume was to contain the *Dictionnaire des idées reçues* (*Dictionary of Received Ideas*), the dictionary of clichés that would, he hoped, shut the mouths of his contemporaries. For Flaubert, hatred was a bracing, sustaining force.

He was at it again on November 20, in a letter, most likely to the Baroness Lepic, in which he claimed that the stubbornness of the Right was going to make of him "a Red! Not out of sympathy for the brutes who make up that lovable party, but from disgust at the others." There followed a summary history of the stupidities of the French Right, which had always hated moderates to the extent that it favored the creation of extremists on the Left. The so-called Conservatives were actually playing the game of their enemies. Thiers, though Flaubert didn't like him, was more intelligent in pushing for a continuation of the republic. This was by no means assured: it was assumed by many French that the ultraconservative Assembly elected in 1871 would restore the monarchy. In fact, France was at this moment a provisional republic ruled largely by anti-republicans, and many believed that the nation could regain stability and greatness only with a monarch. When Thiers fell from power in May 1873, he was replaced by Marshal Patrice de Mac-Mahon, a general, duke, and royalist who believed in the reign of "Moral Order" and was devoted to the restoration of the Bourbon pretender to the throne, the Comte de Chambord, as Henri V. This might well have happened had Chambord been less of an illustration of the adage that the Bourbons learned nothing—and forgot nothing.

In his November 20 letter, Flaubert declared that "the Commune didn't make me despair for France so much as what is happening now. The convulsions of a raging madman are less hideous than the droolings of an idiot old man." He continued his "H-indignation" (in his emphatic form of spelling) against the Right in further letters to Sand—who feared he was turning into an old Benedictine rather than her troubadour—and then turned to a speedy reading of the two books she had just published and sent him, *Nanon*, a novel set during the first French Revolution, and *Francia*, a tale of the Restoration era that followed the fall of Napoleon. Flaubert claimed that reading both had done him good, and proceeded to provide detailed comments, with a distribution of praise and gentle critique. Sand was pleased at his reaction, but also more and more concerned by what she saw—to use anachronistic words—as his chronic depression. She wrote her books for her contemporaries, she said, and they would be forgotten in fifty years, whereas she saw him as writing for future ages, a more difficult task, demanding greater faith. And she became ever more insistent that he visit her in Nohant. Meanwhile, on December 12, Flaubert turned fifty-one. He managed to get himself to Paris by the year's end, where he walked all day and began to sleep decently again.

Sand's insistent invitations finally resulted in a trip to Nohant for a week in April 1873, along with Turgenev, their return on the long train ride fortified by the Russian's flask of brandy. Life was good with her— why couldn't they live together? Flaubert asked in a letter afterward. He then took a resolution to go to Saint-Gervais-les-Bains, in the Alps, to improve his health (and appearance), and signed himself "Reverend Father Cruchard of the Barnabites, Director of the Sisters of Disillusion." Evidently, he was in a good mood, and fully launched into the satiric mode of *Bouvard and Pécuchet*—off, in fact, to find a suitable Norman countryside in which to site their story. He and Sand managed dinner together soon again, in Paris. Back in Croisset, he went to work on a play, *Le Sexe faible* (The weak sex), from beginnings set down by Bouilhet, and then moved on to his own dramatic conception, *Le Candidat* (*The Candidate*). Sand reached her seventieth birthday, still bathing daily in a cold river, and received his warm congratulations. Turgenev finally made his long-postponed visit to Croisset in early October.

The political news in the fall of 1873 concerned the "fusion" of the two monarchist parties, the Legitimists, who gave their allegiance to the Comte de Chambord of the Bourbon family, which had ruled France before the great Revolution, and briefly after the fall of Napoleon, and the Orléanists, the younger branch of the royal family that adhered to the dynasty of the last king to occupy the throne, Louis Philippe, the "bourgeois monarch," who had been dethroned in 1848. Since Chambord had no children, an agreement was reached whereby Chambord would become King Henri V, and upon his death the crown would pass to the Orléanist Comte de Paris. Both Flaubert and Sand feared a return of monarchy. The crisis was unknotted by Chambord himself, when he refused to accept the tricolor flag that had proudly waved in France since the great Revolution, insisting rather on a return to the fleur-de-lys on white ground that had been the flag of the Bourbons.

Further crises were in the offing: in 1875 came the vote that would reaffirm the existence of the republic (by the margin of one vote), but then in 1877 a crisis when Mac-Mahon tried to impose his government against the will of the majority in the Assembly, which led to his dissolution of the Assembly and new elections—that returned a clear republican majority and led to Mac-Mahon's resignation in 1879. The Republic of the Dukes (monarchists at heart) was replaced by a regime of republicans that would endure until 1940. Flaubert and Sand had both long since accepted Thiers's notion of the republic as the regime that divided the French least. And with that, the elongated history of the Terrible Year was just about over.

The year 1874 would bring the decided failure of *The Candidate* on the stage, then the publication of *The Temptation of Saint Anthony* to decidedly mixed reviews. And then in 1875, Flaubert's financial crisis, caused by Caroline's husband's bankruptcy—he calculated that his income had been reduced by half, since, like a good bourgeois, he felt obligated to bail out members of his family. "Honor will be saved, but nothing else," he wrote to Léonie Brainne on October 2. And on May 29, 1876, his announcement that he was working on a story called *Histoire d'un Coeur simple* (*Story of a Simple Heart*), in which Sand would recognize her influence on him. "I think you will find the moral thrust, or rather the human underside of this little work agreeable," he told her. There was no response from Sand, who died, after a week of excruciating pain, on June 8. Flaubert traveled down to the funeral with Ernest Renan and Prince Napoleon, the godfather of Sand's granddaughter Aurore. It was raining. A priest officiated, despite Sand's express wish to the contrary—the work of her estranged daughter, Solange Clésinger. Flaubert did not enter the church or the cemetery. But he cried like a baby twice, first in kissing Aurore (who had her grandmother's eyes) and then when Sand's coffin was carried away.

Not long before the end, they had had a long exchange about why *Sentimental Education* hadn't been a success. That pre-Commune novel had come for Flaubert to have prophetic force. But prophets are not necessarily loved: their messages tend to be gloomy, and Flaubert's is no exception. As we come out of the Terrible Year and its immediate sequels, it is worth asking how Flaubert saw that novel as prophetic, and how he went on to develop his views of human action in history in his final work. It will be interesting as well to set Flaubert's reactions as a writer against other attempts to understand, judge, commemorate, and come to terms with the Terrible Year.

– chapter three –

A Tour of the Ruins

⤚ *Photography Makes History* ⤙

THE PARIS FLAUBERT FOUND ON HIS VISIT IN EARLY JUNE 1871 was a shambles. The western end of the city, Auteuil and its surroundings, showed gaping holes from artillery bombardment, first Prussian, then French. All the way up the Avenue de la Grande Armée to the Arc de Triomphe you saw the scars of shelling. But when you came closer to the center of Paris, on both the Right and the Left banks, you encountered scenes of extreme destruction, buildings and whole quarters laid waste. At the heart of the city—around the Hôtel de Ville and the Tuileries Palace—you came on utter devastation and ruin. Yet, to the surprise of contemporary witnesses, the life of the city revived almost instantly: people went back to work, cafés reopened, strollers reappeared on the boulevards—and many went to have a look at what had happened to their city.

Paris was deeply wounded, and before the scars could be effaced—that, along with punishment of the Communards, was a first order of business for Thiers's government—they became a site of curiosity, in fact a tourist attraction, and the subject of a remarkable photographic record in part created to satisfy the tourist trade. Photography in 1871 was coming of age. The French government had given a first patent on the process to Louis Daguerre in 1839. War and disaster had from early on been a subject demanding record: photos from the Crimean War (1853–1856), and then the famous work of Matthew Brady, Alexander Gardner, and others during the American Civil War in the following decade. Shutter speeds were not yet capable of capturing action shots: the required exposure times were too long. But the aftermath of fighting—as in the rows of the dead in Brady's photographs—held a magnetic attraction for the lens. Théophile Gautier noted the many photographers' vans—their laboratories for developing their plates—parked beside the ruins. These were recorded over and over, for tourist's guidebooks and souvenir postcards.

The ruined Paris Flaubert visited with Maxime du Camp on June 6 was barely freed of smoldering embers and stinking corpses. Many of the hastily dug graves were shallow, leaving parts of bodies exposed. A large effort was under way to cart remains off to other common pits. The two middle-aged men made their way through heaps of destruction comparable to an archaeological dig, but more recent, and yet not excavated. Du Camp, who had remained in Paris throughout the reign of the Commune, railed against the brute beasts of the Commune and told of the hardship and fear of the past seventy-two days. He would continue to fulminate in his four-volume eyewitness report entitled *Les Convulsions de Paris* (The convulsions of Paris), published in the late 1870s. Flaubert's remarks were more philosophical: the reading of his novel, published eighteen months earlier, should have prevented all this. The ruins were for him a subject of meditation.

Ruins had long attracted an attitude of pensiveness and meditation, a mood, you might say, of the *sic transit*. From the time of early Romantic writers such as the Count de Volney, author of *The Ruins of Empire*, and Lord Byron, they had provoked a kind of elegiac philosophizing on glory, vanity, and transience. To Flaubert, they seemed to hold a more severely moral lesson. They were the very incarnation of his contemporaries' stupidity, their failure to learn from their own history. The judgment he had passed in *Sentimental Education* on the cretinizing effect of the June Days and their aftermath lay visible before him.

It's not clear exactly what itinerary through the ruins Flaubert and Du Camp took that June day. The guidebooks that were beginning to appear suggest a number of possibilities, all making their way across the same sites. But before following them in our mind's eye through the ruins, one might look back for a moment from June to March, at the tenuous photographic history of Paris during the Commune, before the cataclysmic days at the end of May. There is in fact this one memorable photo of where it all began: the National Guard's cannon park on Montmartre that was the object of Thiers's worst apprehension, and which he ordered impounded in the action that early on the morning of March 18 sparked the insurrection (see Figure 1, photo insert).

These were the cannon largely bought by public subscription, in an appeal sponsored by Victor Hugo, that held a special place in the hearts of Parisians. They belonged to the people, they were its symbolic last defense. Montmartre was the bastion. It was here that the people of Paris stood their ground when their government tried to disarm them, and where the first blood of the insurrection was shed protecting the cannon, the act that sent Thiers and his ministers packing to Versailles. When Montmartre fell to the Versaillais during the Bloody Week, many Communard leaders knew that their resistance was over.

But in March Montmartre belonged to the insurgents: a photograph showing two National Guardsmen manning a cannon emplacement with a panoramic view of the city beneath them (Figure 2) was very likely taken by Bruno Braquehais, who, deaf and mute, had made a profitable business during the Second Empire photographing "studio" nudes, toney pornography, but seems to have been a Communard sympathizer. He remained in Paris for the duration and would record a crucial moment of its existence.

In photography, that brief existence gave us a number of portraits of the leaders of the Commune, individual or collective, when they were assembled in a group at the Hôtel de Ville. It also produced a number of photos of the barricades built to defend the city against the anticipated invasion from Versailles: barricades that were evidently a source of pride and confidence for their builders and defenders. For instance, for those posing on a barricade constructed in the workers' stronghold of Ménil-montant, in fact part of the last quarter of Paris to fall to the Versaillais in May (Figure 3).

One can see this kind of pride most of all in the creations of Napoléon Gaillard, the Commune's official master-builder of fortifications. He may figure in the background of the picture of what became known as "Châ-teau Gaillard," the barricade of the rue de Castiglione, part of an imposing set of defenses of the Place de la Concorde (Figure 4).

Then, of course, the Place de l'Hôtel de Ville, seat of municipal government, was heavily fortified, as captured in a photograph by Alphonse Liébert, who, along with Braquehais, Jules Andrieu, and Hippolyte Blan-card, would be one of the most notable photographers of the ruins (Figure 5). The barricades were something of a fetish for the Communards, creating a sense of shelter, but they in fact proved largely useless when the invasion took place: the army troops mostly avoided attacking them directly and instead outflanked them, forcing their way through the houses and gardens on either end of the barricades, either to come round on the rear of the defenders and destroy them in cross-fire, or else to force their way up to higher floors and shoot from there. The Communards had an implacable enemy.

The one action of the Commune given an intense historical record—evidently the conscious creation of a *lieu de mémoire* (site of memory), a site needing a record all the more in that it was creating an absence, a hole in the city—was the felling of the column of the Place Vendôme. This event would later be reckoned among the chief "crimes" of the Commune, a sign of its wanton, barbaric, ignorant, and fundamental destructiveness. Destroying this monument was in fact a strange expenditure of energy and political capital. The column (quickly restored after the fall of the Commune) commemorates the first Napoleon, whose gilded statue as Roman emperor stands atop it. It was sheathed originally with brass bas-reliefs made from melted-down cannon captured from the enemy at the Battle

of Austerlitz in 1804. It was re-symbolized, as it were, by the Second Empire, which was always seeking to connect to the glorious Napoleonic past:
Napoleon III replaced an earlier statue of his uncle with what had in fact
been the original conception, an imperial Caesar, in Roman dress. It was
by 1871 a familiar and generally beloved part of the Paris landscape. Yet
it drew the particular ire of the Communards, who declared it "a monument to barbarism, a symbol of brute force and false glory, an affirmation
of militarism, a negation of international law, a permanent insult of the
conquerors to the vanquished, a perpetual attack on one of the three great
principles of the French Republic: Fraternity."

All that in one architectural monument: this act of accusation against
the Vendôme Column gives some sense of the cultural warfare waged by
and against the Commune, its desire (reprised by the student revolts of
1968) to change the cultural conditions of life, to make politics serve a
revolution in ways of seeing and experiencing the world. So the destruction of the Vendôme Column was decreed. Subsequently, blame for this
act was laid squarely upon the artist Gustave Courbet, who was chief of
the Federation of Artists under the Commune. It's not clear that Courbet was in fact mainly responsible for the destruction of the column—
he originally proposed that as an ugly and imperialist monument it be
moved over to the Ecole Militaire. Though his guilt was never clearly established, following the Commune he was imprisoned, then sentenced to
pay financial restitution for the destruction—which he could not do. He
fled the country instead, then died, sad and impoverished, in exile.

The photos in series give nearly a sense of the action of felling the column. Braquehais in particular gives a nearly complete narrative, minus
only the very moment of free fall (recorded in a number of engravings),
making a claim to be one of the first French photojournalists. Among his
photos, first, are Communards at the base of the column (Figure 6), including some women, what looks like a child stretched out at the foot of
one of them, and many in National Guard uniform (since a very large part
of the male population was part of the Guard by this point); and following
that is the column rigged for destruction, along with a bed constructed to

soften its fall, this one probably but not surely by Braquehais (Figure 7). These are followed by a high-angle shot (Figure 8), no doubt taken from a fifth- or sixth-floor balcony, by Jules Andrieu, author of the album *Les Désastres de la guerre* (*The Disasters of the War*), showing the scene of destruction. And to conclude the series there is another Braquehais, a notably evocative picture of Napoleon, got up as Roman emperor fallen in the dust, like an assassinated Julius Caesar, the orb of the world still clutched in his hand (Figure 9).

It is a curious series, in which the Commune and its photographers seem to be intent on making a record of their own folly, willfully creating the kind of scar on Paris that will later be held in evidence against them, anti-monumentalizing the city, so to speak. If they think they are effacing a tribute to militarism and dictatorship, paradoxically they make starkly visible before us what one of the guidebooks will call "a day whose memory will never be effaced."

But mostly the photos are of the ruins created on the final days of the Bloody Week that Flaubert and Du Camp witnessed. Some of the destruction in Paris came from Prussian and then French shelling, especially in the western outskirts of the city around Saint-Cloud, Argenteuil, Neuilly, Auteuil, and Passy. The spectacular explosion of the Cartoucherie Rapp, the munitions factory, probably resulted from a Versaillais shell. But the fires that consumed especially public buildings near the center of Paris mainly were set by the retreating Communards, a wall of flame created in an effort to prevent the advance of the Versaillais troops, perhaps at times also from vengeance and despair. The night of May 24–25, Paris was burning; it was caught in a panoramic lithograph by Michel-Charles Fichot, who I think worked back from the sites of ruin to mark the buildings set afire: it's a good mapping of the destruction (Figure 10). Another popular lithograph shows the Tuileries lit up like a torch. But there is also, quite remarkably, an actual photograph of the fire, taken by Hippolyte Blancard (Figure 11). What Zola's narrator in *The Debacle*, and many other commentators, would moralize as holocaust and purification, here, close up, is life-threatening disaster.

The fires became exhibit number two—after the execution of the hostages—in the detailing of the crimes of the Commune. As Marx said, the bourgeoisie complacently stomached the massacre, but was "convulsed by horror at the desecration of brick and mortar!" If the death of Monsignor Georges Darboy and other clerics murdered during the death throes of the Commune provided strong grounds for retaliation against the Communards, it was the destruction of the capital that reinforced bourgeois indignation. Here was the visible scar, to be cured and revenged.

It was then both paradoxical and inevitable that just as soon as the fighting was over, the ruins of Paris became a tourist industry: the desire for eyewitness of the disaster was intense. "The *ruins of Paris!* What an attraction! Just think!" ironized Malvina Blanchecotte, noting the proper English girls exploring the ruins. Cook's in London quickly offered organized tours of the ruins. There came in fact to be a certain resentment on the part of Parisians at the number of British who came to visit the ruins and, as the locals saw it, gloat over the results of French fratricide. Visitors from the French provinces also flocked to the capital. The ruins created, too, an instant publishing industry. Many of the guidebooks are simple pamphlets, with itineraries through the ruins and comments on the destroyed buildings. Others are heavily illustrated with rotogravures, which one comes to recognize as engravings made from the photographs of the ruins. There was no way of reproducing photographs in printed books at the time—efficient photogravure was still a few years off—but there are some albums, large-format, luxurious affairs, that contain photographic plates. These were produced separately for each edition, then glued by hand into the volume. They are often of astonishing quality, as are many of the individual photographs produced for postcards and other souvenirs. The record of the "crimes of the Commune" (the word returns repeatedly) is paradoxically preserved in images and collections that speak of aesthetic luxury. This in fact will be a central oxymoron of the sites of memory created by the Commune: the castigation of destruction along with an aesthetic and sentimental fascination with the ruins created.

The rhetoric of these guidebooks is routinely anti-Communard. The tropes become familiar: crime, dregs of society, wild beasts, insensate destruction, and so on. As Georges Bell (the pseudonym of Joachim Hounau) writes in his *Paris incendié: Histoire de la Commune de 1871* (Paris burned: History of the Commune of 1871), in many quarters of Paris one finds *vides accusateurs*: emptinesses that accuse the perpetrators. This language of the void becomes interesting. The guide *A travers les ruines de Paris* (Through the ruins of Paris) tells us that "only photography, with its brutal realism and its pitiless precision, can represent these indescribable things that were houses, palaces, cities." Only photography can capture what now is from what once was, since the present form is indescribable, unnameable. Then, Alfred d'Aunay, in his preface to the magnificent album of photographs by Alphonse Liébert, *Les Ruines de Paris* (*The Ruins of Paris*), notes that war and civil war are by now past, and resemble a bad dream half forgotten. But, he adds: "This sight had the sun for witness, and the sun fixed on Bristol paper this lugubrious souvenir." Photography is presented as the work of the sun as eyewitness, and the fixing of the object of witness on paper. Photography is given a quasi-forensic role, producing unforgettable memorializations of sights that one wants to forget like a bad dream. D'Aunay's remark captures a notion that comes back repeatedly in the discourse accompanying the photographs: that the ruins, which themselves record a kind of absence of what once was there, are something to be effaced, blotted out, forgotten. As Georges Bell puts it, "the more one looks at them, the more ardent becomes the desire to see them disappear." Yet they are irresistibly made present by the photographs.

The principal monuments, most notably the Hôtel de Ville and the Tuileries, were nightmarish, unforgettable images of both absence and presence: absences that refer to lost presence, presences that make the absence present. I offer only a selection of the many images of the Hôtel de Ville, the most photographed of all the ruins, the Renaissance building that had for centuries housed the municipal government, and became the headquarters of the Commune. First comes one by the great Charles Marville, the famous photographer of pre-Haussmann Paris, done some weeks after the fire, when the building was already surrounded by hoardings:

clearance and reconstruction had already begun (Figure 12). One taken among the many stark views of the interior ruins is also by Marville (Figure 13). An often reproduced Liébert at first looks like an action photo—firefighters attempting to extinguish the blazing Hôtel de Ville—but on close inspection turns out to be retouched: his photo of the building, done for his great album soon after the event, here has had fire and smoke, firemen, and gushing fire hoses carefully added in with pen and ink (Figure 14). The original Liébert, as presented in his *Les Ruines de Paris*, belongs to the memorial of the ruins (Figure 15).

That retouched photo might be considered relatively innocent compared to a number of photomontages "recording" events of the Commune, especially by one Eugène Appert in his album *Les Crimes de la Commune* (*The Crimes of the Commune*). The album depicted such crucial events as the executions of Generals Clément Thomas and Lecomte on March 18, 1871—the founding violence of the Commune—and the execution of Monsignor Darboy and the hostages of La Roquette Prison, as well as the retributive execution of Commune leaders Louis Rossel, Théophile Ferré, and a sergeant named Bourgeois before a firing squad on the plain of Satory, outside Versailles. These fakes are sometimes clever and were surely taken as "evidence" by many, though their wooden quality is made very evident by the genuine photographs. They do urge a certain caution when using photos as witness to events.

Absence/presence was a crucial issue, too, on the practical level of stone and mortar: in the question of rebuilding the destroyed landmarks. The government that would soon preach "Moral Order" wanted to efface the Commune by ridding the capital of ruins as soon as possible, and most of the functional public buildings, such as the Palais de Justice (here photographed by Blancard, Figure 16), the Ministère des Finances (again by Blancard, Figure 17), and the Cour des Comptes (the Gare d'Orsay was built over its ruins), were quickly rebuilt or replaced. The Théâtre Lyrique, in the Place du Châtelet, (photographed by Liébert, Figure 18), would revive under a different name in 1874.

In addition to specific destroyed buildings—often those crucial to the administration of the city and the nation—there were also whole areas of the city that had suffered heavy damage. On the Right Bank, the length of a major artery, the rue de Rivoli, made for a stunning shot: the depth of field in these photographs is often remarkable (Figure 19). And on the Left, not far from Saint-Germain des Prés, was the Carrefour de la Croix-Rouge, the scene of an intense onslaught against Communard barricades, photographed here by Liébert (Figure 20). These would need to be made whole again—and they were, with notable speed. The rapidity of the French recovery from war, siege, invasion, and then civil war often astonished observers, and the rebuilding of Paris was an urgent part of national restoration.

The Hôtel de Ville, commissioned originally by François I in the sixteenth century (with wings added early in the nineteenth), was crucial both practically and symbolically. Some proposed replacing the ruined building with a new design, but the government quickly opted to reuse what remained of the old façade, creating a replica Renaissance building on the outside while going nineteenth-century for the interior. Work proceeded apace, so that the many haunting images of its ruined condition could become a counterproof of French resolve. It stands today, slightly enlarged from the original, a defiant reproduction.

As for the Tuileries Palace, another of the most dramatic ruins, there ensued a long and heated debate as to whether and how to restore it (shown here in the central Salle des Maréchaux, photographed by Liébert in Figure 21). If the restoration of the monarchy in the person of the Comte de Chambord, crowned as Henri V, had taken place in 1873, as at one time seemed inevitable, it is certain the palace would have risen again. In the failure of that restoration, even the conservative Republic of the Dukes, which followed upon the fall of the Thiers government, led by the monarchist marshal and duke Patrice de Mac-Mahon, had trouble mustering much enthusiasm for rebuilding that which, though briefly a people's palace in the spring of 1871, had come to seem a symbol of tyranny and excess. The debate ended only in 1882—when republicans were firmly in control—with the decision to raze the ruins and remove the debris, thus creating the Place du Carrousel as we know it today. Nonetheless, there is still today an active National Committee for the Reconstruction of the Tuileries. Some insist upon literalizing sites of memory.

The message of the government and the official sources of information was all about forgetfulness and erasure. The Commune would soon become virtually unmentionable, fallen from official history. And yet: there is the phenomenon of these several guidebooks produced precisely to publicize the ruins, and there were the visitors who purchased them and, like Flaubert, toured the city. What did it mean that these symbols of national defeat, class warfare, and heedless destruction became a privileged site of tourism, of sightseeing? The rhetoric of wishing to see and wishing to cover over the sight returns again and again, in a contradiction that cannot be resolved. At work, I suppose, was our inevitable attraction to the sight of cataclysmic happenings, from earthquakes to highway accidents, along with the accompanying wish that they had not happened. But something else seems to be going on here as well. In part, it seems to have been the eerie beauty of the ruins themselves, evoked in a number of guidebooks and commentaries.

Along with the desire to remove the emblems of destruction by making present again the buildings recorded in their absence, as photographed ruins, there was a concurrent discourse of fascination with the uncanny beauty of the ruins, a perverse wish that they might be preserved. Already on June 12 the anti-Communard Blanchecotte lamented the quick turn to restoration of the "splendid horrors," adding, "The Parisian understands nothing about the striking beauty of great disasters." In fact, the imagination of many Parisians was captivated by the images of a living city instantly reduced to lifeless rubble in the manner of Pompeii, the ruin created by an instant cataclysm. *A travers les ruines de Paris* sees the rue Royale as "the street of another Pompeii, shaken by the eruption of the volcano of the populace, blinder in its furies, more stupidly brutal than Vesuvius or Etna."

The comparison becomes a commonplace. And yet the results of volcanic eruption are beautiful. The same guidebook notes of the Hôtel de Ville that it is "black, white, blueish, reddish, rose, so intense was the furnace that cooked and recooked it." Stone set afire with petrol seems to have taken on wonderfully enticing iridescent colors. The poet Théophile Gautier, viewing what remained of the Cour des Comptes: "Above all we were struck by the *beauty* of the ruins." Edmond de Goncourt, wandering through Paris the day after the fighting ended, develops in his *Journal* the full aesthetic of the burned Hôtel de Ville: "The ruin is magnificent, splendid. Ruin in tones of rose, of ash green, of white-hot iron, a ruin shimmering in the agate color taken by stone burnt in petrol, it resembles the ruin of an Italian palace, colored by the sun of many centuries, or better still, the ruin of a magic palace, lit up in an opera with shimmering electric reflections." It is a "marvel of the picturesque, to be preserved," though, alas, it is bound to be restored by Viollet-le-Duc. To which Goncourt, no friend to democracy, appends his notice of an intact marble on the building bearing the "lying legend: Liberty, Equality, Fraternity."

Another work, *Guide à travers les ruines* (Guide through the ruins), written by Ludovic Hans and J.-J. Blanc, notes: "The Ministry of Finance, which in the past was only a mediocre edifice, has become a superb ruin. Fire is a worker of genius." Again we have the Pompeian reference: "It makes one dream of a city swallowed up by a cataclysm." To Gautier, the Ministry of Finance looked like the Colosseum. The ruins have a kind of antique beauty: as in the remains of the Grenier d'Abondance, the storehouse full of substances including wine, oil, and petrol that went up like a torch. Jules Andrieu recorded it in *Les Désastres de la guerre* (Figure 22).

So you have in the rhetoric of the guidebooks, and in tourists' reactions to the ruins, a simultaneous lament on the destruction wrought by the Communards, the work of a kind of human volcano, and a meditation on the seductive beauty of this instant Pompeii. The ruins resurrected the earlier fascination, of Romantics and the Gothic Revival, with the picturesque ruin: the sentiment that led the moneyed to have instant ruins created on their estates, for instance, and to meditations on the slopes of Etna and Vesuvius by Romantic heroes from Chateaubriand to Matthew Arnold. And here, of course, the tourist was in a sense viewing the ruins of an empire—of Napoleon's Second Empire, which had seemed an affluent, powerful, enduring regime until it undid itself in war with Prussia. So to many, the ruins appropriately marked the *sic transit* of empire.

One sees the ruins' aesthetic in full flower in a rare oil painting of the Tuileries done by Ernest Meissonier, famous as a painter of Napoleonic battles and nearly an official court painter under the Second Empire. Look first at Andrieu's photograph of the peristyle in the palace (Figure 23), and then Meissonier's painting (Figure 24). Meissonier, possibly working from the contemporary photographs, uses a sightline through the ruined *Salle des Fêtes* of the palace out toward the Arc de Triomphe du Carrousel, originally part of the palace complex but today standing alone in the Tuileries Garden, itself a kind of evocation of what once was there. Meissonier apparently described the arch with its imperial figure in a chariot drawn by four horses as "Victory on her chariot . . . abandoning us." But others viewed this glimpse of past glory through the ruins as promise of a better future, the rebirth of France.

The painting of course stands in a long tradition of evocative ruins, reaching back to G. B. Piranesi and Hubert Robert, which are often meditations on the transitory nature of human works and aspirations. Meissonier explicitly inserts himself in the tradition of painters of Roman ruins with the Latin inscription he has placed on an escutcheon at the foot of his painting: "Gloria Maiorum per Flammas usque Superstes / Maius MDCCCLXXI" [The glory of our forebears survives through the flames / May 1871], predicting a greater future to the survivors of the flames— that image of purification by fire that would return again and again. And on the walls of the ruins in Meissonier's painting one can detect the inscriptions "Marengo" and "Austerlitz," bearing witness to two of the first Napoleon's great victories. Meissonier's canvas captures that mixture of emotions we find in the guidebooks: a sense of irrecoverable loss, along with a fascination with the ruins left in the wake of that loss, along, also, with an obligatory hope for the future, a call for the resurrection of French glory purged by the flames, as in Zola's account in *The Debacle*.

Since the work of Roland Barthes and Susan Sontag on photography, we have become acutely aware of the cohabitation of the photograph with death, the haunting sense that the instant made present in the image exists no longer. This death effect is strangely redoubled in the case of photographs of the remains of what once was. The point can be starkly underlined by the most famous photo from the Bloody Week, probably taken by Eugène Disdéri (who earlier invented the calling card embellished with a photographic portrait, which expanded photography throughout the middle classes), of the bodies of executed Communards in their coffins (Figure 25).

The circumstances and intention of this stark, haunting, nearly unbearable photo remain conjectural. It somehow looks like an official act of witnessing, and some have suggested that Disdéri took the photo at the behest of the victorious Versaillais, to record the dead—which is not wholly persuasive when one thinks of how most of the dead went wholly unrecorded, thrown into unmarked mass graves. In any event, the photo authenticates, more than any other document I know, the horror of the event. It is, incidentally, just about the only authentic photo of the victims. Most other photos of dead National Guard and troops and civilians appear to be staged, or else photomontages. Whereas Matthew Brady's American Civil War photos record bodies mowed down like wheat fields, with the exception of Disdéri's the bodies are absent from the photos of 1871 Paris, probably because they were carted off the scene so quickly by a government anxious to erase them. Yet there is also an act of artistic witnessing, less horrifying than the photo but equally tragic, in the sketchy lithograph by Edouard Manet—who left Paris after the armistice but returned during the Bloody Week—called, simply, *Guerre Civile* (*Civil War*, Figure 26).

The very lack of photos of the action of the Bloody Week, the way in which emphasis has been thrown instead onto the ruins of Paris, suggests the specific form of intervention of the photograph into the historiography of the moment. The visually recorded history of the life and death of the Commune *is* the ruins left in their wake. The burning of Paris becomes the unforgettable and unpardonable record. That may explain why the image of the largely mythic *pétroleuse*, the proletarian woman running from building to building with a milk can filled with petrol to start a fire, became so dominant in the first journalistic histories of the Commune. The *pétroleuse* is a figure invented to create a dramatic and infernal narrative of the burning of central Paris. She is in a sense a fictional narrative that results from the photographs.

Recall Alfred d'Aunay's words: this sight had the sun for witness, and the sun fixed the image on photographic paper. The witnessing of the Commune is largely in those ruins. Photography inflects history. It produces fictions of the events whose outcome it records. Though the memorialization of historical event was by this point in the nineteenth century clearly a central role for photography—witness the American Civil War, its image fixed for us so much through photographs—the ruins of Paris photographs make a different kind of contribution to the creation of history. They take on a forensic role while the events are still ongoing in public memory—while the trials of the Communards, for instance, go forward at Versailles. They offer a kind of "factual" support for the existence and death of the Commune, its trace left in the destruction of central Paris. Roland Barthes writes: "Perhaps we have an invincible resistance to believing in the past, in History, except in the form of myth. The Photograph, for the first time, puts an end to this resistance: henceforth the past is as certain as the present, what we see on paper is as certain as what we touch. It is the advent of the Photograph—and not, as has been said, of the cinema—which divides the history of the world." In the absence of action photographs, in the aftermath of the massacre of so many of the Communards, including their leaders, the mute testimony of the photographed ruins allows the construction of a history.

Yet the mute photograph of aftermath permits different interpretations, including the fictions concocted by the victors. There will be many of those in the wake of the Commune. Since there was an official wish to silence the history of the Terrible Year, most of the early versions of the event are, like the guidebooks, united in a condemnation of the Communards that makes Flaubert's rhetoric seem almost moderate. A few accounts by participants were published soon after the event, but abroad: no French publisher could have touched them. The crucial *History of the Commune of 1871* (*L'histoire de la Commune de 1871*) by Prosper-Olivier Lissagaray—journalist, editor of *Le Tribun du peuple* in 1871, and a key figure among exiled Communards in London—was published in Brussels in 1876 and translated into English by Eleanor Marx Aveling, Karl Marx's daughter. After the amnesty vote of 1880, and the return of the surviving

Communards from New Caledonia, there are memoirs and histories of the event. One has to await the twentieth century for a commemorative plaque to the dead of the Commune to be affixed to the Mur des Fédérés (Communards' Wall) at the foot of Père Lachaise Cemetery, where in a bloody final showdown, some 127 were shot by the Versaillais and thrown into a mass grave (Figure 27).

The Wall became a site of memory with the annual *montée au mur* (ascent to the wall), which from 1880 onward gathered socialists, communists, and other leftist formations with tributes, oral and floral, every May, in commemoration of the Bloody Week. It reached its apogee during the Popular Front in 1936, with a crowd of 600,000.

There were to be other kinds of commemorations: in Victor Hugo's attempt to reconcile the warring parties in his novel *Ninety-Three*, in the construction of the Basilica of the Sacred Heart on the heights of Montmartre, where the Commune began its resistance. Flaubert's *Sentimental Education*, on the other hand, curiously anticipates the ruins of Paris in 1871. In its portrayal of Flaubert's own generation in its rendezvous with a major historical event, the Revolution of 1848, it may suggest the ruin of our anticipations of desired results from historical action. And like the discourse of ruins, it reaches for a significance beyond the fictional, as an understanding of what happened, in the lives of his contemporaries and the history they lived through. With Flaubert's visit to the ruins and his comment to Maxime Du Camp that *Sentimental Education* should have saved his contemporaries from this tragic folly, we have prepared ourselves to see that novel in its full significance as an act of history making.

– chapter four –

A Generation on Trial

⮝ Sentimental Education ⮞

*L'Education sentimentale is a book that for many years
has been as dear to me as are only two or three people;
whenever and wherever I open it, I am startled and
succumb to it completely, and I always feel as if I were the
author's spiritual son, albeit a weak and awkward one.*

—Franz Kafka, letter to Felice Bauer,
November 15, 1912

PROPHECIES HAVE A MOMENT OF UTTERANCE AND A MOMENT of realization. Flaubert's conviction that his novel of some eighteen months earlier ought to have prevented the devastation he found in Paris in June 1871 makes us want to loop back to that novel, seeing it not so much at its moment of publication as its moment of fulfillment. How could Flaubert claim that the novel should have kept his compatriots from "all this"—by which he no doubt meant at once the insurrection and its suppression, fratricidal violence and the destruction of the heart of the capital? *Sentimental Education* reaches its climax in the Revolution of 1848. But Flaubert is right: it is prophetic of the events of 1871 if you view the earlier revolution as a kind of dress rehearsal for the even more violent occurrences of 1871. To reread *Sentimental Education* from this perspective illuminates the novel in important ways. In particular, it makes us see how much Flaubert's claim to be writing the history of his generation turns on that generation's crucial rendezvous with history in 1848. Far more than any of his earlier work, *Sentimental Education* is deeply imbricated with politics. Its claim to be a generational history includes a claim to historiographical truth. His remark in the ruins of Paris rests on his belief that he had told the truth about his contemporaries as no one else had dared.

Especially in modern France, history was a dominant, an inevitable way of thinking. The Great Revolution of 1789 created a sense of radical break with the past, entry into a new world which, with however many subsequent setbacks, promised ideals of human liberty, equality, and political freedom. History at times appeared to run backward, as when the Bourbon monarchs were restored to the throne in 1815. But eventually they were ousted, and on the whole the movement of history was forward. It was about progress, onward moving time as the vessel of human fulfillment. Flaubert dissents from this faith: even before the great disillusionment of 1870–1871, history just does not seem to be carrying forward the work of humanity. And yet history is the unavoidable context of the characters' actions: it is the only medium in which the individual in the modern world can seek to exercise human agency. Humanity and its destiny have become profoundly historical, to Flaubert as to most of his contemporaries. But what does that mean for the individual in the search for happiness and fulfillment?

Like Kafka's haunted tales of hapless protagonists trapped within incomprehensible social rituals, *Sentimental Education* presents a world in which Romantic perceptions of agency, desire, and progress appear to be hollowed out. The motives that animate Flaubert's Frédéric Moreau are disarmed and thwarted repeatedly within the medium of historical time. It seems that when we think we are exercising agency, we are really caught in an inextricable mass of unenlightened intentions and mistaken actions. A proper reading of Flaubert's novel just might have convinced the generation of the Commune that our historical understanding must be based in *"science"*—the word in French has a wider semantic range than in English, referring to all domains of knowledge acquisition, including the "sciences of man."

The novel's engagement with history strikes us from the very first sentence: "On September 15, 1840, around 6 o'clock in the morning, the steamboat *Ville-de-Montereau*, about to depart, was belching clouds of smoke alongside the Quai Saint-Bernard." That may seem a bit awkward, or amateurish—in a writing seminar you'd be told to revise that opening. The date could come in later, more casually. But Flaubert wanted the flat-footedness of that date at the very outset as a marker of the relation of his novel—subtitled *Story of a Young Man*—to the passage of time, and specifically historical time. The opening may make us want to ask why it is so important that we know the exact moment at which the story begins. What lies ahead? The answer, we will discover, is an event datable in history, a historical milestone. The Revolution of 1848 bursts upon the novel on the very last page of Part 2. Everything up until then, both in "the story of a young man" and in the ambient historical events, has prepared for the moment of 1848, and Part 3 will play out its consequences and sequels. "The moment was coming," as one of the characters tells us some pages earlier—there are other similar premonitory markers—and when it comes, it tests our young man and all his contemporaries.

That first sentence stands as its own paragraph, as a kind of summons to reflect what the young man's travels on September 15, 1840, might come to mean. The second paragraph contains another kind of lesson for reading this novel. "People were arriving, out of breath; barrels, cables, laundry baskets got in their way; the sailors didn't answer anyone; people banged into one another; baggage piled up between the two paddle wheels, and the racket was absorbed in the hissing of the steam, which, escaping from the iron plates, enclosed everything in a whitish cloud, all the while the bell, at the bow, clanged on incessantly."

People are just "people": *des gens, on*—unnamed, unidentified—whereas all the agency is given to things: barrels, cables, laundry baskets, packages. The sailors don't answer any questions put to them. Everything is subject to unpleasant noise and enveloped in a cloud of steam. We're being prepared for a larger problem of agency. When we discover the "young man," eighteen years old, standing near the ship's rudder with an art album under his arm, who has just completed his baccalaureate, who has been visiting his rich uncle in Le Havre and now is on his way home to Nogent-sur-Seine and the boredom of two months of vacation, with this mother, before coming to Paris to study law, we are told: "He found that the happiness merited by the excellence of his soul was long in coming." A treacherous sentence, which places Frédéric Moreau (as the young man is named) in a tradition of romantic longing and belief in the merits of the beautiful soul that the novel will repeatedly question. If things, and noise, and industrial steam have taken precedence at the start—as the subjects of all the verbs—with people reduced to the status of an impersonal crowd, what's to be the place of the beautiful soul in the world?

As with most great novels, this one contains in its early pages the indications of how to read and understand it. There is, for instance, the river journey itself, with the landscape of the shores on either side unfolding in a kind of unedited traveling shot, boringly the same, without human figures. In the sky, immobile clouds. And boredom—*l'ennui*—vaguely pervasive, "seemed to slow the progress of the boat and made the appearance of the voyagers yet more insignificant." On board, Frédéric meets Jacques Arnoux, who directs the "hybrid" enterprise, part art journal and part gallery, known as *L'Art Industriel*. A nicely oxymoronic title: the marriage of art with the industrial regime that in the 1840s was more and more evidently dominant in France. Arnoux attempts to churn out "le sublime à bon marché": the cut-rate sublime.

Then, in the midst of this insignificance and ennui, there is Frédéric's first view of Madame Arnoux, which stands in a paragraph to itself:

It was like an apparition.

She will by the end of the voyage, once Frédéric has gone ashore, have become a "luminous point" in his existence. And so she will remain, for better and for worse. The novel recounts a great love story—of sorts.

So Flaubert sets up in his first chapter the problematics of a young man of romantic temper, fallen in love at first sight with an older and married woman, who somehow is going to have to negotiate the history of the 1840s in France, at a moment where the art to which he is dedicated has become subjected to the industrial, where the Romantic "sublime" has been discounted. If the figure of Madame Arnoux is a luminous point, one that immobilizes much of Frédéric's affective life, Jacques Arnoux is twisted into the fabric of the novel as a figure of movement, of ambition, exploitation, the turning of everything to attempted profit, the degradation of art into commodity. From art merchant and publisher he becomes pottery maker, then in his final decadence seller of religious objects. The other characters who will be introduced—Frédéric's school friend Charles Deslauriers, penniless, ambitious for advancement yet also a malcontent ready for revolution; Hussonnet the bohemian playwright and journalist; Pellerin the talentless artist; Cisy, the traditionalist provincial aristocrat; Dussardier the brave and exploited proletarian; Sénécal the puritanical schoolmaster who will become a pitiless political figure; Dambreuse the capitalist entrepreneur whose goal is to curry favor with whoever is in power—these and many others interweave in a helix around the ongoing movement of history toward and through 1848. Marcel Proust described the novel, affectionately, as a kind of "moving sidewalk," like those in the Paris Métro, that brings the same characters back, again and again, in a way that seems haphazard, due only to chance, but may also reveal the workings of history.

What is a "historical novel"? A classic definition comes from Alessandro Manzoni, author of *The Betrothed* (*I Promessi Sposi*), one of the finest novels in the tradition of Walter Scott, one that sets out "to represent, by means of an invented action, the true state of humanity in a past and historical epoch." That meant, and still means today, an attempt to reconstruct and revivify a period of the past: the Historical Novel Society claims that to fit within the genre a novel must deal with a time at least fifty years prior to the writing. By that definition, Flaubert, writing in the mid-1860s about the mid-1840s, doesn't make the cut. But a broader view of things might note that the realist novel of the nineteenth century, in Honoré de Balzac, for instance, used Scott's example but moved the historical period represented from far-off times to the near-present: Balzac is generally writing about events some fifteen or twenty years prior to the time of writing. Scott and Manzoni's efforts to represent the totality of a society, its spirit—what we sometimes call a novelistic world—may have inspired the realists' desire to represent their own world, the totality and the spirit of contemporary society. Flaubert's novel very much inscribes itself in that tradition, though with striking differences.

For one thing, there is no Olympian narrator to take an overview of events, to synthesize and evoke the historical ensemble. Flaubert's camera eye remains resolutely, restlessly, on the level of his persons and things. What his doctrine of the author's impersonality has become here, more radically than in *Madame Bovary*, is the distribution of most comments on events and sentiments to his characters, via free indirect discourse, used in a way that often makes it difficult for the reader to tell where a character's view ends and authorial comment begins. Flaubert is truly hidden, only a kind of lurking editorial presence. For another, Frédéric lacks the devouring appetite of Balzac's young heroes, who, like Eugène de Rastignac, want to "succeed at any price." That Balzacian ambition promotes almost an oral incorporation of the world: everything is brought together, the whole is seen as a totality, through a young man's wanting love, power, and money. Frédéric is like a Balzacian hero who has lost his ambition, who has lost the force of desperate wanting. Intensity of wanting has been redistributed to Deslauriers, who in fact early in the novel evokes Balzac's paragon of ambition: "Remember Rastignac in the *Human Comedy*! You'll succeed, I'm sure of it!" Too easy a prediction: even in Deslauriers' case, success will prove elusive. It's as if the power of the will had become diffused in the world, the Balzacian capacity to concentrate it on what is wished for no longer available. And then, you might say that something has happened to history itself. It no longer functions as the explanatory narrative that redeems failure and misery in an upward slope of progress.

———

WHAT HAPPENS IN PARTS 1 and 2 of *Sentimental Education*, which lead to the Revolution of 1848 as the event that dominates Part 3? Frédéric returns to Paris after the visit to his mother in Nogent—and his reunion with Deslauriers—ostensibly to study law. Life in Paris becomes fixated on finding a means to make the acquaintance of Madame Arnoux. After finally managing a first dinner in the amiably bohemian Arnoux milieu (though the ménage is riven by Jacques Arnoux's perpetual infidelities and his close to fraudulent financial expedients), Frédéric returns to his apartment and stops in the middle of the Pont-Neuf as 1 o'clock strikes like the voice of his vocation. He is seized by "one of those shivers of the soul which make you think you have been raised into a higher world." And now, "He asked himself, seriously, if he would become a great painter or a great poet; and he decided in favor of painting, since the requirements of that profession would bring him closer to Madame Arnoux. He had found his vocation then! The goal of his existence was clear now, and the future could not fail." That "seriously," set off with commas, appears treacherous, an ironization of Frédéric's moment of conversion (which may parody St. Augustine's), though without narrator or author taking responsibility for it. It is left to the reader to puzzle out what that "seriously" is doing in its parenthetic place in the sentence. Then Frédéric reaches his apartment: "When he had closed the door, he heard someone snoring, in the dark alcove next to his bedroom. It was the other. He thought no more about him." This "other" is his best friend Deslauriers, just arrived to share Frédéric's digs, and deserted on his first night in Paris so Frédéric would not miss the Arnoux dinner. The thought of Deslauriers dismissed, the chapter ends in a moment of narcissistic rapture: "His face appeared before him in the mirror. He thought himself handsome, and stood a moment to gaze at himself."

These three short paragraphs at the end of Chapter 4 of Part 1 capture much of Frédéric's dilemma and his character. He has no deep interest in the law. He has artistic leanings of all sorts—he writes poetry and drama, he wants to paint—but never the self-confidence or willpower to carry through in any of them. His self-mirroring becomes a kind of immobilism, an inability to move forward. Any commitment to a line of action is likely to be interfered with by another contingency. When his best friend comes to join him in Paris, he goes to dine with the Arnoux. When the wealthy capitalist Dambreuse proposes that Frédéric become his private secretary, and buy into new coal mine shares that are bound to return a handsome profit, Frédéric sells an inherited farm and prepares to take the proceeds to Dambreuse. But he then learns that Madame Arnoux is alone at her husband's pottery factory at Creil, and rushes there instead. When that leads to nothing, he comes back to Paris to find a note from the seductive Rosanette Bron, and accompanies her to the races (where his carriage intersects with that of Madame Arnoux, who sees him with the cocotte, creating an "irreparable" harm), which leads to a dinner at Café Anglais, which in turn leads to a duel with the Baron de Cisy, . . . and so on. There is a kind of serial unfolding of the plot, one thing leading to another without a return to any master plot for one's life. When Frédéric has taken 10,000 francs from his capital to fund a new political journal to be edited by Deslauriers, he ends up lending the money—never to be paid back, of course—to Jacques Arnoux. Later, when he becomes the lover of the elegant Madame Dambreuse, he takes on Rosanette as mistress at the same time, living a life of two contrasting desires, "two musics" that interfere without creating harmony. And when he is at last summoned by Deslauriers to participate in the demonstration in February 1848 that will kick off the revolution, he doesn't respond, because he has a tryst arranged, finally, with Madame Arnoux—and has taken and tastefully furnished an apartment to this end. Then, when she fails to show up, retained by her child ill with the croup, he takes Rosanette to bed in the place prepared for his great love.

Frédéric's life—and the novel's plot—seems to be constructed on interferences, if such an idea makes sense. Every decisive crossroads, every crucial moment, produces a distraction more than a decision or a happening. Whereas the Balzacian hero defines the future through his desiring, desire itself in this novel stands under the figure of chiasmus: crossings that hinder rather than enable. But to talk about interferences and chiasmatic desire in terms of Frédéric's character maybe misses the point. Henry James called him an "abject human specimen" and wondered that Flaubert could choose so limited "reflectors and registers" of experience, even of "middling experience." The reader, says James, follows Frédéric's life while asking "Why, why *him?*" James sees acutely the difference between Jamesian and Flaubertian ideas of what a novel should be, but I don't think he can quite grasp what Flaubert is up to. Frédéric's limitations and his abjection in relation to the traditional protagonist's role may be what make him just right for Flaubert's conception of a historical novel. Frédéric is there not to control history, not even truly to participate in historical events, but to undergo happenings of cataclysmic violence and criminal idiocy. He is inadequate as "register and reflector" of history because to offer an adequate consciousness of the event would be a falsification, or else madness. Already in the confrontation of the Revolution of 1848 the greater human horror of the Commune looms as a potentiality.

During his student days in Paris, Frédéric wanders around the city. He resembles the young Balzacian hero newly arrived from the provinces and full of appetite for riches, power, and women, but somehow his desire lacks consistency and leverage on the world. There is a striking demonstration of this when he strolls on the Champs-Elysées, nearly retracing the itinerary of Balzac's Lucien de Rubempré in *Lost Illusions*. (I suspect Flaubert had his predecessor's novel open before him as he wrote the scene.) Lucien has been rejected by his sometime protectress, Madame de Bargeton. She has claimed illness to break off her rendezvous with him. When he then encounters her in perfect health in a carriage on the Champs-Elysées with her fashionable cousin Madame d'Espard (the summit of Parisian society) and they snub him, his alienation at once takes the form of resolve: "I'll roll down the Champs-Elysées in a fine carriage with a footman! I'll have Madame d'Espard's!" Rejection is the springboard of desire, what propels Lucien forward in a quest to have, to devour the world of fashion, whereas Frédéric's promenade leads to his imaginings of Madame Arnoux inserted amid the fashionable women on display in their open carriages—but to nothing more. The sun begins to set, the carriages trot briskly down the avenue, and the passage ends with a description of a scene void of human agents: "Behind the Tuileries, the sky took on the color of the slate roofs.

The trees in the garden formed two enormous masses, become violet at their summit. The gas lamps came on; and the Seine, greenish all along, broke into silvery silk against the pillars of the bridges." The passage is beautiful, far more so than my English rendition. But what has happened to Frédéric, to desire for possession, to the ambition that normally drives the novelistic hero forward? When finally Frédéric enters the world of luxury, and in a fine carriage, along with the fashionable Rosanette, returns down the Champs-Elysées from the races at the Champ de Mars, he recalls his earlier daydreams of happiness. "He now possessed it, that very happiness, and he took no joy from it." Something is amiss with the force of desire itself: it has become less the all-consuming appetency for the world that it was in Balzac and more what the French call a *velléité*, which is not exactly a whim, but a vague and insubstantial desire. He builds himself castles in the air—more precisely, "Moresque palaces," filled with plashing fountains and beautiful girls—and falls into regret when he awakes from his daydreams to find they are not real.

When Frédéric returns to his mother's home in Nogent at the end of his first year of law school, he learns that the family fortune has disappeared in a series of financial lapses and mishaps, and that he can no longer consider himself the rich young gentleman he had been. Chapter 6 of Part 1 of the novel begins melodramatically: "Ruined, undone, lost!" His entire life plan has been destroyed. He acquiesces to his mother's advice and becomes an assistant to the local *notaire*, and begins to sink into the routine boredom of provincial life. Then one morning as he dawdles in bed he receives a letter informing him that his uncle in Le Havre has died intestate, and as nearest relative he has inherited a fortune. He immediately plans a return to Paris, and begins daydreaming of the luxuries with which he will surround his courtship of Madame Arnoux. So in the space of a single chapter, ten pages long, we have covered the whole arc of a Balzacian novel: from dispossession to great wealth, from the provinces to Paris, from deprivation of the loved woman to a renewed courtship. Yet when his mother asks him what he plans to do, exactly, in his Parisian existence, he replies: "Nothing!" Doing nothing appears to be the realization of a dream of happiness.

One more incident is crucial to understanding the mode of the novel as it prepares a generation for its rendezvous with history. Shortly after Frédéric's return to Paris with his inheritance, Arnoux brings him late one night to a masked ball hosted by Rosanette, who is Arnoux's occasional mistress (her favors are widely shared), and who will later become Frédéric's, and briefly the mother of his child. He is dazzled by the garish luxury of her apartment, and by the bizarre and exciting panoply of the costumes he encounters, especially of the women. Flaubert's technique in the chapter is to name all the guests by way of their costumes, as if literalizing the roles they represent for one night. Rosanette herself, for instance, is costumed as a dragoon of the time of Louis XV, complete with wig and spurs, and thus given the military name of Marshal, *la Maréchale*, and will continue under that designation for the evening. And so with the other guests. The result is a surreal *Walpurgisnacht*, bringing before the sharp novelistic lens the nature of "modern love," an eros all the more intense for its artificiality. The masked ball episode extends over several pages. To take just one moment, there is the waltz, a vertiginous, spinning movement that induces in the watching Frédéric a sort of intoxication particularized in each type of eros:

> The Polonaise, who abandoned herself in a languorous manner, inspired in him the wish to hold her against his heart, while gliding together in a sleigh over a snowy plain. Horizons of tranquil voluptuousness, by a lake, in a chalet, unfurled under the feet of the Swiss Maid, who waltzed with her torso straight and her eyelids lowered. Then, suddenly, the Bacchante, flinging back her dark hair, made him dream of devouring kisses, in a copse of flowering laurel, in stormy weather, to the muffled sound of tambourines. The Fishwife, who was out of breath from the beat, too fast for her, was shrieking with laughter; and he would have liked, drinking with her at Porcherons, to have run his hands under the fichu covering her bosom, like in the good old days. But the Stevedore, whose little toes barely touched the floor, seemed to harbor in her supple limbs and her serious face all the refinements of modern love, which has the exactitude of a science and the mobility of a bird. Rosanette was

spinning, her fist on her hip; her rolled wig, bouncing on her ruffled collar, released iris-scented powder in a cloud; and, with each turn, with the tip of her gold spurs, she almost caught Frédéric.

The passage bears comparison with the moment in *Madame Bovary* where Emma daydreams around the word "honeymoon," imagining a series of happy escapes to "lands with sonorous names," where life must be more fully realized. Like Emma's imaginings, the *bal masqué* is marked by the inauthentic, by disguise, a substitution of the fictitious for the real. But here at Rosanette's, the inauthentic reveals something profound about the nature of desire as experienced by Frédéric and his companions: it is always already marked by disguise, by the fictitious, even the fake. That makes it all the more alluring, but not something to rely on.

The underside of desire shows through with the coming of dawn, which lays bare the sordid aftermath of orgy. In particular, the Sphinx, who has been drinking strong liquors, suddenly grabs her napkin, spits up blood, then throws the napkin under the table—but not before Frédéric has witnessed the incident. When he tells her that she should leave and seek medical attention, she shrugs it off: "What's the use? If not this, it'd be something else. Life isn't much fun." Then Frédéric shivers, seized by a glacial sadness "as if he had seen through to whole worlds of misery and despair, a charcoal brazier next to a trundle bed, and the cadavers of the morgue in leather aprons, with the tap of cold water that runs through their hair." The charcoal brazier was a favored means of committing suicide among the Paris poor (used in a Balzac novel, too). Notable here is the move from Flaubert's past narrative tenses—most often, the imperfect tense of repetitive, habitual action—to the present: "le robinet d'eau froide qui coule sur leur cheveux." It gives his vision a kind of eternal present—bringing to the facsimile eros of the ball the underlying reality of death. One is tempted to say that the death drive always underlies the pleasure principle in this novel.

On his return from the ball, Frédéric lies awake with a wine-induced headache, dreaming ardently of women and the luxury of a certain Parisian world. In the hallucination of his first restless sleep, "he saw pass before him, again and again, the shoulders of the Fishwife, the thighs of the Stevedore, the ankles of the Polonaise, the mane of the Savage." Then two grand black eyes—those of Madame Arnoux, but he can't identify them—flutter through the scene. And then the dream overtakes him again: "He seemed to be harnessed next to Arnoux, in the shafts of a cab, and the Marshal, astride him, was ripping open his flanks with her golden spurs." That the discovery of Parisian eros should end with this sadomasochistic dream by this point seems merely self-evident. Frédéric's desire is atomized and incoherent. He can never bring it to bear on the one woman he truly wants, and it scatters among those he doesn't. It is self-defeating and self-wounding.

Frédéric decides that the decisive moment to conquer Madame Arnoux has arrived when he learns that she is at her husband's pottery factory in Creil, and Arnoux himself is absent. The trip to Creil (abandoning his promised meeting with Dambreuse) becomes a full-scale demonstration of the impossibility of a certain kind of romantic passion in the new world of "industrial art." Frédéric stumbles through the new ugly industrializing landscape of Creil—no longer countryside, but not urban, a kind of scar on the landscape—to reach Arnoux's factory, nearby at Montataire. He finds Madame Arnoux in her dressing gown, but this moment of possible intimacy is quickly effaced. And as he follows her around the factory under the guidance of Sénécal, who has become Arnoux's foreman, and a repressive one—in prefiguration of his later incarnation as gendarme—each time he tries to make a declaration of his passion there is an interruption. As he begins one statement with "trembling voice," the "racket of a steam pump drowned out his words"—and so on. Sénécal's demonstration of technique leads to a language of pure cacophony: "les pyroscopes, les alandiers, les englobes, les lustres et les métaux, prodiguant les termes de chimie, chlorure, sulfure, borax, carbonate." The meaning of the terms has no importance (many of them outside the usual lexicon even of the French reader): they represent manufacturing noise; they signify ugliness, industrialism, and the impossibility of romantic love. The visit to Creil ends in a kind of mutism. Frédéric cites the Romantic poetry of Musset. Nothing works. Madame Arnoux concludes that virtuous women must be deaf when it's necessary, and she and Frédéric take their leave without another word. Back in Paris, he turns his pursuit to Rosanette.

The love plot of the novel—that is, Frédéric's only abiding passion, for Madame Arnoux—revives and approaches a promised climax on February 22, 1848. He has spent an idyllic time visiting Madame Arnoux in the country house in Auteuil that Arnoux has rented while pursuing his various business and amorous intrigues in Paris. The idyll is more and more charged with a repressed sexual desire seeking an outlet, and Frédéric finally exacts from her the promise of a rendezvous to walk arm-in-arm in Paris on the afternoon of the 22nd. He then rents a furnished room in the rue Tronchet, decorates it with luxurious accessories, and at the appointed time and place goes to wait for Madame Arnoux, in the hope that their stroll will end in bed. Meanwhile, demonstrations against the government are under way: from fear of civil disorder, it has outlawed a scheduled Reform Banquet designed to promote a broader suffrage (only one of thirty citizens met the property qualifications for voting, and since public assemblies were banned, banquets had become the preferred means of protest). Deslauriers has convoked Frédéric to join his comrades with the phrase "The pear is ripe": King Louis Philippe had come to resemble a pear in the work of caricaturists. But Frédéric can't respond to the summons: he might miss the rendezvous with Madame Arnoux. And as the police start rounding up demonstrators and hauling them off, Frédéric must repress his generous instinct to join them for fear of missing his moment with her. She, meanwhile, is wholly taken up with her infant son, who has fallen ill of the croup, and she passes anxious hours while he seems near death; but then he coughs up the obstructing membrane, and is saved. She never comes to the rendezvous.

Frédéric the next day meets Rosanette, who has been deserted by the prince who kept her, and is terrified by the political crisis. They go to dinner at the Trois Frères Provençaux and have a "long and delicate" meal. As they walk the streets of insurrectionary Paris afterward, they hear "a noise like the crackling of an immense piece of silk torn in two." This is the "massacre" of the Boulevard des Capucines, the evening of February 23, a confrontation of demonstrators and troops that led to firing on the crowd, with about fifty casualties. The bodies were then paraded by torchlight through the streets on carts, as bells rang out the call to arms. By the next day, the situation moved quickly from a revolt to a revolution, and Louis Philippe abdicated in favor of his nine-year-old grandson with an interim Regency—but this solution was quickly overcome by events, and the Second French Republic was proclaimed, with poet Lamartine as provisional head of state. Meanwhile, Frédéric leads Rosanette to the room prepared for Madame Arnoux. At one in the morning, waking to the distant sounds of the insurrection under way, Rosanette finds Frédéric sobbing. When she asks what's the matter, he replies: "It's from too much happiness. . . . I've wanted you for too long!"

———

HERE PART 2 OF the novel ends, on Frédéric's lie—he has possessed the wrong woman in the place meant for the other, the true love. He has missed his rendezvous with Madame Arnoux, a moment that will not come again, and missed also his rendezvous with history: failed to join Deslauriers and the others who have been waiting for years for this moment of political ripeness to arrive. When he awakes on the morning of February 24, he resists Rosanette's entreaties that he stay in bed and goes off to join the insurrection—but as an observer more than a fighter. And from now on the novel will be given over to the revolution, seen mainly through the eyes of Frédéric as a kind of sympathetic but not fully engaged participant/observer, with various other eyewitnesses set in conversation with him: the bohemian Hussonnet, the true participant Dussardier, the painter Pellerin, the fearful banker Dambreuse, and the "citizen" Regimbart, who provides a kind of choral commentary on political events. There is thus a play of different illuminations and political perspectives. Flaubert presents both the participant's perspective, as when Frédéric joins the insurgents in an attack on the police station at the Château d'Eau, and larger integrative views. You can sense Flaubert's desire to be encompassing and evenhanded, yet to tell history from the point of view of those who were on the ground.

What's the Revolution of 1848 like in Flaubert's rendition? He prepared himself thoroughly for his representation of 1848, as I noted earlier: in history books, memoirs, and recollections of acquaintances to complement his own memories. He didn't like to undertake writing about anything without a sense of mastery. His presentation is broad and in many ways dispassionate, clearly the result of an effort to get things right, to give as accurate an account as any that a professional historian could provide. And yet it is shot through with a corrosive doubt about the meaning of any such undertaking. As in other matters of the novel, there is a discrepancy between volition and action, between intention and result, perhaps, more radically, between human agency and the unknown and unmastered forces that truly determine history. Flaubert in my view gives a largely unbiased version of 1848, but his neutrality very often seems to proclaim a curse on both houses: he implies that both sides in the struggle are motivated by delusions.

When, following his night with Rosanette, Frédéric goes off to join the insurgency, he is caught up in the spirit of the moment, and faces the flying musket balls without flinching. But the purpose of this attack on the garrison of the Château d'Eau (in what is now the Place de la République) is to "free fifty prisoners, who weren't there." The comment will prove characteristic: heroic action directed to a meaningless goal. Things become still more complicated. The monarchy of Louis Philippe collapses quickly, the crowd moves to occupy the Tuileries Palace. Here we have an extended set-piece that might stand as a monument to reportage on revolution. It has the virtues of wide-screen cinema, creating a dramatic panorama of the taking of the palace, an event at which Flaubert, along with Maxime Du Camp, had been an eyewitness. Yet by its end it has already suggested the worst that revolution can offer. The scene is witnessed by Frédéric and Hussonnet, who have reached the Salle des Maréchaux on the second floor of the building. Frédéric is caught up in the heroics of the moment, while Hussonnet offers a counterpoint of sarcasm.

> Suddenly the *Marseillaise* rang out. Hussonnet and Frédéric hung over the balustrade. It was the people. They rushed up the staircase, bringing

a flood of bare heads, workers' caps, red bonnets, bayonets and shoulders, so impetuously that individuals disappeared in this seething mass that moved ever upward, like a river pushed backward by a spring tide, with a long roar, driven by irresistible impulse. At the top of the stairs, the crowd dispersed, and the song died down.

It's never easy to translate Flaubert. Here, part of the effect comes from using the singular collective noun *le peuple* as the subject of the following sentence (where I translated "They rushed . . ."), so that it seems as if the mass of the people is for a time a single, elemental force, like a spring tide. As the crowd disperses at the top of the stairway, Hussonnet remarks: "The heroes don't smell good!" To which Frédéric replies: "You're really annoying." They enter the throne room to find a grotesque proletarian seated in the place of power, while others line up to take their turn. "What a myth," Hussonnet comments. "There's the sovereign people!"

The throne is tossed from a window into the courtyard, to be taken to the Bastille and burned. "Then, a frenetic joy broke out, as if, in place of the throne, a future of unlimited happiness had appeared." In demonstration of that future, the mob takes to smashing the furniture, the mirrors, the paintings, pulling out and putting on dresses, shawls, lace. The smashing and breaking is not all: "An obscene curiosity made them search in all the cabinets, all the hiding places, and open all the drawers. Convicts sunk their arms into the beds of princesses and rolled around on them as consolation for not being able to rape them." Others ferret out objects of value to steal. As the air becomes suffocating, Frédéric and Hussonnet move out.

In the antechamber, standing atop a pile of clothing, was a whore, in the pose of a statue of Liberty—unmoving, her eyes wide open, terrifying.

History in Flaubert's rendition has a tendency to resolve into fixed snapshots, as if in imitation of the new art of photography. Here the silent plastic image of the *fille publique* as Liberty remains with the reader as one of those summary representations of revolution, unforgettable and troubling. Whatever else 1848 may be it is a repetition of the great

Revolution—possibly, as Marx would claim, in the mode of farce. But after this debased image of revolution, upon leaving the Tuileries, Frédéric and Hussonnet encounter Dussardier, who has been on his feet for forty-eight hours—a true participant in the revolution who believes in what it has accomplished. "We'll be happy now!" he exclaims, in a remark that suggests both what is worth fighting for and its delusions.

In the following pages we get the reactions of the cast of characters Flaubert has so carefully assembled, from the ambitious Deslauriers, who manages to have himself at once appointed a republican commissioner, replacing a *préfet* of the former regime; to the painter Pellerin, who produces a hideous allegory of "the Republic, or Progress, or Civilization, in the guise of Jesus Christ, driving a locomotive through a virgin forest"; to the banker Dambreuse, who endorses the new republic from fear while studying ways to undermine it. It is Dambreuse who suggests to Frédéric that he stand for *député* from Nogent. Frédéric, encouraged by Deslauriers and Rosanette, accepts: "Frédéric, man of all weaknesses, was won over by the universal madness, and accepted." Here we encounter Flaubert at his most problematic. Frédéric the dreamer and drifter would seem to most readers to have at last made a decision that gives his existence a purpose, an honorable one. Why must Flaubert qualify the decision to seek public office as the result of weakness and unreason? Why must politics in and of itself be condemned as frivolity?

Flaubert carries forward his demonstration over the following pages, as Frédéric's candidacy leads him to visit the various political clubs to seek their backing. This was the moment for clubs, a particularly French way of doing politics. And Flaubert's rendition has the ring of truth, according to an expert historian. "They visited them all, or nearly all, the red and blue, the enraged and the peaceful, the puritan, the licentious, the mystical and the drunken, those where they decreed the death of kings, those where they complained of price-fixing by grocers; and everywhere, tenants cursed landlords, the worker's smock raged against the frockcoat, and the rich conspired against the poor. . . . To show your good sense, you always had to denigrate lawyers, and to use as often as possible the locutions: 'add your stone to the building—social problem—workshop.'"

It's not an inspiring picture of "democracy" at work, though there is occasionally "a lightning flash of intelligence in these clouds of stupidity, apostrophes as sudden as splashes of mud, the law formulated in a swearword, flowers of eloquence on the lips of a cad wearing the strap of his sword on his shirtless torso."

Frédéric finally gets up the courage to present his platform speech to the Club of Intelligence, a hopeful name. In a hall filled largely by workers, he encounters the first of his misfortunes when he sees Sénécal enter and take the chair, offering (we continue in parody of the great Revolution) a kind of imitation Robespierre. After many trivial and futile announcements, the candidates for office begin to present themselves, each more absurd than the last. Finally it is Frédéric's turn to stand up. But before he can deliver his speech, Sénécal—now assuming the role of Antoine Quentin Fouquier-Tinville, the public prosecutor during the Reign of Terror—undertakes to interrogate him on his republican credentials. Was he present at the demonstration of February 22? Can he present a patriot who will testify to his beliefs? When Frédéric pokes the sleeping Regimbart to offer this testimony, Regimbart leaps to his feet and instead introduces a "patriot from Barcelona," who takes over the platform and proceeds to unleash a speech in Spanish. "This is absurd! No one can understand him!" Frédéric calls out—but this simply exasperates the crowd. Sénécal orders Frédéric to leave, and as the scene ends, the speech in Spanish is continuing, no end in sight: "Honor al pueblo francés, que llarmaria yo el primero pueblo del mundo, sino fuese ciudadano de otra nación!" Like the visit to Creil, intelligence ends in verbal cacophony—not industrial this time, but political. Here, as so often in the novel, it is hard to know where to assign blame. The Club de l'Intelligence represents, once again, revolution as farce. Yet Frédéric's credentials as a future representative are in fact null. The whole episode of attempted "representation" seems doomed to failure. The moral seems to be something like: Why bother?

Yet there are other moments that present quite a different picture. In particular, there is Regimbart, "the citizen," who spends his days and evenings moving from one café to another, reading the newspapers and offering political commentary. We come upon a passage of two long paragraphs that begins with him decrying the reaction that was under way by late February and March 1848. He evokes a string of incidents ending with the scarecrow of socialist theories, long debated in enough volumes to fill libraries, but nonetheless: "they terrified the bourgeois like a hail of meteorites." Flaubert interrupts his habitual imperfect here with a past definite: "elles épouvantèrent les bourgeois," as if to turn this terror into something outside of Regimbart's train of thought, making it a factual event, a moment to consign to a historical narrative. He goes on—Is he still following Regimbart's pronouncements in free indirect discourse?—to note that socialism provokes hatred because that is the fate of any idea because it's an idea, a rejection which will later redound to its glory, which means also that however mediocre it may be, it will always be superior to its enemies. As an idea, it appears, socialism stands above its detractors.

If up until now we have putatively been reading reportage of what Regimbart thinks and says (though the final lines of the paragraph create some doubt on that score), the next paragraph surely takes us beyond that speaker, into some kind of more impersonal authorial discourse:

> Now, Property rose in the respect of all to the level of Religion and became identical with God. Attacks on it appeared sacrilegious, almost cannibalistic. Despite the most humane legislation ever, the specter of '93 reappeared, and the blade of the guillotine vibrated in each syllable of the word Republic;—which didn't prevent people from despising it for its weakness. France, no longer sensing that it had a master, began to cry out in terror, like a blind man without his cane, like a toddler who has lost its nurse.

It's a very interesting passage for any discussion of Flaubert's political beliefs. The imperfect tense has been abandoned in favor of the past definite, giving the paragraph the aura of factual reporting rather than reported thought or speech. The worship of property, to Flaubert the provincial property-owner, appears an idolatry worthy of his contempt: recall the letter to Sand in which he execrates the "turdlike" Thiers's panegyric to *La Propriété*. I invoke the author as speaker here because it is difficult not to hear the voice of an author. It certainly is no longer Regimbart, though the transition from Regimbart to whoever speaks here is masked, smuggled away, as is so frequently the case in the novel. Whoever is speaking here does so with a kind of impersonal authority—and such authority suggests authorship. For Flaubert to call the legislation of the short-lived Second Republic the most humane ever may surprise us, though most readers to-day would tend to agree that the work of the provisional assembly was remarkably progressive: it included election by universal manhood suffrage, the abolition of slavery in French colonies, and of the death penalty for political crimes. The conjuring of the specter of the guillotine and the Reign of Terror of 1793 was a spectacular overreaction that would prepare the way for Louis-Napoléon Bonaparte's rise to power as the figure of "order." The final image of France as a blind man without his cane, as a child without its nurse, suggests a kind of Olympian judgment of a missed historical opportunity. Perhaps we are to conclude not only that Frédéric misses his rendezvous with history, but that France herself does—that the country is unequal to the regime of liberty that it opens for itself following the February revolution. That, after all, is something we have seen played out in the subsequent history of the world over and over. Flaubert the reactionary is also Flaubert the idealist, someone ready to salute a new order of freedom, peace, and social harmony. If only one could believe in it.

The promises of February 1848 came to grief in the first instance with the workers' insurrection against the fledgling republic in June. An overwhelming issue in 1848 was known as the *organisation du travail* (organization of work), from the proposal by the socialist Louis Blanc for a state-sponsored system that would guarantee every worker full and fair employment at a living wage. Blanc was a member of the provisional government, and his idea was given shape by the creation of the *ateliers nationaux*, state-run cooperative workshops that turned out to be something of a parody of what Blanc and other socialists had hoped for and proposed— mainly useless make-work jobs in an atmosphere that bred contempt and unrest. The legislative elections of April 23 resulted in a very moderate republican majority, the return to power of a number of figures from the former regime, and a reaction against socialism—*la République*, yes, but not *la République sociale*. The decision was made to disband the *ateliers* and to offer the workers in them a choice between enlistment in the military or work in the provinces on public works projects (such as canal building). The only other choice was starvation, since unemployment was at record levels. The result was the workers' uprising on June 22, which was soon suppressed with a level of pitiless bloodshed that prefigured the reaction to the Commune in 1871.

Here, Flaubert performs an extraordinary balancing act. First, he records the gathering of the proletarian crowd on the eve of the new insurrection. Frédéric witnesses the scene along with Dambreuse and his protégé Martinon. Crowds start to gather toward 9 o'clock in the evening near the Bastille and Châtelet, until they seem to become one moving mass, colored dark blue (the worker's smock), almost black:

> The men that one glimpsed all had ardent eyes, pale skin, faces emaciated from hunger, exalted by injustice. Meanwhile, clouds were gathering; the stormy sky heating the electricity of the crowd, it spun on itself, uncertain, with the wide surge of the ocean swell; and one felt in its depths an incalculable force, something like an elemental energy.

Dambreuse considers it prudent to take his leave at this point. And Frédéric, rather than staying on to witness the sequel, proposes to Rosanette that they leave Paris for Fontainebleau.

The coming bitter and bloody class warfare will thus go unwitnessed by Frédéric—it is not in fact directly recorded by anyone in the novel, which will bring us back to Paris only in the aftermath of the conflict. What we have instead is the "idyll" of Fontainebleau, which will open up other spheres of history, first in the visit to the royal château most closely associated with François I and his favorite woman, Diane de Poitiers (who was later mistress also of his son, Henri II). The château is magnificent, yet melancholic, its "immobile luxury proving by its old age the fugacity of dynasties, the eternal misery of everything." Rosanette yawns. Frédéric, viewing the omnipresence of symbolic representations of Diane de Poitiers, is seized with "a retrospective and inexpressible lust": "une concupiscence rétrospective et inexprimable." That phrase could stand for much of the problem of desire in this novel: it is turned toward the past, not the future; it fixates on impossible objects; it can never reach full expression. A few pages later, when Rosanette recounts the painful story of her youth—she was sold by her alcoholic mother to an old man—there is an exchange of confidences between her and Frédéric ending with the thought that in the midst of the most intimate confidences there are always restrictions. "Each discovers in the other or in himself chasms or swamps that prevent going further; one feels moreover that one wouldn't be understood; it is difficult to express exactly anything whatsoever, thus complete unions are rare." You detect here one of those passages that capture Flaubert's personal view of language, communication, and human relationship. Like a similar passage in *Madame Bovary* that images language as a cracked cauldron on which we beat out tunes for bears to dance to, when we really would wish to wring pity from the stars, this passage, Flaubert's *ars poetica*, suggests his intense self-consciousness about the limits to the medium in which he works.

The melancholy history lesson of the Château de Fontainebleau leads to widening historical gyres when Frédéric and Rosanette hire a carriage for rides in the famous forest. They discover trees—trees that become the object of an extraordinary Flaubertian composition that gives them greater and greater animation as his paragraph unfurls. When, for instance, we come to the oaks: "There were rough oaks, enormous, that twisted convulsively, pulled themselves from the soil, gripping one another and, solid on their trunks, like torsos, threw out with their naked arms calls of despair, furious menaces, like a group of Titans immobilized in their anger." Something has happened to the normally sober premises of Flaubertian description here. It reaches beyond the visual and the aesthetically composed to suggest a history of mythic dimensions, a Titanic earth. This dimension is further enlarged when we pass from trees to rocks, when Frédéric and Rosanette come upon a quarry and an open, rock-filled field. The rocks "ended by filling the whole landscape, cubic like houses, flat like paving stones, piling up, overhanging one another, jumbled together, like the unrecognizable and monstrous ruins of some disappeared city. But the very fury of their chaos makes one think rather of volcanoes, floods, of great unknown cataclysms." This is geo-history, as Frédéric recognizes when he tells Rosanette that the rocks have been there since the beginning of the world and would be there until its end. Rosanette responds that such a thought will drive her mad. And in fact, the effect of the human histories and geo-histories activated by Fontainebleau create a context for thought, for reverie, that pushes current events far into the background. Does all history, like human desire, lead to ruins?

But those current events obtrude in the form of a newspaper article in which Frédéric finds the name of his friend Dussardier on the list of the wounded. Feeling shame at his absence from his nation's agonizing struggle, he resolves to return at once to Paris to care for his friend. The decision (bitterly opposed by Rosanette, who sees self-preservation as the only good) leads to an epic trip back into the city, where he is arrested as a possible spy and passed from one guardhouse to another, but in his displacements has a chance to observe the final act of history in the making that he has missed. In the Latin Quarter, near the Panthéon, he finds an aftermath of civil war that uncannily prefigures that of the Commune:

> On the ruined barricades there remained omnibuses, gas pipes, cart wheels; small black puddles here and there must have been blood. The houses were shot through with projectiles, and their wood framing showed through the damaged plaster. Shutters, holding by a single hook, hung like rags. Where stairs had collapsed, doors opened onto nothing. You saw the interior of rooms with their wallpaper in shreds; delicate things had sometimes been preserved. Frédéric noticed a clock, a parrot's perch, a few engravings.

To be sure, 1871 would be far worse. But this novel, published in 1869, already makes of the class warfare of 1848 an ominous lesson, one that, to Flaubert's disgust, would not be heeded. The lesson is all the more striking in that Dussardier, when Frédéric finally finds him, is tortured by a question of conscience. Perhaps he has fought on the wrong side—he should not have joined the Guard in repressing the workers' uprising, but rather, should have fought alongside his fellow workers. They had been promised so much that then was taken away from them. And those who had put down the uprising heartily hated the republic. All too true, as the rise to power of Louis-Napoléon Bonaparte would soon demonstrate.

From Dussardier's doubts that he chose the right side we move to Sénécal, in the stinking, atrocious prison under the terrace of the Tuileries, where the victorious government stashed prisoners from the insurrection. Here we have one of the most impassioned and evidently personally felt passages in the novel, as Flaubert describes the reaction of the whole range of the bourgeoisie after the victory over the insurgency. The long paragraph begins by describing the National Guard: "They were in general pitiless. Those who had not fought wanted to do something to stand out. There was an overflowing of fear. Revenge was exacted at one and the same time for the newspapers, the clubs, the demonstrations, the doctrines—everything that exasperated them for three months." And then,

> despite victory, equality (as if for the punishment of its partisans and the derision of its enemies) manifested itself triumphant, an equality of brute beasts, a common level of bloody crimes; for the fanaticism of interests balanced the delirium of needs, the aristocracy showed the fury of the rabble, and the cotton nightcap proved itself no less hideous than the red bonnet. Public reason was troubled as after great natural cataclysms. Intelligent men were made idiots for the rest of their lives.

Here again, the voice speaking in the text seems to have gone beyond any one of the characters to assume a magisterial and authorial tone in making what I see as Flaubert's final pronouncement on class struggle and civil war. The effect of civil strife as of natural cataclysm is to destroy public reason and to make otherwise intelligent people into idiots—for the rest of their lives. Which, among other things, means that his claim that *Sentimental Education* ought to have offered a cautionary tale to his compatriots in 1871—ought, if properly understood, to have prevented the greater civil strife of the Commune—has at its very root this contradiction: How are idiots supposed to profit from the lessons of history?

Like the geo-history that Rosanette says will drive her crazy, Flaubert's demonstrations by their very form and nature argue against their intelligent fulfillment. It's not that history is a tale told by an idiot, full of sound and fury and signifying nothing. It's that the eyes and ears to which history is addressed are incapable of seeing and hearing.

The rest of the novel is aftermath, political reaction, and liquidation. Dambreuse assumes a greater importance here, as representative of the wealthy bourgeoisie that dominates in the political reaction. After the reestablishment of order, he and Madame Dambreuse offer a luncheon, where the food itself takes on a political coloration: "Under the green leaves of a pineapple, a bream stretched out, its mouth pointing toward a side of venison while touching with its tail a mound of crayfish. Figs, jumbo cherries, pears and grapes (the first of the season) mounded in pyramids within baskets of delicate porcelain; here and there tufts of flowers mingled with shining silver plate . . . and tall valets in livery served the food. All this seemed better after the emotion of the days just lived through." Frédéric decides to make Madame Dambreuse his mistress, and succeeds with an ease that surprises him, meanwhile maintaining Rosanette, who is pregnant, as his live-in mistress. He finds this life of deception diverting. Dambreuse falls ill and dies, not without causing posthumous pain to his widow, by disinheriting her in favor of his "niece" Cécile, in fact his illegitimate daughter.

His death and funeral offer another opportunity to sum up the politics of an era. As Frédéric sits awake with the corpse, we have this epitaph: "It was over, that life so full of agitation. How often had he run errands in the ministries, made calculations, been a fixer, listened to reports! How many sales pitches, smiles, fawnings! For he had acclaimed Napoleon, then the invading Cossacks, then Louis XVIII, 1830, the workers, all regimes, cherishing Power with such a love that he would have paid to be able to sell himself." When we come to the eulogies spoken at his graveside, they all thunder against socialism, which is somehow held responsible for his premature death.

Now Madame Dambreuse is a widow, not spectacularly rich but affluent enough—and she proposes marriage to Frédéric. The marriage is on the verge of accomplishment when she insists that Frédéric escort her to the auction of the now bankrupt Arnoux household, which is like a kind of living wake for his old love: "The divvying up of these relics, where he perceived vaguely the shapes of her body, seemed to him an atrocity, as if he had seen crows tearing apart her corpse." When Madame Dambreuse insists upon bidding for the small glove box that was so much a part of his life as suitor to Madame Arnoux, she provokes a rupture—he sees her to her carriage and refuses to enter it with her. He calls off the marriage, feeling astonishment at his own action.

The Arnoux auction and the break with Madame Dambreuse take place on December 1, 1851. The next day brings the coup d'état of Louis-Napoléon Bonaparte. Elected president in December 1848—the first presidential election by universal manhood suffrage—on December 2, 1851, he dissolved the Assembly, proscribed leaders of the opposition, and assumed dictatorial powers. On December 4, Frédéric, sore and disillusioned from his episode with Madame Dambreuse (and with the living ghost, as it were, of Madame Arnoux) begins to dream of the countryside, and of a young neighbor in Nogent, Louise Roque, who has long been passionately in love with him, and to whom he was once more or less engaged. Why not her, after all? He takes the train to Nogent, but only to encounter a hallucination: Louise in bridal dress, coming out of the local church on the arm of Deslauriers, now her husband. "Shamed, beaten, crushed," Frédéric returns to Paris that same evening to learn that barricades are up in the city—it's the last resistance to the coup d'état. As he crosses the city on foot under a fine rain, he comes upon a scene near the Opéra, where dragoons are sweeping down the avenue with their sabers drawn. The watching crowd is mute, terrified. Squads of police on foot arrive to push back the crowd into the side streets. But on the steps of Tortoni (famous café on the corner of the Boulevard des Italiens and the rue Taitbout) a lone figure stands, still as a caryatid. It is Dussardier. A policeman menaces him with his sword. Rather than retreating, Dussardier steps forward, crying "Vive la République!" And then he is flat on his back, run through by the sword, and the crowd howls in horror. The policeman circles the crowd with his gaze— and "Frédéric, his jaw dropping, recognized Sénécal."

The conversion of the defender of the proletariat into murderous policeman will become a familiar trope of twentieth-century history, where the betrayal of the people in whose name revolutions were undertaken became monotonously familiar. Fyodor Dostoevsky, writing at just about the same moment as Flaubert, discovered the infernal logic of the passage from libertarian to authoritarian as part of an individual and collective psychology, especially in his *Demons* (known also as *The Possessed*), published in 1870–1871. Flaubert more calmly and coolly sees Sénécal's political biography as part of the history of his generation. The absolutes of political faith result in such a meeting of the extremes. If you put your faith exclusively in politics, you inevitably end up pursuing strange gods and killing in their name.

What is the lesson to be learned? In Frédéric's life, it is one of escape and disengagement. After Sénécal's killing of Dussardier there is a blank—between Chapters 5 and 6 of Part 3—that Marcel Proust claimed to find the most admirable thing in the novel. It's a blank of the unspeakable, followed by a brusque change of gears and temporal mode. We pick up Frédéric at the start of the next chapter with: "He traveled. He knew the melancholy of ocean liners, cold awakenings beneath a tent, the stupefaction of landscapes and ruins, the bitterness of interrupted affections." His loves are made insipid by the memory of his passion for Madame Arnoux. His intellectual ambitions diminish as well. "Years went by; and he endured the disuse of his mind and the inertia of his heart." Then late one afternoon in March 1867—nearly twenty-seven years after the novel's opening—Madame Arnoux pays him a visit, and they together evoke the past and their love. Their conversation becomes a confrontation of verb tenses that signal the impossibility of bringing desire and its realization into accord. She sighs, and after a silence this dialogue ensues, with Madame Arnoux speaking first:

> "It doesn't matter. We will have loved each other well."
> "Without belonging to one another, however!"
> "Perhaps it is better that way," she replied.
> "No, no! What happiness we would have had!"

Her future perfect ("We will have loved each other well") is matched by his past conditional ("What happiness we would have had"). Love is something like the socialist dream, never there in the right place at the right time.

The novel ends with Frédéric and Deslauriers reunited—his marriage to Louise ended with her elopement with a singer—and sitting by the fire, recalling the past and the fates of their friends. They sum up their lives, recognizing that they have both been failures. They reach back to their schooldays in Nogent and their youthful ambitions: "And, exhuming their youth, at each sentence they said to one another, 'Do you remember?'" An exhumation, then, of something dead and buried. Their memories lead them back to the summer of 1837, and their attempted visit to the brothel of La Turque, which ended in failure when Frédéric, floral bouquet in hand, embarrassed by the view of so many women at his disposal, and thinking they were mocking him, turned and ran—and, since Frédéric had the money, Deslauriers was obliged to follow him. We are told this became a story that still was not forgotten three years later—and in fact it is alluded to in the first chapter of the novel, as Frédéric and Deslauriers, meeting again in September 1840, when the novel opens, notice the red light burning on the house of ill repute. And the novel ends on the exchange that many critics found shockingly cynical. After recounting the episode "prolixly" to one another, Frédéric remarks: "That's the best we ever had!" And Deslauriers responds: "Yes, maybe so? That's the best we ever had!"

Designating a youthful (failed) visit to a brothel "the best" life has brought them shocked the critics, who were in any case generally appalled by a book that offered no "hero" at its core and no explicit illumination by life's experiences. Perhaps even more notable than the subject matter of this episode is its temporal status. Frédéric and Deslauriers tell us that the most important experience of their lives happened three years before the novel opened, indicating that everything we have read in this long novel has been somehow off target, mere sequel to the important but unrecorded event. But of course that event takes on its importance only in the two friends' retrospect. At the time, it was an unfulfilled desire that looked forward to many imagined future fulfillments. Seen in narrative retrospect after a life of failed hopes and ambitions, it bathes in the special glow of memory, and of storytelling. In fact, if there is one act or emotion that seems to survive the general wreckage of *Sentimental Education*, it may be storytelling itself, the play of recollection and understanding on the past—a past that cannot be altered, only retold for a present experience of pleasure. It is always too late to change anything: the past is inalterable, and only telling can redeem it. And redeem is surely the wrong word. The past is beyond redemption. The telling has to offer its own reward.

The intractable past baffles us. We don't know how to use it to alter the present. In his *Theory of the Novel*, critic and philosopher Georg Lukács claimed that in the novel, as opposed to the epic, time takes on a new role. It is not simply the time needed for the hero to accomplish his exemplary deeds: "Only in the novel, whose very matter is seeking and failing to find the essence, is time posited together with the form: time is the resistance of the organic . . . to the present meaning. . . . In the novel, meaning is separated from life, and hence the essential from the temporal; we might almost say that the entire inner action of the novel is nothing but a struggle against the power of time." It comes then as no surprise that for Lukács, *Sentimental Education* is the most characteristic of novels, "the only novel that attains true epic objectivity" through the constitutive role of time, and the creative role of memory working on time. To which I would add that the structure of desire and hoped-for fulfillment suggested by the episode of the brothel transmutes by the end into an unfulfillment that can find pleasure only in memory and narration, which themselves cannot alter the historical past. It's not certain that for Flaubert the present can alter the present, either—that there is any point in political action, which seems to lead so inexorably to the betrayal of the ideals that motivate it. "So many crimes have been committed by the ideal in politics," he wrote in October 1871. So watch out how you try to change the world.

Yet Flaubert doesn't appear to me to be the political reactionary he has often been taken for. He is not on the side of the authoritarians, or the puritans, or the censors. His sympathy with the wretched shines through in many a passage of the novel—concerning Rosanette's childhood, for instance, and the dispossession of the workers cast out by the closing of the *ateliers nationaux*. His distaste for wealthy capitalist manipulators is evident in the portrait of Dambreuse. He is not a democrat, in that he sees the people in power as a mockery of expertise and wisdom: he always favored a rule by intellectual elites. But this does not make him a partisan of the current order of things—rule by bankers and speculators and corrupt politicians.

The problem lies not in political ideology, always a ready target for mockery, but in Flaubert's very conception of the limits to human agency. His remark to Maxime Du Camp while viewing the ruins of Paris in 1871, as I understand it, makes the claim that the lesson of *Sentimental Education* should have prevented both the folly of the Commune and the atrocity of its suppression. In his view, the novel makes what historian Carlo Ginzburg has called a "retrospective prophecy": the act of placing oneself back in the past to show how the present outcome was predictable from that standpoint. The structure of prophecy and fulfillment, as in the Christian reading of the Hebrew Bible as a prefiguration of the story of the Gospels, always claims a consonance between earlier and later, what is called for and what is realized. I think Flaubert's view is similar: we know already from the history of our own generation what's going to happen if we attempt a radical revision of the way things are. Therefore we need to refrain, for the sake of humanity. I read this as a kind of moral imperative in Flaubert, perhaps his version of his father's medical imperative: do no harm. It appears to be a solution of passivity, and surely there is much of that in Flaubert's whole stance toward life: he is observer more than participant. Yet the passivity doesn't call for a reactionary politics, merely a smarter one (which may be the most elusive desideratum of all). When in the years following the Commune Flaubert came to accept the republic of Adolphe Thiers as the best solution for France, he claimed it was because it represented a republic without ideology and without ideals. Also without military crusades and bloodshed. It was simply government, getting along and getting by, without any grand ideas or projects. That seemed to him more in line with what life would allow you.

WHAT ABOUT SENTIMENTAL EDUCATION as a historical novel? Flaubert's notes and plans for it show him carefully aligning the plot of his protagonist's actions against the unfolding of historical events, with an evident intention of matching them closely to one another. The fact that Frédéric is largely an observer rather than an active participant in life is helpful in allowing him to be witness at the events Flaubert wishes to record—and absent from those he wants to have refracted or echoed through others' reports, or in direct narratorial presentation. The result is a remarkably seamless integration of a personal biography with national history. It's not quite the Walter Scott or Alessandro Manzoni approach, which involved inventing a fictional character who is then caught up in the large historical forces of the time dramatized, seated, so to speak, at the foot of the banquet table, as kings and captains make world-historical decisions at the other end. Frédéric, through his friends—Deslauriers, Dussardier, Sénécal, and Regimbart, especially—is a kind of informed observer and feeble participant in the history of his time, who experiences directly, though largely passively, its aspirations and disappointments. Henry James's question, "Why, why *him?*" may be answered by noting Frédéric's quasi-anthropological role as someone who exists to witness and annotate history. A more active person with more of his own life might have served less well.

We should take seriously Flaubert's statement that he wished to write the history of his own generation. Frédéric's story of ever unfulfilled romantic passion is of course of great importance, but the historical background of the novel becomes more and more crucial as it progresses until, in the third, final part, it becomes the foreground, so that, for instance, when Frédéric attempts to escape history by the retreat to Fontainebleau, we feel that he, as observer, is missing in action, and we therefore are missing the action. Historian Michel Winock has contrasted Flaubert's famous (perhaps apocryphal) statement of self-identification with Emma Bovary (*"Madame Bovary is me!"*) with what he rightly sees as the collective experience recorded in the later novel: *"Frédéric is us!"* If there is surely, as James claimed, a poverty of experience recorded in the novel, it is essentially the poverty of historical action itself, the tragicomic inability of human beings to produce the results they seek in management of public affairs. Many of the triumphs of historical reporting in this novel come through Flaubert's use of indirect discourse, which is more fully developed here than in *Madame Bovary*. Especially in the Dambreuse salon, where current events are a constant topic of discussion, the voicing of political and ideological commonplaces gives a brilliant (and according to Winock, accurate) picture of the bourgeoisie in its dominant, and momentarily fearful, era of rule. Flaubert's last, unfinished novel, *Bouvard and Pécuchet*, will use indirect discourse to realize a world of stupidities, culminating in the famous *sottisier*, or *Dictionary of Received Ideas*, made up of all the clichés—and clichés defining clichés—that he could collect. Already in *Sentimental Education*, we have a large deployment of stupid commonplaces by which the reigning class justifies its actions and its exploitations of workers and the nation's resources. That Flaubert detested the bourgeoisie is well known. He is of course equally adept at presenting the self-deluding clichés of the insurgents, their repetitive mouthings of the politically correct words of the day. His readings in socialist literature paid off in a corrosively ironic presentation of what he (like Marx) sees as hopelessly utopian schemes for the reform of everything, including relations among men and women. But the novel has a kind of balance because, however self-deluded the proletarians and the revolutionaries may be, the bourgeois are always already more so. In this manner, there is no better history of the midcentury French bourgeoisie than Flaubert's novel.

The great historical writing of the French nineteenth century, best represented by Jules Michelet, strives always for a narrative that is both explanatory and symbolic, that throws up memorable images in representation of key events. Flaubert's sobriety has none of the flamboyance of Michelet, but he is part of what you might call the novelization of history characteristic of his time. He works in the genre of the novel, and wishes to create with it a vivid and significant rendering of history. He wants to direct his reader to a deep understanding of the history of his own generation. History is not background, it is not simply décor, it is the profound subject of the novel. And by the time the Commune has risen and come to its bloody end, more and more the production of significant representations of history will fall to novelists, architects, and artists.

Literary and cultural critic Edmund Wilson many years ago published an essay, "Flaubert's Politics," that starts from the unusual but accurate recognition that Flaubert "seems always to see humanity in social terms and historical perspective." That is a very important corrective to the critical tradition that sees Flaubert as an ivory-tower artist concerned only with the perfection of his style. Wilson goes on to consider the parallel between Flaubert and Marx, especially in their reaction to 1848 and its sequel in Louis-Napoléon Bonaparte's seizure of power. Both focused their analytic attention and their hatred on the bourgeoisie as the class that turns everything, including culture, including human relations, into the cash nexus. Dambreuse is possibly the most loathsome character in Flaubert's novel: the Latin motto emblazoned with his coat of arms on his carriage says it all: *Quibiscum viis* (By any means)—Get ahead by any means possible. More sympathy goes to two figures from the proletariat, the honest and conscientious Dussardier, and, curiously, the courtesan Rosanette, who is portrayed as venal and mendacious but essentially as a sympathetic character who has made the best of the bad hand life has dealt her. The triumph of the bourgeoisie is captured in the kind of inexcusable oxymoron of Arnoux's *L'Art Industriel*. The notion that art can be industrialized is an idea deeply antipathetic to Flaubert. When Arnoux establishes his ceramics factory at Creil, his work falls between stools: the products are neither popular enough to make money nor original enough to become art, "so that, without pleasing anyone, he was ruining himself." He eventually declines further into selling religious knickknacks. Better either to be a starving artist or an exploited worker than to ruin art in a forced marriage with commerce.

Wilson cites Ford Madox Ford's opinion that one must read *Sentimental Education* fourteen times in order to appreciate it fully. He notes that a first reading (in college, for instance, in my own experience) baffles and even repels. Later on, with the accumulated experience we sometimes tell ourselves is wisdom, it comes to seem one of the truly indispensable books. As Wilson writes:

We are amazed to find that the tone no longer seems really satiric and that we are listening to a sort of muted symphony of which the timbres had been inaudible before. There are no hero, no villain, to arouse us, no clowns to amuse us, no scenes to wring our hearts. Yet the effect is deeply moving. It is the tragedy of nobody in particular, but of the poor human race itself reduced to such ineptitude, such cowardice, such commonness, such weak irresolution—arriving, with so many fine notions in its head, so many noble words on its lips, at a failure which is all the more miserable because those who have failed are hardly conscious of having done so.

The failure of 1871, then, was very plausibly a failure to understand the failure recorded in *Sentimental Education* and published for all to read and learn from in 1869. Flaubert the impassible partisan of artistic impersonality and perfection sees his novel as some version of St. Augustine's *tolle, lege*: take up and read this book, it will change your life. The failure to read will doom you to repeat the tragic errors of the past—and repeat them not as Marx would have it, as farce, but as a deeper tragedy. The farcical presentation would come later, in *Bouvard and Pécuchet*. For all its despair of human ideals and the supposed cynicism of its final summing up, *Sentimental Education* strikes me as a deeply moral book, completely engaged in the ethical substance of choices in life. It has no morally sensitive protagonist in the manner of Henry James's Lambert Strether or Maggie Verver. That role is passed on to the reader, who must ultimately draw the lessons from the colossal failure of a generation unequal to its rendezvous with history.

I have worked myself around to thinking that Flaubert's comment to Maxime Du Camp in the ruins of Paris was not so fantastical as it at first seemed. To claim that a reading and an understanding of his novel would have saved his contemporaries from the disaster of the Commune and its repression, from the whole story of the Terrible Year, invests literature with a force of moral suasion that seems excessive. Yet the claim is simply a reaffirmation of the extraordinarily high value Flaubert attached to serious literature, which was not simply an aesthetic value. The tendency to defend his novels on the ground of artistic merit alone—as if he were a practitioner of art for art's sake—falsifies his ambition. He really meant it when he said the errors of the Terrible Year could have been avoided by an intelligent reading of his novel. The inexcusable fault of his contemporaries was stupidity. The true antidote to stupidity is learning, which means knowing how to read. If you don't know how to read—a novel by Flaubert, for instance—you are condemned to repeat the stupidities of the past. There is no cure for society other than in what he called *science*, including those human sciences, psychology and sociology, that analyze human motive and behavior. Access to the human sciences is through reading, which can include novels of the analytic exactitude sought by Flaubert. If you don't know how to read, in the fullest sense of the term, you are doomed.

If the reading of *Sentimental Education* presented in this chapter (possibly trying the reader's patience, but it could have been extended into a whole book!) has been at all persuasive, it may point us from 1848 to 1871. Flaubert's lesson in reading past history engages the effort in the immediate wake of the Terrible Year to say what these events in contemporary history mean. Once the Commune had been put to the sword, where was the nation headed? How was one to make the lessons of civil war operative? Next to the political history that ensued from the Terrible Year—largely a story of reaction, though not ending in monarchy as it might have—there is a cultural struggle to say what the events meant and how they should be remembered. The ruins of Paris set off a conflict of hearts and minds, a symbolic battle for the control of history.

FIGURE 1. Cannon Park Montmartre, March 1871. Photographer unknown. Paris, Musée Carnavalet. © Musée Carnavalet/Roger-Viollet/The Image Works.

FIGURE 2. Cannon on Montmartre, rue Chevalier de la Barre (formerly rue des Rosiers). Photo probably by Bruno Braquehais. Bibliothèque Historique de la Ville de Paris. © BHVP/Roger-Viollet/The Image Works.

FIGURE 3. Barricade, Chausée de Ménilmontant. Photographer unknown. Musée Carnavalet, Paris. © Musée Carnavalet/Roger-Viollet/The Image Works.

FIGURE 4. Barricade, rue de Castiglione. Photo by Bruno Braquehais. Adhoc-photos/Art Resource, New York.

FIGURE 5. Barricade in front of the Hôtel de Ville. Photo by Alphonse Liébert. © Alinari Archive/The Image Works.

FIGURE 6. Vendôme Column, with Communards gathered at the base. Photo by Bruno Braquehais. Musée Carnavalet, Paris. © Bruno Braquehais/Musée Carnavalet/Roger-Viollet/The Image Works.

FIGURE 7. Vendôme Column rigged for destruction. Photo perhaps by Bruno Braquehais. © Roger-Viollet/The Image Works.

FIGURE 8. Fallen column from on high. Photo by Jules Andrieu, from *Les Désastres de la guerre*. © BnF, Dist. RMN–Grand Palais/Art Resource, New York.

FIGURE 9. Statue of Napoleon, fallen. Photo by Bruno Braquehais. Paris: Bibliothèque Nationale de France. © BnF, Dist. RMN–Grand Palais/Art Resource, New York.

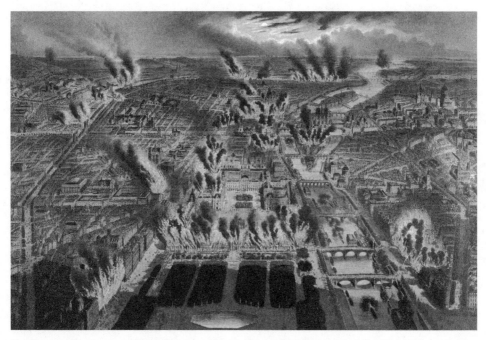

FIGURE 10. Panorama of Paris burning during the night of May 24–25, 1871. Lithograph by Michel-Charles Fichot. Paris: Musée Carnavalet. Erich Lessing/Art Resource, New York.

FIGURE 11. Paris burning: the Préfecture de Police, as seen from the Left Bank. Photo by Hippolyte Blancard. Bibliothèque Historique de la Ville de Paris. © Hippolyte Blancard/ BHVP/Roger-Viollet/ The Image Works.

FIGURE 12. Hôtel de Ville, façade, after the fire, 1871. Photo by Charles Marville. © Beaux-Arts de Paris, Dist. RMN–Grand Palais/Art Resource, New York.

Figure 13. Hôtel de Ville, interior. Photo by Charles Marville. Bibliothèque Historique de la Ville de Paris. © Charles Marville/BHVP/Roger-Viollet/The Image Works.

Figure 14. Hôtel de Ville on fire. Retouched photo by Alphonse Liébert. © BHVP/Roger-Viollet/The Image Works.

FIGURE 15. Hôtel de Ville. Photo by Alphonse Liébert, from *Les Ruines de Paris et de ses environs*. Library of Congress.

FIGURE 16. Palais de Justice. Photo by Hippolyte Blancard. Bibliothèque Historique de la Ville de Paris. © Hippolyte Blancard/BHVP/Roger-Viollet/The Image Works.

FIGURE 17. Ministère des Finances. Photo by Hippolyte Blancard. Bibliothèque Historique de la Ville de Paris. © Hippolyte Blancard/ BHVP/Roger-Viollet/ The Image Works.

FIGURE 18. Théâtre Lyrique. Photo by Alphonse Liébert, from *Les Ruines de Paris et de ses environs*. Library of Congress.

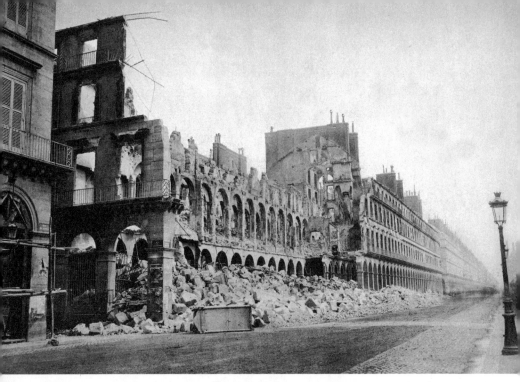

FIGURE 19. Rue de Rivoli, with ruined Ministère des Finances on the left. Photographer unknown (possibly Charles Marville or Hippolyte Blancard). Bibliothèque Historique de la Ville de Paris. © BHVP/Roger-Viollet/The Image Works.

FIGURE 20. Carrefour de la Croix-Rouge. Photo by Alphonse Liébert, from *Les Ruines de Paris et de ses environs*. Library of Congress.

FIGURE 21. Palais des Tuileries, Salle des Maréchaux. Photo by Alphonse Liébert, from *Les Ruines de Paris et de ses environs*. Metropolitan Museum of Art, New York–OASC.

FIGURE 22. Grenier d'Abondance. Photo by Jules Andrieu, from *Les Désastres de la guerre*. © Beaux-Arts de Paris, Dist. RMN–Grand Palais/Art Resource, New York.

FIGURE 23. Palais des Tuileries, peristyle. Photo by Jules Andrieu, from *Les Désastres de la guerre*. © Beaux-Arts de Paris, Dist. RMN–Grand Palais/ Art Resource, New York.

FIGURE 24. The Ruins of Tuileries Palace. Painting by Ernest Meissonier. Oil on canvas, 136 cm x 96 cm. Paris: Musée d'Orsay. Erich Lessing/Art Resource, New York.

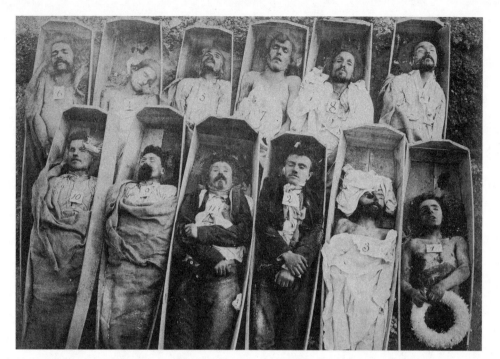

FIGURE 25. Communards in their coffins. Photo by Eugène Disdéri. 1871. Paris: Bibliothèque Nationale de France, EO-19-FOL. © BnF, Dist. RMN–Grand Palais/Art Resource, New York.

FIGURE 26. Guerre Civile. Lithograph by Edouard Manet, 1871–1873, published 1874. On chine collé, final state (II). Metropolitan Museum of Art, New York–OASC.

FIGURE 27. Mur des Fédérés (Communards' Wall), Père Lachaise Cemetery, Paris. Photo by Luther Bissett. Wiki Commons.

FIGURE 28. Basilique du Sacré-Coeur (Basilica of the Sacred Heart), Montmartre. Photo by Jimmy Baikovicius. Wiki Commons.

FIGURE 29. Saint-Front de Périgueux. Photo by Père Igor. Wiki Commons.

FIGURE 30. Mosaics, "Hommage à la France," Basilica of the Sacred Heart, by Luc-Olivier Merson. Erich Lessing/Art Resource, New York.

FIGURE 31. Jeanne d'Arc, statue by Emmanuel Frémiet, 1874. Place des Pyramides, Paris. Archive Timothy McCarthy/Art Resource, New York.

FIGURE 32. Jeanne d'Arc, by Jules Bastien-Lepage, 1879. Metropolitan Museum of Art, New York-OASC.

– chapter five –

Hearts and Minds

Flaubert's trip to Paris in June 1871 provided matter for a large number of fulminating letters on the criminal stupidity of his contemporaries, which he sent to several different correspondents. It also allowed for his continuing work in the library as he pushed ahead with *The Temptation of Saint Anthony*. Back in Croisset, that labor became the antidote to the black bile that contemporary affairs had provoked in him. As he wrote to Sand during another Paris trip in July: "The immense disgust that my contemporaries give me throws me back into the past—And I am working on my good *Saint Anthony*, with all my force." He made another research trip to Paris in August, and then another from November to March, putting in four to five hours daily at the library. After that he resumed the mantle of the hermit of Croisset. Then came his mother's death in April 1872. With *Saint Anthony* finished (it would be published in 1874), he began taking notes for the book in which, he said, "I will try to *vomit my bile* on my contemporaries"—*Bouvard and Pécuchet*.

The political aftermath of the Terrible Year would keep intruding, especially when the "fusion" of Bourbons and Orléanists in the fall of 1873 threatened—as he now saw it—the return of monarchy. Never the participant, Flaubert had nonetheless discovered a need to comment on public affairs. More than in the prewar past, which now seemed so long ago, he was caught up in the political, social, and moral evolution of his country, which was at a difficult moment of self-assessment. And eventually he would have to return to writing about it, and provide his own symbolic commentary on the question of who should write the history of his time, and interpret its meanings. Before returning to him once more in his study looking out on the Seine—lamenting that fewer of the locals bathed nude than in the past—we need to look toward Paris.

The Commune seemed to be fixed in its aftermath by that fallen column of the Place Vendôme, symbolic of all its other "crimes." Public memory was for many years to come decisively, dismissively anti-Communard. Nonetheless, recent events provoked a period of intense reflection and debate in France over the causes of the Terrible Year and possible future remedies. The partisans of a new "Moral Order" predominated in the debate when Marshal Mac-Mahon rose to the presidency in 1873. Flaubert, who thought him a dangerous fool, dubbed him "the Bayard of modern times," capturing in the allusion to the pure knight of legend the fatuous hypocrisy of the preachers of morality and repression who now ruled France. He had predicted this victory of the reactionaries.

Mac-Mahon decreed the restoration of the Vendôme Column, begun in 1873 and finished in 1875. But well before Mac-Mahon's presidency, the most reactionary elements in France undertook the incarnation of its anti-Communard (and anti-republican) sentiments in the stone of the Basilique du Sacré-Coeur, or Basilica of the Sacred Heart. It would rise on the height of Montmartre, just about where the National Guard cannons had stood, those cannons whose attempted capture had ignited the Commune insurgency. The basilica dominates the Paris skyline still today; it's the sight that generally meets your eyes first in arriving or last when leaving the city. It's a building hard to place architecturally or historically. Tourists flock to it as to one of the wonders of the world on a par with the cathedral of Notre Dame de Paris, possibly without much attention to its place in French history and the political message that it conveys. Frommer's travel guide to Paris offers this capsule version: "After France's 1870 defeat by the Prussians, the basilica was planned as a votive offering to cure France's misfortunes." That's a considerable bowdlerization. The builders of Sacré-Coeur saw it as expiation for the sins of republican France, most egregiously represented in the Commune.

The story of the basilica may evoke incredulity, so improbable and even perverse it may seem. The idea for the church originated in 1870 with two laymen, Alexandre Legentil and Hubert Rohault de Fleury, who attributed France's defeat by Prussia to French decadence and secularism, its falling away from the way of Christ. They called for a "national vow" to rededicate France to the Sacred Heart of Jesus. This was the extreme version of a popular story that wanted to see 1870–1871 as divine chastisement. We encountered a left, secular version in Zola's vision of Paris burning in expiation of the luxury and corruption of the Second Empire, in *The Debacle*. Such a thorough catastrophe had to be justified as the wages of sin. France's moral failure was evidenced not only in defeat by Prussia, but also in its inability to rescue Pope Pius IX from Italian insurgents who were intent on stripping the Vatican of its temporal power. Napoleon III's Italian and papal politics amounted to a doomed balancing act: he was attempting at once to promote Italian unity and to protect the pope's rule over Rome—which the insurgents insisted must be the capital of Italy.

Part of the complex story in which the emperor managed to make enemies on both sides was the formation of the Papal Zouaves, an international volunteer corps in the defense of the pope that recruited from France many unredeemed reactionaries, especially from the Vendée region, in Brittany, that had long resisted republican rule during the original Revolution. These Zouaves, commanded by Athanase de Charette, great-nephew of a famous Vendée general, joined the French Army of the Loire in which Flaubert, like many of his contemporaries, placed their last hope for reversing the fortune of war and breaking the siege of Paris. Charette, though, insisted that his Zouaves retain a separate identity within an army officially dedicated to republicanism. Along with Louis-Gaston de Sonis, a famously pious Catholic general, he led a heroic, though vain—and somewhat absurd—charge at the Battle of Loigny, in the Loire Valley, on December 2, 1870. Toward evening, as light was fading on that cold and bloody engagement of what remained of the French Army, de Sonis ordered a charge on Prussian positions. His troops hesitated, and he turned to Charette and his Zouaves to lead the charge. The standard-bearer of the Zouaves unfurled their white royalist banner with its emblem of the bleeding heart and the words, "Sacré Coeur de Jésus, Sauvez la France," reflecting the belief that only the Sacred Heart of Jesus could work the miracle of French salvation. The charge resounded not only with the cry "Vive la France!" but also with "Vive Pie IX!" More than half the legion fell dead. Both Charette and de Sonis were wounded; de Sonis had to have a leg amputated the next day. Neither ever reconciled to the republic. The cult of the Sacred Heart in which they had enlisted brought together the irreconcilables of modern France.

For Legentil, Rohault de Fleury, and others who joined in the national vow, 1870 was not only a failure but also a sin that needed expiation, which could best be symbolized in a new religious edifice that made evident a rededication of the French nation to the Sacred Heart of Jesus. "This temple," declared Monsignor Joseph-Hippolyte Guibert, archbishop of Paris, "will stand among us as a protest against other monuments and works of art erected for the glorification of vice and impiety." There were early proposals that the basilica be constructed on the foundations of the Opéra, designed by Charles Garnier under Napoleon III but not yet finished, which was considered by many to be the very incarnation of Second Empire excess and decadence. What would be more appropriate than a severe church in its place? But nothing could equal the allure of Montmartre, especially its height: the foundations of the church would stand higher than the top of the Panthéon, home of such impious ancestors of the republic as Voltaire and Jean-Jacques Rousseau.

The Butte Montmartre was highly symbolic, and not only because of its elevation above Paris. Its name originally meant "mountain of martyrs," from the travails of early Christians. St. Denis, bishop of the city, is supposed to have been seized, tortured, and decapitated by the heathen Gauls there in 327. A chapel to his memory was destroyed in the French Revolution. Archbishop Guibert was persuaded in 1872 that Montmartre was the place for the expiatory church. His predecessor, Monsignor Darboy, had resisted the idea as unnecessarily confrontational; but the relatively liberal Darboy had been shot as a hostage of the Commune, and had been replaced by the hard-liner Guibert. Climbing the Butte in October, Guibert exclaimed: "It is here, it is here where the martyrs are, it is here that the Sacred Heart must reign so that it can beckon all to it!" So in 1873 the National Assembly, dominated by non-Parisians—*les ruraux*—who were largely conservatives, monarchists, and Catholics, voted, 382 to 138, to declare the site on Montmartre "of public utility," which in France means you can then take the land by the equivalent of our eminent domain, and raise funds for the project.

There followed, inevitably, a story of intense conflict. Here were the most reactionary elements of France intent upon creating a monument that would overtop the Panthéon, symbol of secular greatness (the Eiffel Tower was still in the future). The cult of the Sacred Heart of Jesus had an interesting and, from a secular point of view, sinister history. It dated to a relatively recent candidate for sainthood, Marguerite-Marie Alacoque, who in the seventeenth century had visions of the wounds of Christ—of what he was made to suffer by humanity—which, with the support of the Jesuits, was proclaimed a symbol of divine love for humanity. She was beatified by Pope Pius IX in 1864 (and canonized by Benedict XV in 1920). Wearing the image of the bleeding Sacred Heart of Jesus was thought to ward off danger. During the resistance to the Jacobin republic in the Vendée, peasant soldiers stitched the emblem to their jackets to protect against republican bullets. It became the symbol of allegiance to the monarchy and the Church and rejection of the republic—a conflict that would play itself out all through the nineteenth century in France. There arose a legend that Louis XVI, imprisoned by the Jacobins, vowed to dedicate France to the cult of the Sacred Heart were he to be delivered from captivity. When instead he died on the guillotine, the cult only grew stronger, uniting those intent on counter-revolution. (When Stendhal, for instance, wants a symbol of Restoration reaction, he has his women characters educated in convents of the Sacred Heart.) So by the time of the Terrible Year, the proposition to crown impious and insurrectional Paris with a church dedicated to the Sacred Heart was an audacious gesture of anti-republicanism and clerical potency. And it was clearly seen as such by its opponents. Had Darboy survived the Bloody Week, it is unlikely the basilica ever would have risen on the heights of Paris; but Guibert strongly supported it, and in 1873, the legislature had few members willing to oppose the clergy. In a phrase that seemed to sum up the thinking of the right-wing majority, the bishop of Perpignan declared that the church high on Montmartre would be a lightning rod "to protect us against the lightning bolts of divine anger."

So work began. In 1876 a provisional chapel was completed, and became important as a place of pilgrimage for the faithful from all over France, and hence for the collection of donations for the construction of the permanent church, itself conceived from the start as a pilgrim's goal. Although the state had authorized the taking of the land, construction was to be funded by private donations. In addition to the contributions of large donors, there were provisions for modest ones. You could over time fill up a card ruled off in squares, the "carte du Sacré-Coeur," for ten centimes a square, and when you had filled in all the squares, you had purchased a stone for the church. You could then write out a vow on parchment that would be sealed in a glass tube and placed within a hollow that was cut into the stone (in order to secure the tongs that lifted it into place). Your vow, sealed in the glass, would be cemented into place before the next row of stones was laid. The basilica is literally filled with such texts, as if in representation of its self-conscious creation as itself a message to the people of France. Pilgrimage to the site became an important rite for provincial French who held fast to the beliefs that so many Parisians had abandoned. This divide between leftist, nonbelieving Parisians and devout denizens of rural and small-town France was also part of the story: Paris needed to be chastised and brought to heel.

After the fledgling republic survived the restoration crisis, thanks to the intransigence of the Comte de Chambord, and President Mac-Mahon's failed attempt to override the Assembly in 1877, it began to secularize and to emerge from the rigors of "Moral Order." Successive governments tried to kill the basilica project, but without success. The Radicals led by Georges Clemenceau in fact by 1882 won a vote, 261 to 199, to stop the building, but their action never took effect, largely because the government feared the loss of jobs for the workers on the project. It moved forward despite the fact that the Montmartre site proved to be a difficult and expensive one on which to build. It turned out there were gypsum mines, for the material used in making plaster of Paris, honeycombing the hill. Any substantial edifice would subside and then collapse. Before the real building could begin, it would be necessary to sink masonry pillars deep into the hill as supports for the edifice. Eighty-three pillars were driven into the Butte. This was costly and time-consuming. Still the project continued. Between 1876 and 1910, 76 billion francs were spent on it. Meanwhile, in 1898, Zola's novel *Paris* dramatized a (failed) anarchist plot to blow up the Sacré-Coeur. The basilica was finished by 1914, but its consecration was delayed by another war with Germany—the Great War—until 1919. France had by then officially voted for the separation of church and state (in 1905), but that perhaps made the emblem dominating the secular city all the more powerful.

The strange architecture of the Sacré-Coeur has significance as well. A competition for the design of the church attracted seventy-eight entries, which were put on public display at the Palais de l'Industrie in February 1874. There was a curious deficit of designs in the indigenous tradition of the Île-de-France, the Gothic cathedral, probably because the small, squarish plot on Montmartre didn't lend itself to a long Gothic nave. The Romanesque style, newly popular, predominated. Many entries proposed domes. The winner—in the judgment of a panel that consisted half of architects and half of clergy, with Archbishop Guibert reserving the final decision to himself—had many domes. It was the work of a relatively obscure but well-connected architect from the southwest of France, Paul Abadie, considered to be a disciple of Viollet-le-Duc, the great restorer, many would say simultaneously the destroyer, of Gothic monuments throughout France. Abadie was a diocesan architect, and hence held the advantage of enjoying long-standing relations with a number of bishops.

His model for the Sacré-Coeur was apparently the cathedral of Saint-Front in Périgueux, which he had restored starting in 1852, or, more accurately, reconstructed (see Figures 28 and 29).

Saint-Front dates mainly from the twelfth century, though with earlier foundations and many later restorations, including Abadie's own, which was a complete makeover that regularized the cathedral. It had gained its importance in large part as a way station for pilgrims on the famous route to Santiago de Compostela. It has always been something of a stylistic mystery, since it resembles so little the indigenous French tradition (but that was true of a number of other churches in the southwest as well). Its dome is thought to derive from St. Mark's in Venice, and there is a generally "eastern" feel to the structure—more Byzantine than French. Some have cited the Hagia Sophia in Istanbul as its source. So far as one can tell from photographs taken pre-restoration, Abadie's makeover, regularizing and multiplying the domes, increases the Byzantine feel. So while the Basilique du Sacré-Coeur is often referred to as "eclectic" in style (the campanile, for instance, is clearly of Italian inspiration), it strikes the viewer, still today, as a radical and unwelcome break in the stylistic traditions of the Île-de-France. Perhaps, it has been suggested, it is supposed to represent a self-conscious hearkening back to an earlier moment in Christian inspiration, a renewal of the tradition of proselytism that was part of the Catholic revival of the post-Commune years. St. Front, first bishop of Périgueux—appointed by St. Peter himself, in some versions of the legend—is held to have converted much of Périgord in the fourth or fifth century. The conversion of unbelieving French was on the minds of the basilica's sponsors.

On the fronton of the completed basilica one reads the inscription *Gallia poenitens et devota* (France repentant and faithful), which expresses the intent of the authors of the original national vow of expiation for a sinful France. The aim was "to efface by this work of expiation, the crimes which have crowned our sorrows," as Hubert Rohault de Fleury put it. Archbishop Guibert offered up a prayer that God "redeem once again this France that you loved and who, turning from her many errors, wishes to return to her Christian vocation." How strange, when one thinks about it, that glorious Paris should be crowned with this image of repentance and expiation. Although the national vow was formulated following defeat by the Prussians in December 1870 and January 1871, the crimes of the Commune would soon take the dominant place in the complex of sins to be expiated. By the time the Assembly voted—over strenuous objections—for the enabling legislation of 1873, it was clearly the Commune that was to be exorcised by the building. After the laying of the cornerstone, Rohault de Fleury, who had joined with Legentil in devising the original national vow, declared: "Yes, it is here where the Commune began, here where Generals Clément Thomas and Lecomte were assassinated, that the church of the Sacred Heart will rise! Despite ourselves, this thought would not leave us during the ceremony you have just read an account of. We remembered this hill furnished with cannons, overrun by inebriated fanatics, inhabited by a population hostile to any religious idea and seemingly animated most of all by a hatred of the Church." Republican France, though now holding political power, would have to see rise before all eyes a symbolic refusal of all that the republic stood for. The basilica was from the start "at war with the spirit of modern times," as a dissenting deputy put it: an appeal to those who rejected modern French history, and perhaps modernity itself.

Inside, the church is richly decorated with mosaics, some of them quite extraordinary in subject matter to anyone who bothers to look closely. High above the altar, the mosaics of the cupola, executed by Luc-Olivier Merson, represent the national vow, with the presentation of a replica of the basilica by four successive archbishops of Paris, along with its lay sponsors. The latter include a kneeling Alexandre Legentil, and standing next to him Hubert Rohault de Fleury and Emile Keller, the Legitimist deputy who floor-managed the legislation enabling the project, and then behind them Generals de Sonis and Charette, the futile heroes of the Battle of Loigny, with swords and battle flag, Charette in his Papal Zouave uniform. Next we have the family of Louis XVI, the king kneeling in a posture of devotion, dedicating France to the cult of the Sacred Heart. There is also in the background a proletarian *sans-culotte* from the time of the great Revolution, leaning with indifference against a pillar. The mosaics offer a celebration of the most radically reactionary figures of modern French history; they also constitute an illustration of a claim to the continuity of Catholic France, interrupted by revolution, contested by a radicalized proletariat, but nonetheless the interpretation of French history to be celebrated (see Figure 30). If you descend to the crypt of the basilica, you will find an urn holding the heart of Legentil, the first to propose the vow.

The basilica participates fully in that crucial battle of emblems that followed the Terrible Year. The Comte de Chambord on his deathbed asked that the banner of the Sacred Heart that had been unfurled by Charette during the unavailing charge at the Battle of Loigny—the one we see in the mosaics—be placed over his body. It was a sacred relic. The church in Loigny-la-Bataille holds a stained-glass window where St. Henri is represented in the likeness of Chambord, the King Henri V who never was. As René Rémond writes in *Sites of Memory*, still today the Sacré-Coeur is "the symbol and the rallying sign of all those who refuse the Revolution." A site of memory, indeed: a place of pilgrimage explicitly designed to call to mind the long tradition of Church opposition to irreligious France and its attempts to upset the reigning political order. France in this view is an apostate nation that must be brought back into the fold. The victory of this ultraconservative, Catholic, monarchic France is perpetuated in the white stone of the basilica. One can by this point say it is only a symbolic victory, since France followed the course of republican perdition ever more resolutely into the future.

Yet symbolic victories are not without importance, especially in France. The Right showed its force again at the end of the century in the Dreyfus Affair, which turned on an accusation of treason against Captain Alfred Dreyfus of the French Army, a Jew and scapegoat for the army general staff, which led to another virulent contest between republicans and antirepublicans. The latter were emblematized by the army elite, mainly aristocrats and wannabes, who demonstrated a strong continuity with the generals who suppressed the Commune and, at least in republican legend, surrendered to Prussians in preference to fighting for the republic, and who had been trained in brutal repression in colonial campaigns in North Africa. Purging the army of its anti-republicanism proved a long and arduous campaign.

Along with the Basilica of the Sacré-Coeur, the time following the Terrible Year saw a revival of the cult of Joan of Arc, which would still prove potent three-quarters of a century later when Charles de Gaulle used the Cross of Lorraine as the insignia of Free French forces in World War II. Joan of course was revived because the peace treaty with Prussia entailed the loss of Alsace and much of Lorraine, the two provinces "sacrificed" to the Hun, and the historical Jeanne d'Arc came from the village of Domrémy in Lorraine. Her image became a rallying point and symbol for a claim to French revival that included *revanchisme*, the politically potent drive to retake the lost provinces, and beyond that, a mystical emblem of French greatness. The Battle of Loigny took place in close proximity to Patay, where in 1429 Joan routed the English. But Joan also was claimed by the Left, as a woman of the people who was abandoned by her king and burned by her church. The left-leaning historian Jules Michelet made her the very fountainhead of the nation in his book of 1853: "Always remember, compatriots, that our homeland is born from the heart of a woman, from her tenderness, her tears, from the blood she gave for us."

In fact, as Michel Winock has shown, Joan was a symbol disputed between Left and Right: herself a humble peasant and a saint (she would be canonized in 1920), a liberator of her people and a daughter of the Church, both warrior and martyr, she lent herself to multiple symbolizations, and became perhaps more than anything an emblem of the need for emblematization—the way that both of the irreconcilable parties in the fight to say to whom France belonged post 1871 used the symbolic in their conflict. The gilded statue of Joan, designed by Emmanuel Frémiet, commissioned by the state, and erected in 1874 (later altered by the sculptor himself), still stands in the Place des Pyramides in Paris, legible as an incarnation of the French spirit by both sides—not the reconciliation that Victor Hugo sought so much as a sullen agreement to disagree (see Figure 31). The attempt in 1879 by the painter Jules Bastien-Lepage, himself a native of Lorraine, to capture Joan as both peasant and visionary as she first hears saintly voices outside her parents' home in Domrémy, predictably sparked disparate appreciations of the attempted marriage of real and sacred (see Figure 32). A later statue of

Joan stands, along with King Louis IX—St. Louis—at the very entrance to the basilica of the Sacré-Coeur.

Flaubert found the devotion to the Sacred Heart sponsored by Pius IX "hideous." He understood better than most that an attachment to Jeanne d'Arc, the cult of the Sacred Heart, the insulted army, and the thirst for revenge against Germany for the lost provinces all militated for the restoration of the monarchy. He detested Marshal Mac-Mahon, who succeeded Thiers as chief of state in 1873, and assumed that his role as president of the jittery provisional republic was to transition to the reign of Henri V, who called himself Comte de Chambord, but in the belief of his backers had been the one and only legitimate king of France since the death of Louis Philippe in 1836, or possibly since his birth in 1820. He was at birth known as the "miracle child," since he was born seven months after the assassination of his father, the Duc de Berry, the younger son of Charles X, the last Bourbon king. The Legitimists, who rejected the Orléanist line as usurpers, believed in Chambord, and were known as *henriquinquistes*, "Henry the Fifthers." Chambord himself seems to have been convinced not only of his right to be king, but indeed that he *was* king, and simply awaiting recognition as such. The speeches and open letters that he dispatched during the war, the Commune, and the ensuing uncertainties about the regime are signed simply "Henri," the way a king signs ("Louis," his ancestor wrote). In his "Manifesto After Sedan"—following the fall of the Empire and the declaration of the republic—he proclaimed that it was only by "a return to its traditions of faith and honor that a great nation, momentarily weakened, will recover its power and its glory." He continued: "Don't allow yourselves to be taken in by fatal illusions. Republican institutions, which may correspond to the aspirations of modern societies, will never take root on our old monarchical soil." He announced that he was ready to be a constitutional monarch and expressed both his sympathy with the working class and the need to reorganize society on more just bases. He was not in his own eyes a reactionary: his thinking was consonant with respectable right-wing paternalistic social ideologies. But he was sincerely convinced of the unimpeachable right and authority of hereditary kings. Because he believed (along with many of his French contemporaries, especially in the Church) that France was essentially and irreducibly a monarchy, he continued to insist that he alone dictate the terms of restoration.

"I believe that we will have the Henri V," Sand wrote to Flaubert on October 3, 1873. "I am told I see things too much in black. I don't see anything, but I smell an odor of the sacristy making head." Flaubert replied on October 30 that he believed people *feared* the return of monarchy—public opinion was against it, the army was either Bonapartist or republican, and leading French businessmen preferred the republic as well. Mac-Mahon's effort to restore the monarchy was dangerous. Flaubert was made anxious by it: he had forced himself to read the extremist pamphlets published by Chambord's supporters and claimed that they had the mentality of men from the twelfth century. If they came to power, they would turn back the clock to an unimaginable past.

It was on May 8, 1871—during the reign of the Commune—that Chambord had lamented the false choices offered the French people, saying: "A Christian nation cannot with impunity shred the pages of her history, break the chain of her traditions, inscribe at the head of her constitution the negation of the rights of God, banish all religious thought from her laws and her public education. In these conditions, she will never have more than a respite from disorder: she will oscillate perpetually between Caesarism and anarchy, those two equally shameful forms of pagan decadence, and will not escape from the fate of people unfaithful to their mission." Napoleon III's Second Empire was one form of "pagan decadence." Like the supporters of the Basilica of the Sacré-Coeur, Chambord thought the work of the Commune, its rejection of authority in favor of anarchy, its claim to a godless state, to be diabolical and unnatural, bound to lead only to further divine chastisement. He ended his letter with the declaration, "The word is with France and the moment is with God." A pomposity that Flaubert was ready to skewer, though he feared it.

Then came Chambord's most famous manifesto, on July 5, 1871, when he announced that his return from his Austrian exile to the Château de Chambord, in anticipation of his triumphal return to Paris, had ended with his once again taking the path to exile. The reason: while he was ready for every sacrifice, he could not sacrifice his honor. That honor was bound up with the flag. "I am and I want to be a man of my time," he declared. Nonetheless, in a sentence that led ever deeper into the past: "I will not allow the banner of Henri IV, of François I, of Jeanne d'Arc to be snatched from my hands." And in a final flourish: "Henri V cannot abandon the white flag of Henri IV." Better exile than the tricolor flag of revolutionary France.

But after this failure, by the fall of 1873 Chambord had the competing Orléanist branch of the family—the branch of Louis Philippe, king of the French from 1830 to the Revolution of 1848—won over to his cause with the "fusion" they agreed upon in August, whereby following the death of the childless Chambord, Henri V, kingship would pass to the Orléans' Comte de Paris. France was now nearer than ever to restoration. Thiers had fallen and Mac-Mahon was in power. Emissaries from the royalist camp in France made embassies to Chambord, urging him to relent on the question of the flag. A compromise was proposed: the white flag of the Bourbons would continue as the king's personal standard, while the tricolor remained the flag of the nation. Not acceptable, said Chambord. As he wrote to the bishop of Orléans in 1873, the flag question was simply "a pretext invented by those who, while recognizing the need to return to traditional monarchy, wish to preserve at least the symbol of revolution." An honest fellow, Flaubert declared him, in relief, writing to Caroline in November: "Does anyone think you can rub a whole people the wrong way! Deny 80 years of democratic developments, and return to rights granted by the king!" What he found truly comic was the anger of Chambord's partisans against their leader: they seemed to have forgotten the divine right of kings that they claimed to be defending. Chambord himself went back into exile. You can to this day see, in the stables of the great Château de Chambord, in the Loire Valley, the coach prepared for his triumphal entry as king into Paris—and never used.

Chambord could not understand the revolutionary tradition other than as a break with all that France truly was. He remained convinced, even as the republic settled in to endure, that he was the "indispensable pilot" of France. But no compromise was possible on questions of symbolism. The white flag with its fleur-de-lys, the banner of the Sacred Heart, the basilica: these appeared at least as important as what they represented. Chambord's refusal to accept the terms of kingship made Flaubert write "*hosannah!*" to the Princess Mathilde for deliverance from "the nightmare of Monarchy!"

That republic only truly became the overtly declared form of government when the Wallon Amendment, concerning the election of the president of the republic, passed by a one-vote majority on January 30, 1875. Its continued existence as a republic was then confirmed in the crisis of May 16, 1877, when Mac-Mahon tried to counter the wishes of the Assembly, which he dissolved, but then elections brought a more resolutely republican majority; Mac-Mahon capitulated, and then in 1879, he resigned. If, as Thiers famously said, the republic was the regime that divided the French least, its emergence was slow, uncertain, and constantly threatened. Only after 1877 did it seem more or less assured of survival. And later crises, including the threat of General Georges Boulanger in the late 1880s and the fall of France in 1940, would show that there was always a part of the nation that did not accept republicanism, that still longed for an authoritarian state.

All this is context for the battle following the Terrible Year to say what it meant, what sector of the French nation should write its meaning. Although support for the Commune was little in evidence, and there seemed to be something of a conspiracy of silence to keep anything but the reactionary interpretation from public discourse, there was a group, which included Victor Hugo and Léon Gambetta, working for an amnesty for those Communards who had not been killed during the Bloody Week or judicially executed in its aftermath. Amnesty came on July 11, 1880, in a republic now dominated by republicans, and the banished in New Caledonia were allowed to return home. From then on, the Commune became an intensely debated subject, with no consensus as to its meaning. The site of the Communards' last stand (at least symbolically) at the Mur des Fédérés, at the foot of Père Lachaise Cemetery, itself emerged as a "site of memory" to the political Left in the 1880s.

Flaubert was of course never a participant in homage to the Commune, but he continued to rail against the repressive and imbecilic reaction that followed. In February and March 1872, he reported dinners with Victor Hugo, whom he found more and more lovable. This might not seem entirely predictable, since Hugo was one of the very few public figures to speak out in sympathy with the Communards and to work actively for their amnesty; and Flaubert might legitimately have judged Hugo's writing to be marred by inflated rhetoric and bombast. But he declared his solidarity with Hugo on many occasions—recall his outraged letter to the *Nouvelliste de Rouen*, which had attacked Hugo the poet because of his political views. While not espousing Hugo's politics, Flaubert accepts them, and unreservedly admires the writer and the man.

Then, in February 1874, he wrote to Sand: "Have you read 93 by old Hugo? I like this book better than his two previous ones. There are truly beautiful moments in the first volume. But all his characters speak like Hugo. He doesn't have the gift of creating real characters." The two previous books are *L'Homme qui rit* (*The Man Who Laughs*), a historical novel, and *L'Année terrible*, Hugo's chronicle in verse of war, defeat, siege, the Commune, and repression. That effort at immediate history of the event—in verse!—reads like fragments of an epic poem recounted by an angry and compassionate Olympian deity. But it was not Hugo's definitive word on the Commune. That came in 1874, in the novel Flaubert praised, *Quatrevingt-treize* (*Ninety-Three*) named for the year of the Terror during the great Revolution. Rather than a direct commentary on the events of 1871, Hugo offers a return to a crucial conflict of the original Revolution in an effort to sort out the claims of the opposing parties in modern French history. He wrote the novel with the explicit intent of reconciling those parties, bringing an end to the seemingly insoluble standoff between Blues and Whites, those who belonged in one way or another to the republican tradition, on the one hand, and the partisans of authoritarianism and monarchy on the other. Written in the immediate aftermath of the Commune, from December 1872 to June 1873, on the eve of the restoration crisis, Hugo's novel seeks an Olympian overview, and an acceptance of a society of the future that acknowledges the claims of the past while seeking a synthesis of opposites. It is a utopian vision.

Hugo appears to reverse the situation of 1871—the Paris insurgency besieged by the Versaillais—since *Ninety-Three* focuses initially on the insurgency of the Vendée, royalist Brittany pitted against the revolutionary government in Paris, and the efforts of the republican expeditionary force to quell it. The novel sets the Marquis de Lantenac, a Breton aristocrat who has himself smuggled from England back into his homeland to organize the insurgency, against his young great-nephew, Gauvain, sometime *vicomte*, who has become a general in the republican army. Behind Gauvain stands Cimourdain, a *ci-devant* (a much-used term of the revolutionary period meaning "former": a former aristocrat or priest), a sometime priest who has now become an incorruptible partisan of revolution. With this symbolic distribution of roles ready to unfold, the story opens with a republican army battalion moving cautiously through the thick Breton forest, in which rebels can go to ground and remain undetectable, and coming upon a peasant woman, Michelle Fléchard. She has three young children—one still suckling at her breast—and has sought refuge after the burning of her village.

The opening scene brilliantly demonstrates what is in contest in the very uses of language. When Sergeant Radoub, a fast-talking Parisian, demands to know her *patrie*, Fléchard doesn't understand. It's only when he glosses *patrie* as *pays*, here meaning locality, that she replies with the name of her sharecrop and parish. Although she has been taught French by the local priest—she is not confined to Breton—Fléchard considers that she is from Brittany, not France, which to Radoub is incomprehensible and unacceptable, all the more so when she tells her story, which involves her father's incapacitation from a beating by his lord (he had poached a rabbit), her husband's father's hanging by the same lord for running contraband, and her husband's death in the fighting. It is a tale of utter woe in which the family has nonetheless remained loyal to lord and priest. By the end of the chapter, the Bataillon du Bonnet-Rouge adopts Fléchard's children as its own, and Sergeant Radoub invites her to come with them: "Venez, citoyenne." The term "citizen," of course, speaks to her changed status within the republican ranks and is emblematic of

the whole linguistic drama that Hugo has created in representation of
the forces in conflict.

How can these peasants fight for the lord and church that have oppressed them for centuries? How can they accept their status as beasts of
burden when a new age of freedom has dawned? This is what a worldview
is like, including the linguistic and symbolic world one inhabits, and why
you can't easily change it, in 1871 as in 1793. On the monarchist side, the
Marquis de Lantenac invokes the beliefs that led to the building of the
basilica on Montmartre. In claiming the obedience of the Breton peas-
antry, he appeals to the sacrificed king, and his son the Child of the Temple
(he who should have become Louis XVII but instead died as prisoner of
the Jacobins), the suffering of the bleeding, wounded Church, its places
of worship sacked, its priests banished—precisely the pathos evoked in
the bleeding Sacred Heart of Jesus. Opposed to him is that great-nephew
named after the knight of the Holy Grail, Gauvain—pure of heart and
devoted to the new ideals of liberty, equality, and fraternity. It is Gauvain's
name that one reads on the bills posted on the walls calling for the capture
and execution of Lantenac. And seconding Gauvain is the *ci-devant*, who
has converted his religious fervor into a belief in the republic. The national
drama is also a familial and a theological drama.

As Flaubert wrote to Sand, quite rightly, Hugo does not know how
to invest characters with independent life: they are all projections of the
author himself, parts of his internal dialogue. But as Flaubert also seems
to think, that doesn't matter here: if *Ninety-Three* is not great as a novel,
it is an extraordinary rhetorical creation. Hugo's love of grand symbolic
gestures leads him, in the second part of the novel, to a staging of the
very political heart of the tumultuous year 1793, when the three leaders
Danton, Marat, and Robespierre sit in solemn conclave making life-and-
death decisions. At times it's like something from a child's history book,
with illustrations of famous "moments," or even a comic-strip version of
history. Hugo then takes us to the revolutionary legislature, the Convention Nationale, which he sees as a kind of culminating point of history, a
deliberative body intent on remaking the world in impassioned debate and
sublime oratory. It is then with a return to Brittany in Part 3—entitled

En Vendée—that we come back to the plot of the novel and the series of antitheses to be worked out.

To come directly to the confrontations and debates of the last pages of the novel: Cimourdain has been sent as commissioner of the republic to oversee Gauvain, his former pupil, because Gauvain is known to have a penchant for clemency, and that must be stopped. Meanwhile, a massacre in the village of l'Herbe-en-Pail ordered by Lantenac has left Michelle Fléchard wounded, and her children lost—taken hostage, in fact, by Lantenac's forces, and brought to his fortress. Everything comes to climax deep in the Breton forest, in the medieval fortress of La Tourgue, its name a deformation of La Tour Gauvain, hence named for Gauvain's ancestors, and the stronghold of Lantenac. Here, Lantenac and his force of nineteen men retreat for their last stand, as Gauvain lays siege, and Michelle Fléchard will at the critical moment arrive on the scene in search of her lost children.

Hugo uses this dramatic moment to stage a series of debates on the meaning of the Revolution, of the Old Regime and its contestation, on social justice, on mercy, and on the society that must be created in the future. Earlier, we have had Gauvain and Cimourdain on the great Revolution. To Cimourdain's view that the Reign of Terror was the necessary salvation of the Revolution, Gauvain replies: "We don't overthrow the throne in order to keep the scaffold standing." Here, Hugo reaches back over forty years to his novel about a man about to be executed, *Le dernier jour d'un condamné* (*The Last Day of a Condemned Man*), published in 1829, then reissued in 1832 with a preface in which Hugo denounces capital punishment. "The scaffold is the only edifice that revolutions do not demolish," he wrote in the preface. Why should this be? A true revolution must enter an absolute plea of refusal to capital punishment. In a sweeping historical gesture, Hugo proclaims: "In the past the social edifice was supported on three pillars, priest, king, and executioner. Already long ago a voice said: *the gods are leaving!* More recently another voice was raised to cry out: *the kings are leaving!* Now it is time that a third voice be raised to say: *the executioner is leaving!*" But here we are three-quarters of the way through the nineteenth century and the executioner still is very much present—indeed, especially visible in the aftermath of the Commune. When will his compatriots learn that they have an imperative not to kill?

The debates undergo transformations. The climactic scenes of the novel begin with the republican assault on La Tourgue. A mine opens a breach in the tower. Lantenac and his faithful band, including the monstrous peasant l'Imânus, prepare their last stand. Sergeant Radoub leads the bloody assault. The end of Lantenac has almost come—when a hidden door in the tower opens, and the peasant Halmalo, who knows the secrets of La Tourgue better than its lord does, appears to lead the marquis down a hidden staircase to safety. The prey has escaped—but not before l'Imânus has set fire to the library that houses the three children of Michelle Fléchard, to kill them in retaliation for the child-king locked in the prison of the Temple, the dauphin who should be Louis XVII. The only access to the library is through an iron door from the tower, and the key to that door is in Lantenac's pocket. Then, as the library leaps into flames, Michelle Fléchard arrives on the scene, sees her children at the library window, and screams, in a maternal anguish that anticipates Bertolt Brecht's Mother Courage lamenting her dead children. Fléchard's scream brings the republicans' consternation—and Lantenac's moral turnaround. He returns to the tower he just escaped, unlocks the door, saves the children—and then is seized by Cimourdain. He is to be guillotined at dawn.

The debate now is between Gauvain and his conscience: Has Lantenac been redeemed by his act of loving-kindness? Should he be executed for the sake of the Revolution that he has put in jeopardy, or spared as a noble human being? Where is the moral imperative here? Gauvain goes to visit his great-uncle in his cell, the dungeon of La Tourgue, where we listen to Lantenac's rant against the Revolution as the destruction of everything that made life worth living, and his indictment of the *philosophes* and the other scribblers who undermined the Old Regime: "Books make crimes," he declares. Gauvain responds by placing his general's cape over Lantenac's head and shoulders, and giving him his freedom. In the morning, Cimourdain will discover Gauvain alone in Lantenac's cell. Against his deepest sentiments, but in the name of an inflexible law, Cimourdain will court-martial Gauvain and cast the deciding vote for his death on the guillotine.

Now, with Gauvain imprisoned and awaiting execution at dawn, Cimourdain pays him a last visit in the dungeon, and these two debate the meaning of revolution. Cimourdain upholds the idea (famously articulated by John Adams in the American founding) of a republic of laws, not of men: that law must inexorably prevail. To which Gauvain replies that to justice he prefers "equity"—and he develops a vision of a social democracy founded on true equality, with respect for the capacities of all, including the liberation of women and universal education. It is a brave position for Hugo to develop in 1874, when the post-Commune government proclaimed that "Moral Order" was the foundation of society. Gauvain sums up all the generous dreams of 1848 and the Commune at its most idealistic. In response to Cimourdain's ideal of perfect justice, he proposes that "Above the scales [of justice], there is the poet's harp" ("Au dessus de la balance, il y a la lyre"). Justice alone, to Hugo, cannot take you the next step, into a visionary future, into a world truly designed for human happiness.

These debates eventuate—Hugo is now deep into the visionary—in a dialogue, at sunrise, between La Tourgue and the guillotine: the representation of monarchy, feudalism, and a society based on hierarchy and a sense of class prerogative, on the one hand, and the instrument invented to cut all that off at the root, on the other: "On one hand, inextricable gothic complexity, serf, lord, slave, master, commoner, nobility, the abstruse code multiplied by customs, the judge and the priest together . . . the royal privilege of bankruptcy, the scepter, the throne, the arbitrary will of kings, divine right; on the other hand this simple thing, a blade. On one side the knot; on the other the axe." Perhaps most succinctly: "On the one hand the debt, on the other the payment come due." In the course of the debate, the guillotine will say to La Tourgue: "I am your daughter" ("Je suis ta fille"). The guillotine is engendered by the wrongs of centuries of feudalism. Hugo seems to adopt here the view expressed by Gauvain in dialogue with Cimourdain, when he says that he absolves the present moment. The moment of Terror needs absolution, and it may be absolved by what it has had to correct. But that is only a moment: revolutions in the name of humanity cannot go on killing without destroying themselves. Hugo summons his contemporaries to contemplate not just the meaning of the Revolution but the sweep of its bloody aftermath in a country where neither side has ever accepted an outcome as final.

The novel ends with Gauvain's execution, and at the same moment Cimourdain's suicide: "And these two souls, tragic sisters, flew off together, the shadow of the one mingled with the light of the other." Hugo's rhetorical antitheses resolve here in the chiaroscuro (another of his favorite rhetorical devices) of the dark and illuminated souls clasped together. We are supposed to read this as a rhetorical claim to the end of the long struggle to say to whom France belongs. The image is not black or white but the two embraced together. If you have understood the argument of *Ninety-Three*, you cannot go out and continue the old conflicts. You must accept that peace and reconciliation will come not through justice alone, but only with social justice. Flaubert by this point was prepared to hear that message.

If *Sentimental Education* makes a claim to understanding history, and might have offered a prophetic guide to future political events, *Ninety-Three* wants to exercise a more direct action on the political moment, a novelistic equivalent to the action that Hugo had undertaken in the Assembly for Communard amnesty. Hugo, the exile returned after his banishment by Napoleon III—who had refused to come back to France during the Empire even when offered amnesty, and then chose exile again following the Bloody Week—was well on his way to becoming a national hero. Elected to the Senate, he had in 1876 made a resounding speech in favor of amnesty for the Communards, contrasting the harsh treatment meted out in the wake of March 18, 1871, to the shower of governmental favors given to those who endorsed the crime of December 2, 1851, the coup d'état. Hugo then published, in 1877–1878, his *Histoire d'un crime* (*The Story of a Crime*), his final judgment on Louis-Napoléon's seizure of power. The campaign for amnesty would succeed by 1880. Hugo's seventy-ninth birthday (his entry into his eightieth year) was the occasion for a *fête* orchestrated by (and much commented on by) the republican press.

His funeral in 1885 was grandiose, one of those national manifestations that the French can make of a hero's burial.

Ninety-Three was a best seller. But it is hard to see that its message of fraternity and reconciliation had much effect. The republic endured until its collapse in defeat in 1940, and it became ever more secular. It voted for the separation of church and state, and for the creation of free, universal, secular education. The remaining Communards were amnestied. Chambord died in exile in 1883. Much was done to remake France as a single country. But one can't say that Hugo's vision of fraternity and the end to hostilities between the Blues and the Whites was fully realized. On the contrary, the Dreyfus Affair brought to the surface again, viciously, the irreconcilable conflicts of French society. And that affair in turn looked forward to the polarizations of the 1930s: on the one hand the Popular Front, spectacularly though briefly in power, on the other the rise of the right-wing leagues that triumphed when the Nazis took over. Hugo's visionary socialism may never have been a likely candidate for realization. There was one cause for which he had pleaded passionately that did eventually succeed: the abolition of capital punishment, which was enacted by the French Assembly in 1981.

What the Basilica of the Sacré-Coeur, Frémiet's statue of Jeanne d'Arc, and Hugo's *Ninety-Three* have in common is their symbolic response to invasion, defeat, and civil war. They are attempts from different political compass points to claim an interpretation of historical event by way of symbolic languages. This may seem to us a particularly French and particularly modern phenomenon: only the French would have conceived the grand collective publication called *Les Lieux de mémoire* (*Realms of Memory*), using places, monuments, and myths to write a collective history. The attachment of memory to chosen symbolic places and monuments is not exclusively French, of course; it surely has something to do with a "modern" conception of memory, including the form of memory we call nostalgia, which in many ways seems to belong to a modern world moving at a speed such that it creates, and mourns over, the past repeatedly. And this has no doubt been especially marked in a France divided between avant-garde Paris and a countryside that still lived by the church bell. The need to grasp the meaning of history in various symbols and genres assumes new and great importance in these last decades of the nineteenth century. The claim to discern and articulate historical meanings is very much on people's minds. If the historical novel is an invention of the early nineteenth century—in such as Scott and Manzoni—by the end of that century it has become a crucial arena for the debate of historical interpretations, an important arena for symbolic representations.

Flaubert's novel very much participates in the debate about the meanings of history—the national history experienced by Flaubert's own generation, and how it interweaves with the individual's life. The retrospective reading of *Sentimental Education* proposed in Flaubert's remark to Du Camp in the ruins of Paris suggests that we see that novel not only as the history of the generation that met its rendezvous with destiny in the Revolution of 1848 and its tragic aftermaths, but as a kind of prospective guide to what history will do to your life. Here, Flaubert and Marx join in a kind of strange alliance, the latter claiming that the Commune lighted the way to future proletarian revolution, the former that it confirmed his prediction of savagery and reaction. If Marx's lesson learned is that the workers of the world must unite in militant activity, Flaubert's seems to border on quietism, the sense that no political action is worth the cost. Yet there is some humanist convergence in their reactions to the ruins of Paris, the sentence they both pass on a complacent and stupid bourgeoisie.

Flaubert went on to explore stupidity and mental abjection in *Bouvard and Pécuchet*, a novel in which the Revolution of 1848 will reappear, in a provincial Norman setting, as a kind of arbitrary and incomprehensible series of events. Yet we will find in that novel clear signs of his progress toward a position far more sympathetic to the Left, and to republicanism. Meanwhile, he gives a certain displaced version of the struggle for the hearts and minds of his compatriots in one of his last completed works, the tale "Un Coeur simple" ("A Simple Heart"), written for George Sand but reaching her too late. It may not be far-fetched to suggest that the imagery of the heart has something to do with the Sacred Heart of Jesus worshiped by right-wing France—but how very different a heart it is.

– chapter six –

"A Simple Heart"

IN THE AFTERMATH OF THE COMMUNE, FLAUBERT—PERHAPS without quite realizing it—became a republican. For all his belief in rule by intellectual elites—"mandarins," as he liked to call them—his horror and disgust at what reactionaries and monarchists were up to drove him into alliance with the liberal bourgeoisie. He feared Chambord and his partisans. He detested the regime of "Moral Order," and mobilized a public protest when the heavy hand of the censor fell on his friend and disciple Guy de Maupassant. He claimed, too, that the local *préfet* in Normandy had banned a lecture on François Rabelais—and one on geology: "crimes," he called these acts of censorship, writing to Edma Roger des Genettes in September 1877. President Mac-Mahon's attempt to abrogate parliamentary democracy in the crisis of May 16, 1877, enraged him. "After five minutes thinking about it, it puts me into a paroxysm of Fury," he told Léonie Brainne in August. "Stupidity wounds me. And I don't know of anything in history more *inept* than the men of May 16. Their stupidity makes me dizzy." In October he put it more simply to Maupassant: "Merde pour Mac-Mahon"; and to Zola: "Merde pour l'Ordre moral." All during the summer of 1877, he was deeply anxious about the outcome of the elections that would follow the dissolution of the Assembly by the "Bayard of modern times," in his ironic epithet. When a republican majority resulted, he was relieved. Though Mac-Mahon was likely to commit further mischief, the republic now seemed assured; it would be the best bulwark against the imposition of religion and the suppression of free thought represented by monarchists and clergy.

Discreet milestones along Flaubert's path to republicanism can be found, and one of them was his decision on September 8, 1877, to attend the grandiose funeral procession for Adolphe Thiers, that incarnation of the bourgeoisie whom he once described as turdlike. Flaubert was moved as he joined the million marchers who made up the cortège in what he felt to be a truly national demonstration. "I didn't like this king of Prud-hommes,—no matter! Compared to those around him, he's a giant. And he had a rare virtue: Patriotism. No one summed up France like him," he wrote to Edma Roger des Genettes. So if not the man, he appreciated Thiers as symbol of a nation determined to move forward after the Terrible Year. He saluted the publication of Victor Hugo's scathing narrative of the coup d'état of 1851, *The Story of a Crime*: "a *very* good book," he told Maupassant. Then, even more telling: on January 19, 1878, at the house of his publisher Georges Charpentier, he dined with Léon Gambetta, the foremost French republican leader. "We now are great friends," Flaubert wrote to Edmond Laporte. "We had a private meeting. Three more like that and we will say *tu* to one another!" Edmond de Goncourt, who also took part in the dinner, described with his customary acidity Flaubert taking Gambetta off for private conversation after dinner. That Flaubert sought to closet himself with the man who embodied the rise of a new political caste and a new social class (he came from the petite bourgeoisie) to republican rule speaks forcefully to his own evolution. Much as he might rail against modern times and claim the role of hermit, Flaubert was too much the historian to stand aside from the world. His consciousness of life was profoundly historical.

Between the immediate aftermath of the Commune in the summer of 1871 and the constitutional crisis of the summer of 1877 and its republican sequel, much had happened in Flaubert's professional and personal lives. He probably began a liaison, of infrequent meetings, with the young Rouennais widow Léonie Brainne, and continued his rare but prized arch-secret meetings with the English governess Juliet Herbert. His doctors sent him to take the waters at Kaltbad in Switzerland. His mother died. He wrote a play, *The Candidate*, which had its premiere at the Théâtre du Vaudeville in March 1874, and was a total failure. In April the same year, he published the long-gestated *Temptation of Saint Anthony*, and this was, with the exception of some appreciation, less than a success. He went back to work on *Bouvard and Pécuchet*. Then, in the fall of 1875, retrieving an old idea, he composed "La Légende de Saint Julien l'Hospitalier" ("The Legend of Saint Julian the Hospitaller")—inspired, he claimed, by a stained-glass window in the Cathedral of Rouen. It would be the first of three stories, along with "A Simple Heart" and "Hérodias," published in April 1877 as *Trois Contes* (*Three Tales*), to favorable reviews this time and a generally warm public reception. "A Simple Heart," in particular, was well received, and it has endured as one of his masterworks, one quite different from all the others.

The turn to writing the three short stories, one medieval, one modern, one set in antiquity, seems to have been self-therapy. The year 1875 was a particularly bleak one: following the death of friends, and especially his mother, and continuing troubles with his health that his physician called "neuropathic," came the crisis of rescuing Caroline's husband from bankruptcy. He and his mother had invested in Commanville's lumber import enterprise, and the crisis reduced Flaubert to a state of constant financial anxiety in a life that had largely been protected from money worries. He sold his principal source of income, a farm at Deauville, for 200,000 francs to satisfy Commanville's creditors, and announced to his friends that he was ruined. Declaring Commanville bankrupt would have made more sense—but Flaubert saw that as a dishonorable action. He detested asking for public favors, but he nonetheless began to solicit a sinecure of some sort—the most likely idea seemed to be the post of librarian at the

Bibliothèque Mazarine, in Paris, but it turned out that had been promised to Frédéric Baudry, an old friend of Flaubert's. Eventually, a secondary post was created at the Mazarine with an annual stipend of 3,000 francs, which he would reluctantly accept.

In his work on *Bouvard and Pécuchet*, which entailed volumes of reading and extensive notes, Flaubert was not making good progress. In September, he made a sudden decision to go spend some time in Concarneau, in Brittany, with a friend, the naturalist Georges Pouchet. It was in Concarneau, when he was without his library and his dossiers of notes, that he revived the long dormant "Legend of Saint Julian the Hospitaller." By December he was back in Paris, looking for documentation he thought he needed for the tale. He completed the research quickly (for him) and then moved on to "A Simple Heart," which he finished in August 1876. It was then the turn of "Hérodias," which he completed after two months of intense labor. Meanwhile, on June 10, 1876, he traveled to Nohant for George Sand's funeral.

It was for his old and beloved "*chère Maître*" that he wrote "A Simple Heart." It was she, after all, who had told him, repeatedly, that he had a good heart, and lamented that he hid his humanity too much behind the mask of impersonality that he assumed for his fiction. In that long and eloquent letter from October 25, 1871, where Sand told of her childhood and the making of her political beliefs, she said to her old troubadour: "You will understand me, you who are goodness from head to toe" ("Tu dois me comprendre, toi qui es bonté de la tête aux pieds"). It's a characterization that a reader wouldn't necessarily derive from his novels. Then, in her very long letter of January 12, 1876, Sand came back to the judgment that *Sentimental Education* failed because of Flaubert's refusal in the book to clarify his own moral stance: "To withdraw your soul from what you write, what kind of an unhealthy fantasy is that? To hide your own opinion on the characters you present, thus to leave the reader uncertain about the opinion he should have of them, that's to wish not to be understood, and then the reader parts company with you; for, if he wishes to understand the story you have to tell him, it's on condition that you show him clearly that this character is strong and this other one a weakling." This advice of course stands opposed to everything Flaubert believed as an artist. Sand continues: "So, you need to go directly to the highest morality that you have in yourself, and not make a mystery of the moral sense and profit to be found in the work." The whole letter is harshly critical of his literary practice, anti-Flaubertian in its advice to the point that he might have taken offense, were it not that they had long vowed to say anything they wished to one another without fear of offense and misunderstanding.

In response, Flaubert, then at work on "Saint Julian," contrasts their temperaments: her idealism and his position stuck on the earth: "There is no point in preaching to me, I can't have another temperament than what I have. Nor another aesthetic, which is its consequence. . . . As for showing my personal opinion on the characters I dramatize, no, no! a thousand times no! I don't recognize that I have *the right*. If the reader can't draw out the moral that should be found there, it's because the reader is an imbecile, or that the book is *false* from the point of view of exactitude. Because from the moment something is True it is good." At the end of his letter, he mentions that after completing the short story he is now working on, he'll do another, since he is too deeply upset to undertake longer work.

The second short story would be "A Simple Heart"—when the *Three Tales* were published, it would stand first. He mentions the story in a letter to Sand on May 29, 1876. What he says almost sounds like a conversion to her understanding of art: "You will see by my *Story of a Simple Heart*, where you will recognize your direct influence, that I am not as stubborn as you think. I believe that the moral tendency, or rather the human underside of this little work will please you!" There was no reply; she was already slipping from consciousness. Flaubert wrote anxiously to her daughter-in-law Lina and to Prince Napoléon for news. Sand died on June 8. A last skirmish about belief and orthodoxy took place around her funeral, since her estranged daughter Solange Clésinger insisted upon a church, a priest, and burial in sanctified ground. Flaubert refused to enter the church or the cemetery, and shed his tears as the coffin passed by. He reported to Turgenev: "In order not to offend 'public opinion,' the eternal and execrable *them* [in French: *on*], they had her carried to the church!

I'll give you the details of this tawdriness." "Goodness" to Flaubert and to Sand, to the very end, had nothing to do with religion.

The moral and emotional depth of "A Simple Heart" isn't so easy to define, though any thoughtful reading of the tale feels its presence. Some readers have found the treatment of the peasant Félicité, the drudge of a servant to Madame Aubain in the Norman town of Pont-l'Évêque, to be characterized by a condescending irony. I would instead agree with Flaubert's declaration to Edma Roger des Genettes shortly after Sand's death: "The *Story of a Simple Heart* is quite simply the narrative of a hidden life, that of a poor girl from the country, a believer but not a mystic, devoted without exaltation and tender like fresh bread. She loves in succession a man, the children of her mistress, a nephew, an old fellow she takes care of, then her parrot,—and when the parrot dies, she has him stuffed,—and when dying in her turn, confuses the parrot with the Holy Spirit. It is not at all ironic, as you presume, but on the contrary very serious and very sad." Flaubert reserves his irony for those who hold power, who think they are entitled to the world's riches and favors, and claim to master its languages. No need to be ironic with his poor country girl.

Félicité is beyond irony. As other commentators have noted, she has a precursor in one of the few wholly sympathetic characters in *Madame Bovary*, Catherine Leroux, who receives a medal at the agricultural fair for a half-century of servitude on the same farm. Catherine Leroux scarcely understands what the pompous bourgeois officials want of her: her senses and her understanding are like those of the farm animals with whom she has passed her life. It is this state of "servitude" that Flaubert quite remarkably explores—remarkably, because in his own existence he appears to have been a privileged bourgeois who never, at least until the Commanville financial disaster, thought much about his entitlements, including the servants who prepared his food every day, cleaned his clothes, and generally performed those tasks that the nineteenth-century bourgeoisie took for granted that they didn't perform themselves. The brilliant first sentence of "A Simple Heart" makes the point without stating it: "For half a century, the bourgeois housewives of Pont-l'Évêque envied Madame Aubain her servant Félicité." The French is even more telling, since the locution for "to envy" is followed

by a preposition: you envy to someone. "Pendant un demi-siècle, les bour-
geoises de Pont-l'Évêque envièrent à Mme Aubain sa servante Félicité." The
"heroine" of the story appears to be only the object of envy directed to her
possessor, Madame Aubain. And the next line tells us why: "For one hundred francs a year, she cooked and cleaned, sewed, washed, ironed, could
bridle a horse, fatten poultry, churn butter, and remained faithful to her
mistress,—who moreover was not an agreeable person."

The story of servitude is in part one of repetition, of a kind of time-
less sameness. We learn of Félicité in the first chapter: "At the age of
twenty-five, one would have thought she was forty. And after passing
fifty, she no longer showed any ageing;—and, always silent, her back
straight and her movements restrained, seemed a woman made of wood,
functioning like an automaton." Against this apparent timelessness there
is a movement of history, summed up in a paragraph that seems nearly
to deny historical process:

> Then years went by, all the same and without incidents other than the
> return of the major holy days: Easter, Assumption, All Saints. Domestic
> events made a date, to which one referred later. So in 1825, two glaziers
> plastered the vestibule; in 1827, a piece of the roof, falling in the court-
> yard, almost killed a man. The summer of 1828, it was Madame's turn
> to give the holy bread; Bourais around this time mysteriously vanished;
> and old acquaintances passed away one by one: Guyot, Liébard, Mme
> Lechaptois, Robelin, uncle Gremanville, long since paralyzed.

And then we have what is just about the one punctual historical event in
the novel: "One night, the stage coach driver announced in Pont-l'Evêque
the July Revolution." The only consequence of this change of regime in
1830 is the appointment of a new *sous-préfet*, a former consul in America
whose family possesses "a negro and a parrot." The only reason to mark the
historical event at all would seem to be the parrot, which will be passed
on to Madame Aubain when its owner is promoted to a *préfecture*—and
which then will become Félicité's possession, her only possession following
the deaths of her nephew Victor and Madame Aubain's daughter Virginie.

Early on, we are told of Félicité: "She had had, like anyone else, her love story" ("Elle avait eu, comme une autre, son histoire d'amour"). That story—one of seduction (though she preserved her virginity), promise of marriage, and then abandonment—is over and done with when the story of the simple heart begins: it's in the past perfect tense, a prelude to the timelessness of her servitude. When Madame Aubain falls ill after learning of the fraud practiced on her by her business agent, Bourais, we learn that "in March, 1853, she was seized with chest pains": the whole history of the Revolution of 1848, including its aftermath and the coming of the Second Empire, has been elided. It has been of no importance in Félicité's life. The repetitive gestures of servitude take the place of what we think of as the succession of significant events. Félicité's history is one of natural process, mainly loss and death.

If "history" as a domain of knowledge is tied to instruction, Félicité's knowledge comes from the animals in her life. When she is being courted during her "love story," we are told: "She wasn't innocent in the manner of proper young women—animals had instructed her." The life of animals is everywhere, instructing, giving meaning to what she would not otherwise comprehend. When she accompanies Virginie to her catechism, she acquires a knowledge of religion: "Sowing, harvesting, cider presses, all these familiar things the Gospels speak of were part of her life; God's passage had sanctified them; and she loved lambs more tenderly because of the Lamb, doves because of the Holy Spirit." There is here the beginnings of a confusion of representation and represented, of symbol and symbolized, that is central to her experience. In church, she gazes long at the dove, as representation of the Holy Spirit, and observes that there is something of the parrot in his appearance. The resemblance is even more striking on a popular print of the Holy Spirit, which she buys and hangs on the wall in her attic room. When the parrot Loulou, now dead and stuffed by the taxidermist, stands next to the religious icon, she takes them in with the same glance: "They became associated in her mind, the parrot becoming sanctified by its relation to the Holy Spirit, which became more living in her eyes and intelligible. God the Father for his annunciation couldn't have chosen a dove, since those animals don't have tongues, but rather one of Loulou's ancestors."

To find this treatment of Félicité's intellect ironic would be to give Flaubert little credit. Beyond irony there is something you might call stupidity, *bêtise*. Here, that does not mean the stupidity of the bourgeoisie that Flaubert rails against throughout his life, and which will be the exclusive concern of his *Dictionnaire des idées reçues* (*Dictionary of Received Ideas*). Félicité's *bêtise* is that of the *bêtes* amidst whom she lives, whom she understands. In the episode in which she saves Madame Aubain and her children from a charging bull, it is as if she perfectly seizes the bull's way of "thinking," placing herself in so close a relation that she knows how to baffle the animal. When Loulou suffers a disease, she discovers the abscess and removes it with her fingers. This is a wisdom of the natural world that contrasts with the book learning represented by the atlas that Bourais uses to show her the location of her nephew Victor, who has sailed to Havana:

> He reached for his atlas, then began explanations on longitudes; and he had the smug smile of a pedant faced with Félicité's stupefaction. Finally, with his pencil holder, within the ragged edges of an oval spot he pointed to an imperceptible black dot, adding: "There." She bent over the map; this network of colored lines tired her sight, without teaching her anything; and when Bourais asked her to say what was bothering her, she asked him to show her the house where Victor was staying. Bourais raised his hands, sneezed, laughed out loud; such ingenuousness excited his joy; and Félcité didn't understand the reason— she who was expecting to see maybe even the portrait of her nephew, so limited was her intelligence!

Bourais's assumption that the system of representation used by maps, including scale and the markings of latitude and longitude, is self-evident and self-explanatory is an excellent example of self-satisfied bourgeois stupidity: stupid because it cannot step outside the limits of its own systems of knowledge, see them as systems that are arbitrary and depend upon codes that require decoding. Félicité's expectation of a more literal representation of Victor's place on the globe isn't stupider, it simply assumes another order of representation, one where—as in the passages on the Holy Spirit—there is an intimacy of representation with the represented, a tactile and sensuous alliance of the two. As in her sexual instruction from animals, Félicité knows in ways that are closed to Bourais. And it will be the parrot Loulou who first takes Bourais as a figure of mockery, laughing wildly when it sees him, so that Bourais must sneak around to the back door to make his entrance. Bourais of course will later be revealed as a con man who ruins Madame Aubain: the parrot is the first to detect his fraudulence.

Our assumptions about Flaubertian irony can cloud our understanding of what he is up to in "A Simple Heart." Recall what he wrote to Edma Roger des Genettes: "It is not at all ironic, as you presume, but on the contrary very serious and very sad." One needs to set aside the presumption of irony. But when you do, it is not so easy to say what the tone and the mode of the story are. I think the answer is to be sought in the very title of the tale: it is about simplicity, almost in the sense present in "simpleton": a limited understanding, by the world's standards. "Lord! how stupid you are," Madame Aubain tells her; and she replies, "Yes, Madame." Her language is consonant with Loulou's. When she grows deaf in old age, it's only the parrot's talk that reaches her. "As if to distract her, he reproduced the tick-tock of the turning spit, the raspy cry of the fishmonger, the saw of the cabinetmaker who lived across the way, and, when the bell rang, imitated Madame Aubain,—'Félicité, the door! The door!'" This is speech that imitates understanding, a kind of primary mimesis of the world, which in its way is no less meaningful than Bourais's bourgeois pedantry.

It may in some sense be a language of the heart, as the organ of feeling and also of knowledge. Flaubert seems to be attempting to imagine the world from the point of view of a simple and loving apprehension of the world, one that progressively invests its love into a seeming fiancé, into Madame Aubain's children, her nephew, the parrot live and then stuffed. I don't claim any intended dialogue with the project for the Basilique du Sacré-Coeur that was in the news at the time that Flaubert was composing what he calls in his letters his *Story of a Simple Heart*. He was of course very much aware of what he called the "hideous" cult of the Sacred Heart meant in France in 1875, its use as emblem by the forces of clerical and monarchist reaction. Whatever his conscious intentions, his simple heart stands in stark opposition to the bleeding heart envisioned by Marguerite-Marie Alacoque and those who persuaded the pope to beatify her in 1866. That was an elaborate, baroque heart, one ensconced in rhetoric both sugary and apocalyptic, something embroidered on silk robes and banners, and ultimately political. The simple heart is a counter-emblem.

It is hard to know what to make of the religiosity of "A Simple Heart" in the work of a declared nonbeliever. The other two stories of the *Three Tales* also touch on religious subjects: the story of Saint Julian, which ends with his embrace by Jesus Christ and his assumption into heaven, and the claim that the author has transcribed the legend as it is depicted in a stained-glass window of a church in his hometown, along with that of Salome demanding the head of John the Baptist. Certainly the tales make no claim to orthodoxy or to an allegiance to the Church as such. The ending of "A Simple Heart," in particular, takes us into a kind of religious experience that must seem heresy to the orthodox, perhaps even in a way that is satirical of religious belief, yet undeniably spiritual. Félicité lies dying as the ceremony of the Lord's Feast—with Loulou part of the altar decoration—unfolds in the courtyard below her window.

> The azure vapor of incense rose to Félicité's room. She opened her nostrils, taking it in with a mystic sensuality; then closed her eyelids. Her lips were smiling. The movements of her heart slowed one by one, more uncertain each time, softer, as a fountain runs dry, as an echo fades away; and, when she exhaled her last breath, she thought she saw, in the opening heavens, a gigantic parrot, soaring over her head.

The paragraph takes us over the threshold from life, and with the final "she thought she saw"—"elle crut voir"—claims a final vision in which the Holy Spirit becomes a gigantic Loulou. Once again, the standard terms of representation are reversed and confused. The spiritual stands for the literal, it seems, rather than the reverse. The passage does not affirm Christian belief, but it calls upon the symbols of belief to create its own form of simple religious experience.

A contention that the stories represent a return of their author toward Christian belief can't really be sustained. Flaubert was amused to find *Three Tales* on the recommended reading list of a Catholic bookstore, approved for "family reading." "I'm becoming a Father of the Church!" he told Léonie Brainne in August 1877. One gets closer to the spirit of "A Simple Heart" in recalling its intended ideal reader. He reiterated to Maurice Sand that he wrote the tale for his late mother: "I had begun *Un Coeur simple* with her in mind exclusively, only in order to please her. She died while I was in the middle of my work. Thus it is with all our dreams." The tale returns us to all of George Sand's pleas for a good and loving heart, and her repeated diagnosis that her seemingly misanthropic friend in fact was the essence of goodness. Defining what she meant by goodness never was easy. It certainly did not mean traditional religious belief—she was even more militant in her atheism than Flaubert. It had to do, simply, with having a good heart. And that seems to be what Flaubert is getting at in his story of Félicité, the story of someone so simple that she knows and understands and lives and dies only by her heart. It's not much of an existence when you think of those fifty years of servitude, yet it's the life of an affirmatively good person.

There is a curious moment that Flaubert recounts—labeling it "an extraordinary event"—in a letter to Caroline from the fall of 1871. He tells of taking a walk on a glorious October afternoon and finding himself in contemplation of nature. "I was overtaken by such tenderness for the little calf that was lying beside its mother, on the dried leaves lit up by the sunshine, that I kissed, on the forehead, the said calf!" No further commentary is provided. Flaubert seems astonished at himself. Sand would have understood.

The writing of the *Three Tales* was a parenthesis in Flaubert's long labor on *Bouvard and Pécuchet*, the enigmatic "novel" left unfinished at his death. As with his previous books, Flaubert read enormously to write this one. But whereas the reading for *Sentimental Education* was to furnish background information, here book reading itself stands in the foreground of the novel. Flaubert's two scriveners give up copying to move to the country, where they read many books on a succession of topics, from gardening to childrearing, and attempt to use them as guides to practice. Book learning is taken to be a faithful representation of the world, to the point that it can be put to use in the world. Yet the results are inevitably dire. For instance, the garden they construct with great labor fails to represent any of the effects it has attempted to put into symbolic form. Their source of instruction here is *L'Architecte des jardins* (The garden architect), not Flaubert's invention but an actual book published in 1852, one of the many volumes he used in preparation of the novel. It proposes a typology of gardens:

> There is, first of all, the melancholic and romantic type, signaled by forget-me-nots, ruins, tombs, and "a shrine to the Virgin, indicating the place where a lord fell under an assassin's dagger." One constructs the dreadful type with overhanging rock, splintered trees, burnt-down huts, the exotic type by planting torch thistle "to inspire memories for the traveler or the colonist." The pensive type should offer, as at Ermenonville, a temple to philosophy. Obelisks and triumphal arches characterize the majestic type, moss and grottos the mysterious type, a lake the dreamy type. There is even a fantastic type, the most beautiful example of which could once upon a time be seen in a Wurttemberg garden—for there one successively encountered a wild boar, a hermit, several sepulchers, and a skiff that by itself left the shore and took you to a boudoir, where fountains soaked you when you sat on the sofa.

If you are Bouvard and Pécuchet, you marvel at this description: "Faced with this horizon of marvels, Bouvard and Pécuchet were nearly bedazzled." And nothing in the passage prevents one from taking it "straight." Yet the way Flaubert has chosen and set the words from *L'Architecte des jardins*—"mounted" them, one might say, as of jewelry—they offer Flaubert's deadpan humor in full force.

Bouvard and Pécuchet not only take straight the descriptions of these genres of garden, they read them as instructions for their do-it-yourself project. They ravage their existing garden in order to construct an eclectic version of what they have read in *L'Architecte des jardins*, making use of what lies to hand. They build an "Etruscan tomb": a quadrilateral of black plaster "looking like a dog kennel." The "great rock" that they cement together from pieces of granite found in a riverbed looks like "a giant potato." Four squared-off tree trunks holding up a tin hat with its corners bent up "signifies" a Chinese pagoda. They chop down a tree to figure one "struck by lightning." When their work is done, they unveil it to their invited guests after dinner: "In the twilight it was something terrifying." It is met with incomprehension.

Turgenev had written Flaubert to express doubt about the projected novel as Flaubert described it, recommending instead that he should treat his topic "*presto*, in the manner of Swift, of Voltaire." In reply, Flaubert, despite his immense respect for Turgenev's critical judgment, argued that he didn't want to do a "more or less witty fantasy," but a detailed, developed narrative, one where he appears to believe in the story—which might result in "something serious and even terrifying." The two copyists seem to have achieved that terror with their garden, and, also like the Flaubert of *Sentimental Education*, to have provoked incomprehension in their audience. That is to say that while the efforts of Bouvard and Pécuchet are clearly ludicrous, in another reading their constructive results appear to them sublime. The perspective of reading is what matters. If it "signifies" a Chinese pagoda to me, who are you to say it isn't that? The book is radical Flaubert—radical in the manner Sand deplored—in its refusal to give the reader any sure sense of how to take it, of where to stand in evaluating its story.

The story is largely one of trial and failure, as Bouvard and Pécuchet move through different domains of knowledge, attempting to apply what they learn from instructional manuals to real-world experience. When they attempt to improve their wheat crop, they cut it too soon and the stacks go up in flames from spontaneous combustion. When they attempt to put up preserves, the contents of their jars go bad, or else explode. When they study history, they find so many opposing opinions that they give up in confusion. When, more ambitiously, they adopt a boy and a girl and attempt to educate them according to the treatises, they fail again, signally: the girl is seduced by a criminal, the boy becomes a rogue. Flaubert appears to be undertaking a demonstration of the uselessness of several branches of human knowledge—or perhaps, rather, the inapplicability of human knowledge to the conduct of existence.

And then there is the *Dictionary of Received Ideas*. When Flaubert's niece, Caroline, rushed *Bouvard and Pécuchet* into print in the year following his death in 1880—she and her husband were desperate for money—it was in a single volume without any clear ending. Caroline then asked Guy de Maupassant to work the manuscripts left at death into a coherent second volume. Maupassant's study of the manuscripts soon led him to the conclusion that nothing could be done with them: there was both too much and too little, too many versions and no clear outline. What did seem to be clear enough, though, was Flaubert's intention to include within the second volume his collection of stupidities, the *sottisier* on which he had been working for years, which would be published at last as the *Dictionary*.

This is one of the most baffling works not only in Flaubert's oeuvre but in modern literature as a whole. It also appears to be central to his project as a writer. He seems to have collected, throughout his life, examples of stupidity, bourgeois complacency, and bad faith. The collection is a compendium of clichés, but that's not the end of it. The clichés are such as to demonstrate both the expressive and the intellectual limitations of those who use them: they capture a worldview. In an early explanation of the project, in a letter to Louise Colet of 1852, he says: "One thus would find there, in alphabetical order, on all possible subjects, *everything one is supposed to say in society in order to be a proper and amiable person. . . .* It would have to be that in the course of the whole book not a word would be my own, and that once one had read it you wouldn't dare to speak, for fear of uttering one of the phrases in the book." It would be in this manner a book to end all books, indeed to end all utterance, since you would fear that anything you said would fall into the category of the cliché. So that cataloging the world's dumb utterances would have the effect of reducing the world to silence. If only. But notice that the political climax of *Sentimental Education*—the moment, in the wake of Louis-Napoléon's coup d'état, when Sénécal kills Dussardier—results in silence, a kind of speechlessness at what History has produced. It's as if, not able to bring his contemporaries to renounce speech altogether, he maneuvers his historical account to a moment that silences the crowd as well as the novel.

His other famous statement about the *Dictionary of Received Ideas* comes in a letter to Louis Bouilhet from 1850. Here, the context is more cultural-political: he foresees a "substantial preface" in which "one would indicate how the work was created in the goal of bringing the public back to tradition, to order, to reigning convention, arranged in such a manner that the reader would not know whether he was being made fun of or not." Here, he gleefully foresees producing a reaction of uncertainty on the part of the reader: Am I within the tradition of the commonplace, or outside it? Where should I be? The "commonplace" (as Sartre has well noted) is where we can all meet, in the exchange of what we call "small talk," that which indicates an interest in belonging to the exchange and the society it represents. When the commonplace is revealed as such, as dominant convention, as the place of non-thinking, either we don't see the revelation, indicating our inability to step out of the common place, or we are rejected to some uninhabitable outside, a non-common place, where we may not be able to speak at all.

For the historian, Michel Winock tells us, the *Dictionary* is a mine, since it offers a collective portrait of the nineteenth-century bourgeois, a satiric "ideal type." It does so, though, without ever clearly indicating the place or stance of the satirist. To make that stance clear would be to violate the very principle of the collection, which is to prevent the reader from knowing whether he is being mocked or not: to offer no place outside the commonplace. Readers must establish the satiric position for themselves, create their own margins outside the discourse of the cliché. When George Sand told Flaubert that *Sentimental Education* failed because there was no clear normative position in the novel—or outside of it, in an authorial preface, for instance—she made the point. And many another reader has reacted in the same way: Henry James, for instance, felt threatened by a novel that so completely eschewed any apparent normativity. (Though James did seem to understand, in a hesitant way, what Flaubert was up to in *Bouvard and Pécuchet*, and what might be gained by the exploration of language itself.) Flaubert moves from what are recognizably novels, *Madame Bovary*, *Salammbô*, *Sentimental Education*, to something that appears to use the novel form in order to explore the mimetic function of language itself. He is in this manner close to a younger generation of painters who were moving beyond representation to an exploration of its very means, the language of their art. That language both entices Flaubert, since it can be the medium of beauty and truth, and also disgusts him, since it is equally the medium of clichés, complacencies, lies, and the political deformation of reality.

That makes of such a work as "A Simple Heart," I think, a radical dissent. It labors to create (this took pages and pages of drafts, about four times the length of the final version) a language so simplified and limpid that it keeps us close to the natural world, to sensation, to smell and touch. Abstraction in language and thought can only be approached by way of the everyday. Any attempt to understand symbolization returns us to the object itself used to symbolize, not what it may refer to. There is no distinction between the lamb and the Lamb, the parrot and the Holy Spirit. As for this latter, the abstraction par excellence: "She had trouble imagining his person; for he was not only a bird, but also a fire, and other times a breath of air. It's perhaps his light that flares at night along the edges of the swamp, his breath that pushes the clouds, his voice that makes the harmony of the church bells; and she remained in adoration, ecstatic in the cool of the walls and the tranquility of the church." Simplicity, yes; stupidity, even, since she fails to understand the process of symbolization, reading backward from symbol to its literalization in the common things of her life. But nonetheless perfection in its realization of a world inhabited by spirit. If, as the philosopher Charles Taylor has argued, one of the contributions of the nineteenth-century novel to our culture was its finding significance in the everyday, Flaubert outdoes even such as George Eliot and George Sand. The dignity of the everyday is a kind of absolute, despite the utter poverty of Félicité's experience of life.

The artful simplicity of "A Simple Heart" is wholly different from the bourgeois commonplace. The story lies beyond irony: to treat Félicité and her story with irony is to take a position like that of Bourais, who mocks her lack of understanding of the representative system of maps. Bourais, as the parrot Loulou first appears to understand, is a fraud, the perfect type of the bourgeois (he is a *notaire*, that indispensable acolyte of bourgeois property and pretension) who takes for granted his entitled position in bourgeois society and finance, yet becomes the very figure of falsity and cheating. Even more than the complacent Madame Aubain (whose name suggests a gift, a windfall), Bourais offers a lesson in reading the bourgeois. And the response of the parrot, part mechanical parrotry and part almost knowing parody, suggests that against the pretentious commonplaces of the bourgeoisie, the language one uses needs to exercise a kind of hygiene, a taking apart of language by language. Since there is no such thing as a true metalanguage, one that would dominate language analytically, you need to undermine language from within.

That's what seems to be happening in the *Dictionary of Received Ideas*. Sometimes this is on the level of the standard social response. For instance:

BUDGET. Never balanced.

HOTELS. Good only in Switzerland.

OYSTERS. You can't eat them anymore! They're too expensive!

But the accepted responses often contain sinister political assumptions:

CENSORSHIP: Useful, no matter what they say!

POACHERS: All ex-convicts.—Responsible for all the crimes committed in the countryside.—Should excite a frenetic anger: "No pity, Sir! No pity!"

REPUBLICANS: Republicans aren't all thieves, but all thieves are republicans.

BACHELORS: Mad, selfish, and debauched.—Should be taxed.— Are preparing a sad old age for themselves.

Commonplace wisdom can be perfectly self-canceling:

> HORSEBACK RIDING: Good exercise for losing weight. Example: all cavalry officers are slim. For gaining weight. Example: all cavalry officers have a large belly.

Or, in this famous suite of definitions:

> BLONDES: Hotter than brunettes (see Brunettes)
> BRUNETTES: Are hotter than blondes (see Blondes)
> NEGRESSES: Hotter than whites (see Blondes and Brunettes)
> REDHEADS: (See Blondes, Brunettes, and Negresses)

By the time you reach the end of this series, the perfectly stupid answer presents itself, thus demonstrating that you—and I and everyone—are steeped in stupidity. Like any dictionary, this one is circular, defining a word by other words. In this case, however, the circularity of the definitions leads us back to a kind of basic impossibility of speech itself. We recall Flaubert's early ambition, expressed in the letter to Louise Colet, to make it impossible for anyone to open his mouth from fear of uttering clichés. Silence may be the only answer. The solution of Bouvard and Pécuchet, after the failure of all their self-educative projects, and their attempts to educate Victor and Victorine and their fellow townspeople, is to return to copying. Anything that comes to hand. They become comparable to the parrot Loulou, simply regurgitating the already said and already written, without visible intention other than keeping language going. They are already a couple from a Samuel Beckett play.

We have then at once in these years close to Flaubert's death both the unfinished and perhaps interminable project of *Bouvard and Pécuchet* and the *Dictionary* that was to be its culmination, and the achieved perfection of his tale of the simple heart. There is no point in trying to reconcile the two. If *Bouvard* seems a counsel of despair—or at best a kind of cosmic secular comedy—"A Simple Heart" offers something even more difficult to grasp. The story of Félicité offers no optimism about life. Even she can sense the despair of its losses. On her way to Honfleur to take the dead Loulou to the taxidermist, after she has been knocked into a ditch by the passing coachman, she reaches the hill above the town. Flaubert writes: "When she reached the heights of Écquemauville, she saw the lights of Honfleur shining in the night like a bunch of stars; the sea, farther on, spread out haphazardly. Then a weakness stopped her; and the misery of her childhood, the disappointment of her first love, the departure of her nephew, the death of Virginie, like the waves of the tide came back all at once, and rising in her throat suffocated her." It is only as she loses her senses and retreats more and more into deafness and insentience that life takes on a more benign aspect. The beauty of the tale is not the beauty of her life. It lies rather in the narrative's evocative power in simulating and understanding that life.

That is not unlike the very end of *Sentimental Education*, where Frédéric and Deslauriers find in the collective retrospective narration of their lives a pleasure that they did not experience in living it. But whereas Frédéric and Deslauriers stand as figures of admitted failure, one can't speak of Félicité's life in such an idiom: there have been no choices, only circumstances and occurrences. History is not something she can even imagine, much less attempt to inflect—its only outcome seems to be the delivery of Loulou as a sub-prefect moves up to the rank of prefect. The solution to the problem of life, as Flaubert would often repeat to those, including Louise Colet and George Sand, who wanted him to become more engaged, is that of withdrawal. But not into the realm of the dandy or the aesthete, two possible responses of the time, but rather into the ascesis of art.

The two retreats need distinguishing. Flaubert has too often been seen as fleeing reality. On the contrary, he sees himself engaging reality from the only place that matters: that of understanding. When he claims that *Sentimental Education* ought to have offered a political lesson to his contemporaries, he was not being frivolous or self-serving. He meant that understanding, intelligence, what he often called *science*, was the only way to respond to life. Like Hegel's owl of Minerva, that science, that knowledge of how to conduct oneself in life, only takes flight at nightfall. Flaubert's generation experienced a whole series of nightfalls in the political upheavals of the nineteenth century. But in his view, they did not learn the lessons that they might have. In that sense, the testament of "A Simple Heart," if we can take it as such, speaks to an absolute pathos of life in regard to its understanding. Life, too, is both subject to history and also nonhistorical in its repeated patterns of servitude and loss. That's what life has to offer. Only the storyteller can make you see and understand it.

In these last years of his life, Flaubert's correspondence continued unabated, with a greater frequency of letters to the rising star Zola, and the declared disciple, Maupassant. And all the other usual correspondents, including Léonie Brainne in more and more intimate tones. He and Maxime Du Camp made the decision to burn letters to one another after noting the fate of Prosper Mérimée (the author of *Carmen*), whose love letters were published posthumously in 1873. Flaubert and Du Camp had many youthful indiscretions to hide—the word "indiscretions" is clearly one of those bourgeois clichés used to cover up a scabrous reality. Best of all among the faithful correspondents was Turgenev, who translated *Saint Julian* into Russian, and who, in July 1877, sent him a magnificent Bokhara dressing gown: "This royal garment plunges me into dreams of absolutism—and sensuality! I'd like to be naked in it, and sheltering Circassian women with me!" But one senses the loss of Sand: there was no one else who quite understood his sensibility, no one else, perhaps, who understood that, despite the "between men" flourishes of the correspondence with Du Camp, Maupassant, and other guys, there was what you might see as a sweet and "feminine" side to him. Not even Léonie Brainne, who certainly loved him, and appears to have proposed marriage to him in 1878 (he had to explain his utter unsuitability as putative husband), was quite able to produce the same vibrant response. No one other than Sand seems to have been able to bring his "heart" out in the open.

– chapter seven –

The Historical Imagination

A LONG WITH THE INTERMINABLE COMPOSITION OF *BOUVARD and Pécuchet* and the punctual writing of *Three Tales*, Flaubert was dreaming of yet another novel, this one explicitly historical and political. "The *subject* of the novel *Sous Napoléon III* finally came to me!" he wrote to Edma Roger des Genettes in 1878. The first mention of this project came in a letter to the same correspondent in 1874. Only fragmentary sketches for the book were set down in his notebooks, giving tantalizing indications of what was to be a major social novel. It seems to have been intended as a retrospective look at life in the Second Empire—its title implies its root-edness in a historical moment, viewed from the perspective of its demise. He set it aside to work on *Bouvard and Pécuchet*, but he clearly intended to return to it. His notes suggest that the novel was to have dealt with the worlds of business, the church, and sex, and to have involved three couples, three studies of women and their men. What I find especially intriguing are these words about one of the three couples:

The hero, a *democrat*, man of letters, free thinker and poor, in love with a great *catholic lady*. Philosophy and modern religion in opposition, and seeping into one another.

At first he is virtuous in order to be worthy of her. She is for him the ideal. Then seeing that doesn't get him anywhere he lets himself go. And redeems himself at the end by an act of devotion. He saves her during the Commune of which he is a part and then turns against the Commune and has himself killed by the Versaillais.

Scholars of Flaubert's notes for the project have suggested that the novel was to reach its climax in the Great Exhibition of 1867. But here Flaubert appears to push to the very end of Empire, and beyond, in the Commune and its suppression by the Versaillais. It sets one dreaming to think that Flaubert might have chosen as hero a democrat who joined the Commune, even if to turn against it in the end. How to imagine the worldview that Flaubert would have bestowed on such a creation! Clearly something that would have been impossible for him before the Terrible Year forced a re-evaluation of his understanding of politics and society. Interesting, too, that against the democrat he would have set the "*grande dame catholique*," as if, in the manner of Victor Hugo, to bring together the political extremes of France in a romance that at first fails to find fulfillment and then at the moment of political paroxysm brings rescue and self-sacrifice. One scholar who has studied the notes for the novel reports that the word "catholic" appears far more frequently than in any other Flaubert novel. That may reflect his disdain for the postwar and post-Commune France of Mac-Mahon and the *Ordre Moral*, possibly including the planned basilica on Montmartre. Whether there is a moment of happiness for this couple before his death at the hands of the Versaillais is unclear, though the notes don't suggest it, and from our readings in Flaubert we would not expect to find lovers happily reunited: that is not generally part of his novelistic vocabulary.

Maxime Du Camp reported that Flaubert told him he regretted having completed and published *Sentimental Education* before the coming of the Terrible Year: he imagined that the defeat at Sedan could have furnished an impressive final scene in his narrative of dissolution, with the emperor slouched in a corner of his carriage while French troops captured by the Prussians marched past. That would have been an appropriate alternative ending to the historical drama that comes to its bitter climax, in the novel as published, with the coup d'état of 1851. In any event, *Sous Napoléon III* appears to be the unwritten sequel that would have extended the earlier novel through the Second Empire. The scenario, especially the man of the Left in love with a woman of the Right, leaves us with an unassuageable thirst for more. Flaubert's notes, referring to various corrupt public officials of the regime, make it clear that the novel would imply the kind of judgment on the Empire expressed repeatedly in his letters from the Terrible Year—the one, for instance, to George Sand on April 30, 1871: "It was all fake: fake realism, fake army, fake credit, even fake whores." That letter was written during the reign of the Commune in Paris on the brink of the class war and massacre. The possibility that his novel was to have reached its climax at this moment, at the bloody demise of the Commune and painful birth of the regime in which he spent his final years, registers a remarkable commitment not only to fiction concerned with historical circumstance and event but even fiction that is deeply entwined in the political. The scarce fragments of *Sous Napoléon III* give us a Flaubert who has at the last chosen not the distanced archaeological-historical novel (such is *Salammbô*), but the intersection of individual lives and loves with event, as in the third part of *Sentimental Education*, but now possibly with a more ideologically mature protagonist.

Reading proof for a new edition of *Sentimental Education* in 1879, Flaubert noted that its lack of success might have come from a lack of *"the falsity of perspective,"* by which he seems to mean a lack of traditional novelistic construction that would focus the reader's attention more narrowly and bring the story to overt climax and resolution. That doesn't exist in real life, he continued: "But Art isn't nature!" He has been too honest and pure in his depiction of life. What Flaubert came to realize by this point—how might it have inflected his writing of *Sous Napoléon III?*—was that his de-dramatization of the novel, while a result of his artistic probity, made his most ambitious novel difficult reading. Perhaps

Frédéric's narrative should have been more like that of a Balzac hero, such as Lucien de Rubempré.

I suggested that the story of Frédéric Moreau's flawed ambition and ineffective desire often reads as a negative print of Lucien de Rubempré's meteoric rise and fall. If Flaubert sits as critic of Balzac's appetencies and especially the hyperbolic terms of their fulfillment, he nonetheless remains the emancipated disciple of the first master of the realist novel devoted to contemporary history. *Sentimental Education*, and before it *Salammbô*, and the notes for *Sous Napoléon III*, suggest Flaubert's place, untraditional as it may be, in the nineteenth-century tradition of the historical novel.

Balzac's Lucien de Rubempré is himself the author of a historical novel that he brings with him to Paris in search of a publisher. *L'Archer de Charles IX* (The archer of Charles IX) it is titled, evoking a soldier loyal to the Valois king who reigned from 1560 to 1574 (he ascended the throne at age eleven) during the Wars of Religion, including their nadir in the St. Bartholomew's Massacre. The Valois monarchs and the powerful figure of Catherine de Medici (Charles's mother and the regent during his minority) behind the throne had long attracted historical novelists as marking a period of glamour, gallantry, intrigue, and heroism. (Madame de Lafayette's seventeenth-century masterpiece *La Princesse de Clèves* takes place in the Valois court.) Lucien's youthful effort is apparently rather unformed, poorly designed and rendered, until Daniel d'Arthez gets his hands on the novel and transforms it into something remarkable that will later on, with a "magnificent" preface written by d'Arthez, become a posthumous success. D'Arthez is the universally acknowledged leader of the "Cénacle of the rue des Quatre-Vents," a group of young thinkers and artists who have devoted themselves to study and the slow realization of tremendous projects, including Michel Chrestien's European government and d'Arthez's ideal of the historical novel.

In the lessons he gives Lucien on how to write a novel, d'Arthez holds up for emulation the master recognized by Balzac himself, Walter Scott, who stands at the inception of the historical novel as we know it. D'Arthez's admiration for Scott is more or less boundless, but he wants Lucien to do something new. Where Scott introduces his characters through long dialogues, Lucien needs to use description. He needs to get to his action quicker, and vary his approaches. Scott was constrained by English Protestant prudery to present boringly virtuous women. France has the advantage of brilliant Catholic women guilty of lapses from virtue, to set in contrast to the somber Calvinism at contest during the Wars of Religion, the most passionate period of national history. *L'Archer de Charles IX* could be but the first in a long series of novels that would depict France from Charlemagne onward. "You'll thus do a picturesque history of France, in which you'll paint costumes, furniture, houses, interiors, private life, all the while creating the spirit of the time, instead of painfully recounting the well-known facts." And he recommends that Lucien start by rehabilitating Catherine de Medici from the weight of Protestant prejudice that hangs over her reputation.

One can perhaps feel some relief that Lucien doesn't manage to execute d'Arthez's master plan. But that plan very much catches the preoccupation of many a novelist of the French 1820s and 1830s, including Balzac himself, and it stretches past novelists to historians. We are at the moment that presides at the birth of narrative national history, and the novel takes its place in that enterprise: some would claim that it is Scott and his novels that spark the revival of history writing. One could say that the nineteenth century discovered the need for narrative explanation with a new urgency, that the new "sciences of man" would be dominated by a historical understanding of how and what we are through an inquiry into how we got that way. Darwin, Marx, Freud: these dominant intellectual figures all claim that the understanding of individuals, societies, and the natural environment implicate narrative histories. Archaeology, geology, paleontology, linguistics, paleography: all these disciplines that constituted themselves essentially during the nineteenth century similarly call upon an evolutionary, time-defined context of explanation. The enormously influential writings of Henri de Saint-Simon on work, industrialism, and the structure of society, and the many varieties of socialism that it inspired, offer an evolutionary understanding of production and social organization.

History comes to seem the dominant discourse of the time, perhaps most clearly so in France because the Revolution—and then its many reprises throughout the century—made history a lived experience, and its understanding a vital task. Jules Michelet (who was a friend of Flaubert), in his histories of the French Revolution and of the nation, became a national hero. The prohibition of his lectures at the Collège de France in January 1848 was a spark of the revolution. Augustin Thierry's histories of early France, inspired by Scott, provided a template for national history in the ancient struggle of Gauls and Franks. A newly invigorated French nationalism claimed the centrality of the country's intellectual and cultural history to all of Europe: François Guizot—minister of education and then prime minister in the 1840s—declared at the outset of his *Histoire de la civilisation en Europe* (*The History of Civilization in Europe*): "There is almost no great idea, no great principle of civilization which, in order to expand everywhere, hasn't first taken place in France."

Writing history was deeply connected to political life. Guizot, the most powerful political figure in France up until the Revolution of 1848, alternated between governing and writing history, as well as publishing editions of historical documents; Alphonse de Lamartine laid out his political agenda in large part in his history of the Girondin party (the moderate revolutionaries who lost out in struggle with the Jacobins) before becoming leader of the short-lived Second Republic in 1848. The man who emerged as ruler of France following the defeat of 1870, Adolphe Thiers, wrote his own history of the French Revolution, in ten volumes published from 1823 to 1827, and a number of other historical works. The list of publicly influential historians could be extended; notably, it would include, in Flaubert's time, Alexis de Tocqueville, Ernest Renan, and then Hippolyte Taine, who laid out the three principles of historical explanation common to much of his century: "race, milieu, moment."

Revolutionary historiography, in particular, holds a key place in French understanding of French history and identity. Rare were the thinkers of the time who did not feel that the French Revolution began a new epoch in human history, and historians have continued to ratify that judgment. What the Revolution meant was of course in dispute from the outset, and has not ceased to be since, for all the talk of a peace settlement among clashing views at the time of the Bicentennial in 1989. For Frenchmen growing up in the nineteenth century (recall that Flaubert was born in 1821), the meaning of the great rupture that put an end to centuries of an Old Regime that claimed to be founded in God as well as nature was crucial. Tocqueville's *L'Ancien Régime et la Révolution* (*The Old Regime and the Revolution*, 1856) in its need to understand the social and administrative structures that led to revolution may be the most intellectually probing account of what it meant to live in the postrevolutionary order, but that is also a theme dear to poets and novelists, not only Balzac but also Stendhal, Hugo, Alfred de Musset, Alfred de Vigny, Alexandre Dumas (père), and a host of others who return to it again and again.

Michelet, born the same year as Balzac, set aside the chronological progression of his monumental *Histoire de France* during the political ferment leading up to 1848 in order to write that part (in seven volumes) devoted to the Revolution, published from 1847 to 1853, an impassioned classic that continued for generations to define a national epic. Michelet's Old Regime, developed in volumes written subsequently, is shown in retrospect to make revolution necessary. In general, the narrative of the great French nineteenth-century histories is one of emancipation, of progress from a society dominated by arbitrary force: first that of feudal lord and then of monarch, seconded by an ignorance imposed by the Church. One might judge with different degrees of severity the excesses of the Revolution in the time of the Terror, but on the whole the work of the Revolution was necessary, even inevitable, and the attempts to reverse it in the Restoration and then the Second Empire were temporary setbacks in a history of progress. Although the Terrible Year would cause thinking people such as Flaubert to question the overarching narrative of progress, it survived as a dominant frame of thought until the guns of August 1914, and perhaps even beyond, though greatly tempered.

The historical novel mattered because it appeared to be a genre in which one could attempt to capture the totality of a historical moment, which is very much part of the advice d'Arthez gives to Lucien. Scott's understanding of the historical novel is well captured by Georg Lukács in his study of the genre, *The Historical Novel*. Contrasting the picturesque use of history in some Romantics, Lukács comments: "But for Scott the historical characterization of time and place, the historical 'here and now' is something much deeper. For him it means that certain crises in the personal destinies of a number of human beings coincide and interweave within the determining context of an historical crisis." That is, history is a lived context of personal existence, and its rendering crucial to understanding both national and individual destinies. The goal was perhaps best expounded by Scott's Italian disciple Alessandro Manzoni, in his essay *On the Historical Novel* (*Del Romanzo Storico*, 1830), which presented the theory of his quite Scott-like (but possibly better than Scott) novel *The Betrothed* (*I Promessi Sposi*, 1827). Manzoni worried about the promiscuous mixing of fact and fiction and the deceptive effect on a reader of fiction presented in factual historical context. The aim of his kind of historical novel, as I have noted, is "to represent, by means of an invented action, the true state of humanity in a past and historical epoch." On this definition, fiction is used to reveal historical truth: "invention," as it was classically called, is a tool for opening up historical reality. That is very much what d'Arthez has in mind in his didactic moments with Lucien. The historical novel is not supposed to be merely costume drama or historical flight of fancy. It is meant to get at a kind of truth of everyday life—customs and ways of being—that political histories tend to scant. Manzoni, for instance, cites within his novel a number of the seventeenth-century *gride*, the legal declarations that give insight into contemporary abuses of power and attempts of the humble to deal with them. In some manner, one could say that kind of twentieth-century historiography associated with the scholarly review *Annales* learned the lesson of the historical novel: that the most interesting history tries to uncover people and ways of life that do not "make" history, that do not reach overt political enactment.

I have suggested that the "realist" novel of the nineteenth century comes about when Balzac shortens the distance between the represented historical moment and the moment of writing—reduces it to some ten or twenty years, looking back from the 1830s and 1840s to the 1820s, so that he is writing about near-contemporary society, attempting to see it in the same totality as the earlier periods represented in the historical novel.

The realist novel, that is, seeks to see modern life itself as a historicized concept, as a whole that will be illuminated by the novelist's fictive plot and characters. This is a persuasive view throughout the heyday of the novel, and it surely has something to do with our love of and need for the novel as a cognitive instrument.

The great French novels of the nineteenth century are all historical novels in some manner, in that they are largely concerned with the struggle to say to whom France belongs in the wake of Revolution, Napoleonic epic, Restoration, and then repeated insurrections. Stendhal's *The Red and the Black* (*Le Rouge et le noir*, 1830), for instance, uses the usurping figure of Julien Sorel (at times evocative of Danton) to pose the question of who shall inherit France. Stendhal then turned to an explicitly historical novel in *The Charterhouse of Parma* (*La Chartreuse de Parme*, 1837), albeit one with a large measure of fantasy and myth, describing a despotic principality where alienated youthful "ardent souls" spend their days reading histories of the French Revolution. He found the historical documents issued by various contemporary publishers more interesting reading than most fiction, and in his *Italian Chronicles* (*Chroniques italiennes*, 1836–1839) he took to transcribing manuscripts from the past, transforming them into passionate short stories. Eugène Sue's last serial novel, *The Mysteries of the People* (*Les Mystères du peuple*, 1849–1856), resurrects Augustin Thierry's Merovingian historical legends to structure his plot as a conflict between conquering Franks and conquered but restless Gauls, who have become a proletariat struggling to overthrow its vicious masters. The elder Alexandre Dumas's yet more fanciful historical romances, especially his masterpiece *The Count of Monte Cristo* (*Le Comte de Monte-Cristo*, 1844–1845), nonetheless evoke a struggle for liberation against evil occult powers of repression. More explicitly political and more historical, Balzac claims to represent a total picture of society—rivaling, he said, with the Civil Registry—written from the point of view of someone who largely deplored the results of the Revolution. The success of Balzac's undertaking was such that the Marxists, starting with Marx and Engels themselves, were the first to salute his synthetic portrait of the contradictions of nascent capitalist society, with its exploitation of the working poor, its fraudulent bankers and rapacious entrepreneurs, and its transformations of intellectual production into a commodity that, to Lukács, represented "the capitalization of spirit."

Another way to put this would be to say that in nineteenth-century France, history was simply an inescapable context of life in a way that it wasn't before the Revolution. To be a peasant or a provincial bourgeois under the Old Regime was to live in an essentially history-less world, following long-standing patterns of existence, or the eternal cycles of nature. An emblem might be found in the scarcity of timepieces: for peasants and inhabitants of small towns, the bells of the local church kept the time. All that changed with the Revolution. Even if peasant life remained subject to natural rhythms, the Napoleonic Wars, with their constant demand for men and for horses to be sent into battle, made an awareness of history inevitable. Conscription reached everywhere. If nothing else, the French of the nineteenth century knew Napoleon, his battles, his conquests.

French Romantic drama, which began in the 1820s and triumphantly captured the Comédie-Française with Hugo's *Hernani* in 1830, also immersed itself in history, following Stendhal's call for plays about national history in his polemical pamphlet *Racine et Shakespeare*, composed in the wake of the French rediscovery of Shakespeare, who would become an enabling figure in the break with classical French traditions. The most prolific of all playwrights, the elder Dumas, even created his own theater, the Théâtre de la Renaissance, to produce his sprawling and blood-curdling historical dramas, which were often akin to the more plebeian genre of melodrama, which also often took up a habitus in sixteenth- and seventeenth-century court intrigues. Melodrama and Romantic drama lent themselves well to adaptation by opera librettists—just add music—and a number of operas, by Donizetti, Rossini, Meyerbeer, Verdi, and others, take us back to dramatic historical moments. Past history could be made to speak to the present. And when present political affairs were protected by censorship, you could try to use past history to take a stand. This was most obviously the case for Verdi, who repeatedly encountered the heavy hand of the censor, and was forced to find often implausible dodges (the action of *Un Ballo in Maschera* resituated from

Stockholm to Boston, for instance) in order to veil his intentions. Yet Verdi usually managed to get the message of Italian liberation and unification through. From *Nabucco* to *I Vespri Siciliani* to *Aida*, the voice of the oppressed resonates insistently and unforgettably.

Painting, too, joins the historiographical movement, striving for liberation from the dominance of the biblical and classical historical subjects imposed by the academies in favor of subjects drawn from national history, and from Scott. Eugène Delacroix entered enthusiastically into painting historical moments, chosen for their illustrative value in history, some for the Museum of French History that King Louis Philippe installed at Versailles starting in 1833. Paul Delaroche became the master of the melodramatic illustration of history in such tableaux as *The Children of Edward in the Tower of London* and *The Execution of Lady Jane Grey*. History in Romantic drama, melodrama, opera, and painting makes us realize how present, how immediate the historical imagination was for generations of nineteenth-century Europeans who understood their own lives as part of history, as determined by history in a way that earlier generations' existence had not been. Erich Auerbach in his study of realism makes the point that in Stendhal for the first time (though to argue precedence here is not the point) representation is bound up with "time perspective." *The Red and the Black* is inherently historical: every move, every thought, attributed to Julien Sorel, to his admirers and detractors, takes on meaning as part of a system of Restoration conceived to counter and suppress the recent revolutionary and Napoleonic past. It's not so much a deterministic picture of man within historical time—Julien stands in revolt against all determinisms—but rather that every word and gesture is by its nature part of a history to which it contributes and which gives it meaning. As Stendhal's narrator explicitly tells us, politics has become the context of everyday life in a country excruciatingly aware of an underlying class warfare. In the famous debate between "author" and "publisher" on the place of politics in the novel—"like a pistol-shot at a concert," says the author—the publisher has the final word: "If your characters don't talk politics, they are not Frenchmen of 1830, and your novel is not a mirror, as you claim it to be." An understanding of politics is necessary to grasp one's current place in history, and then to make an attempt to inflect life's future unfolding. In between *The Red and the Black* and *The Charterhouse of Parma*, Stendhal worked on another novel, *Lucien Leuwen*, never completed, which was almost wholly devoted to the political life of the 1830s.

Stendhal's novels and so many others give the impression of a country up for grabs: a country that has seen such extremes in its history, from 1789 on, with still more on the way, that all sorts of possible upheavals may lie ahead. That is not to say that change comes easily, and the end of *The Red and the Black* records the victory of an older generation over the young: Julien goes to the guillotine, and his loathsome father inherits the fortune he has accumulated. The victory of fathers over sons appears also in Hugo's *Hernani*, which was staged a few months earlier than Stendhal's novel. You might be able to draw up a list of defeated aspiring young men (Don Carlo in Verdi's opera on a text by Schiller, for instance) that would seem to represent the anxiety of history, the fear of its moving backward, as it appeared to do for the French with Restoration in 1815, then with the increasing conservatism of the July Monarchy, which came to power in 1830 and went down to defeat in the Revolution of 1848, and then, perhaps most depressing of all, the collapse of the Second Republic born of that revolution in Louis-Napoléon's coup d'état, and the revival of empire. To follow the career of a long-lived and politically engaged writer such as Victor Hugo is to marvel at repeated reversals of fortune—political triumph, threat of arrest, exile, return, more exile, eventually a funeral that was a national event. To live in the history of postrevolutionary France is to be aware of the roulette wheel of history, surely one of the allusions of Stendhal's title.

If you are a writer or an "intellectual," a word the French would coin toward the end of the century, then you want to understand your life in a history full of upheavals, reversals, false hopes, disillusions, and a sense of constant struggle. The contentious historiography of the French Revolution makes the point: thinking people feel the need to try to understand cataclysmic events, and they do so in writing about them: histories, memoirs, novels. The outpouring is vast. By the 1860s, books on the French Revolution had become commonplace. Everyone seemed to claim a right to analyze and recount the past, remote or recent, in order to define his or her place in relation to it. If the Goncourt brothers in their famous preface to *Germinie Lacerteux* in 1865 claimed a "right to the novel" for all social strata of society, there was also an implicit claim abroad of a right to historiography. We all have the right, maybe even the duty, to write history from our own perspective. And of course making the claim to that right extends beyond France, to James Fenimore Cooper in America and Leo Tolstoy in Russia, to name the most obvious instances. The defeat of France by Prussia would itself set off an agonized debate about causes, and calls for national regeneration; many questioned French education as compared to the more research-oriented German model, which led to the creation of more teaching positions in many subjects, very much including history. By 1885, a Chair in the History of the French Revolution had been established at the Sorbonne.

The claim of a right to and a need for historiography brought as well a new attention to the sources of history and the methods for understanding and evaluating them. The Convention Nationale, during the great Revolution, instituted sweeping changes in French education at all levels and in all branches and created national archives open, for the first time, to the public. The documents of national history took on prime importance: Thierry and Guizot, for instance, spent much of their careers gathering, annotating, and publishing such documents, and Michelet's great *History* derived from his post as head of the historical section of the National Archives: it is history conscientiously and overtly written from a close study of original sources. Emblematic of this new documentary basis of historiography is the foundation of the École des Chartes in 1821, a *grande école* created for the learned study of documentation through training in such disciplines as paleography, numismatics, philology, different legal systems, and so on. It became an example to all of Europe. History henceforth could not be the mythological construction of sacred history, bound to a teleology of redemption, or the philosophical overview of a Voltaire or Montesquieu, or the imaginative radical genealogy of Rousseau. It needed to be patiently constructed from the retrieval, decipherment, and interpretation of original documents. One finds novelists, Manzoni and others, offering commentary on the sources of their fictions and the historical context of their characters' words.

Before Flaubert took up the task of writing the history of his generation in *Sentimental Education*, he published a massive historical novel of his own, one written from the archives, that has nothing to do with the historiography of France but rather with ancient Carthage. *Salammbô*, published in 1862, curiously looks forward to the ruins of Paris in 1871. It concerns the wars between Carthage and its mercenary armies that lasted from 241 to 238 BCE. After those struggles, Carthage itself, founded in the ninth century BCE, only lasted until 146 BCE, when, following Rome's victory over this great rival in the Third Punic War, it was razed to the ground. Only the most fragmentary ruins remained—and these Flaubert visited in the spring of 1858. One of the attractions of the subject for Flaubert was precisely how little was known about ancient Carthage: the novel would have to be an archaeological reconstruction. Upon its publication, the poet Leconte de Lisle understood the attraction: the novel, he said, is "penetrated especially with this singular genius, characteristic of our century, that reconstructs piece by piece long-gone eras, by what is most powerful and ideally true in them." To make Carthage arise from her ruins in an operatic spectacle: such was Flaubert's concern. He began by reading ninety-eight books, he tells us, and that was just the beginning of his labor.

Salammbô belongs to the project of the nineteenth-century historical novel in its meticulous reconstruction of daily life at a given historical moment. But unlike Scott's or Manzoni's resurrection of early times of European history with recognizable genetic ties to the present—of interest because they blend familiarity with strangeness—Flaubert's ancient North Africa was strange beyond recognition. Its ties to common humanity seemed missing. Flaubert's reconstructions are often brilliant, and his fidelity to the historical record, such as it was, impressive. It's almost like the work of a science fiction writer determined to create a fully coherent alternative world. Yet the very detail of his picture, detail that in *Madame Bovary* and *Sentimental Education* can be revelatory of the essential, often seems to stand in the way of any overall understanding. The novel is evocative, exotic, barbaric, spectacular, but often laborious reading because its created world remains so alien. Like Hugo's *Ninety-Three*, it achieves a certain epic grandeur, though with very different materials and means. Charles Baudelaire noted that only Flaubert could have written such a novel. "Much too much bric-à-brac, but many grandeurs, epic, historical, political, even animal."

The temptation to quote from the novel is great, since so many individual passages are astonishing in their evocative detail. Just one example, from the visit to the generally well-ordered camp of the Mercenaries, who come from a variety of countries:

> In the midst of the servants and strolling vendors circulated women of all nations, brown like ripe dates, greenish like olives, yellow like oranges, sold by sailors, picked up in dives, stolen from caravans, taken in the sack of cities, who when young were worn out from lovemaking, beaten when old, and who lay dying in alleys off the pathways, along with baggage and abandoned beasts of burden. The wives of the Nomads swayed over their high heels in dresses of camel skin, square and wild in color; Cyrenaic musicians, swathed in violet veils and with painted eyebrows, sang while squatting on woven mats: old negresses with hanging teats gathered, for their fires, animal dung which they dried in the sun: the Syracusians had gold plaques in their headdresses, the wives of the Lusitanians collars of seashells, the Gauls wolf skins on their white breasts; and robust children, covered with vermin, naked, uncircumcised, gave the passersby blows with the head to their bellies or came at them from behind, like young tigers, to bite their hands.

It's as good a descriptive passage as many in *Madame Bovary*, and far more exotic, evocative of a world neither the reader nor Flaubert has seen, a world created in the imagination. Yet perhaps it is lacking in the essential: a sense of why this story matters to the reader. Its persons are conceived with a fidelity to the archaeological record that makes them too foreign for understanding. Salammbô herself, the daughter of Hamilcar Barca, is fundamentally exotic, an object of our contemplation rather than someone through whom we can experience a historical period. Flaubert does not, in the manner of Scott (the manner recommended by d'Arthez to Lucien), find a middling type of character to serve as our guide into this ancient world. *Salammbô* at times seems an object lesson in the dangers of writing historical fiction. The greater the realism of detail, the more the meaning of the large historical evocation seems to be questionable. Our understanding is at issue.

If *Salammbô* instances Flaubert's fascination with "the historical," it doesn't make the claim to personal historiography that we find at the origin of *Sentimental Education*, begun just after the publication of the former novel explicitly to capture the moral and sentimental history of his own generation. Here he claims with a new and personal urgency the right to historiography: a right not to manage history (the illusion of political actors) but to try to understand it. The bafflement and hostility that greeted the novel upon publication, and that often still confront it today, did not result despite its historiographical claim but because of it. If it were only Frédéric's story of aspiration and failure that was at stake, both appreciation and dismissal of the novel would be easier. Everything would rest on the story of one disillusioned young romantic. But it is impossible not to see that more is at stake once the Revolution of 1848 takes center stage in Part 3 of the novel. One has to recognize the historicity of the novel at this point: one can perfectly apply to it the words Lukács uses to characterize Scott: "Certain crises in the personal destinies of a number of human beings coincide and interweave within the determining context of an historical crisis."

And yet (surely this is one of the prime sources of bafflement for readers of the novel) this historical crisis is not presented in the manner of any previous historical novel. There is no Olympian narrative viewpoint, there is no authoritative voice to help us understand history in the making, there is no normative perspective. Stendhal famously inserted the hero of *The Charterhouse of Parma*, Fabrice del Dongo, into the Battle of Waterloo as a confused participant-observer who understands nothing in the unfolding carnage and keeps asking himself for weeks afterward if it was a real battle, and if it bore the name Waterloo. But the narration of that novel begins with a kind of world-historical sweep in describing the triumphant entry of the French armies under the young Bonaparte into Lombardy and Milanese territory at the start of the novel. However elusive, witty, and unpredictable the Stendhalian narrator may be, he nonetheless provides us with a normative view of historical happening. That is far more emphatically the case with the narrators of Balzac's or Hugo's or Sand's novels, and true also of Tolstoy's *War and Peace*, published in its original Russian in the same year as *Sentimental Education*.

Flaubert gives us little to hold on to in understanding the very genre of his novel. When it opens, in 1840, it appears to be (as the subtitle indicates) "the story of a young man." Only gradually during Part 1 do political and historical allusions accumulate. Issues of class consciousness come to the fore as the cast of characters swells, reaching from Dambreuse (formerly d'Ambreuse: he has found it expedient to disguise his aristocratic origins) at the apex of society to the proletarian Dussardier. In the political agitations and subterranean plotting especially associated with Sénécal and Deslauriers, we begin to see, but only very tentatively and obliquely, the formation of a political opposition to the regime. Warnings that "the moment is coming" and then "the pear is ripe" plant clues of what is to come, but they are slender, submerged in the ongoing story of Frédéric's loves and ambitions. When the revolution breaks out, Frédéric does his best to hide from it, because he finally has a rendezvous with Madame Arnoux. Her failure to come leads to her substitution by a Rosanette made fearful by the insurgency. By the time, the next day, that Frédéric goes out to join the insurgents, History has already eluded him. And he will spend the rest of the revolutionary moment playing a kind of catch-up—including his attempted candidacy for the Assembly—that never quite works. When the crucial showdown of the June Days arrives, he is off to Fontainebleau with Rosanette, in a kind of shabby idyll.

In other words, despite preparatory warnings, the revolution simply occurs in the novel. It is an event that begins, in the novel's representation of it, around the corner, as a noise, like the tearing of a sheet of silk, that needs interpretation. That is the fusillade of the Boulevard des Capucines, a "massacre" of citizens by the police that triggers the formidable insurgency that Frédéric discovers in the morning. There is no overview here, no announcement that we are about to witness a historical event. "History" just happens, as one more event of daily life. It's down the street, around the corner. Eventually you can catch up with its happenings, even join them. But the owl of historical understanding only flies long after the event, and even then, it's not clear what there is to understand.

As Flaubert appeared to recognize by 1878, Sand had given an accurate diagnosis of why his novel was so little understood and appreciated. He has pushed the limited perspectival view of history created by Stendhal for Fabrice on the battlefield of Waterloo to the point where overview and understanding appear almost to disappear completely. He has given his reader a radical form of historical consciousness that never can reach total understanding. If in this generational history the Revolution of 1848 clearly stands as his generation's major rendezvous with history, Frédéric misses that rendezvous in a profound way. And Flaubert has given himself no perspective to compensate for his character's failure in a more comprehensive and normative overview. The novel is a bit like a piece of music with no indication of its key. Where major historical event is concerned, that may be a problem.

Flaubert strives to record the presence of history over Frédéric's shoulder, so to speak. When Frédéric returns from Fontainebleau to Paris toward the end of the June Days, we encounter this brief and haunting evocation of military action:

> The rue Saint-Victor was completely dark, without a streetlamp or a lighted window. Every ten minutes you heard:
> "Sentinels! On the alert."
> And the cry, thrown into the midst of silence, echoed on like the sound of a stone falling into an abyss.
> Sometimes the heavy tread of feet approached. It was a patrol of a hundred men, at least; whispers, the click of metal on metal came from this confused mass; and moving on, swinging rhythmically, it was lost in the shadows.

> There was at the center of crossroads a dragoon on horseback, immobile.

Such a passage is as if to say that historical Event is there, even if the protagonist can only dimly apprehend its significance. "The heart shrank from these noises, so different from those of every day," we read just a few lines later. That heart is presumably everybody's and Frédéric's too. The heart's reaction to history in its bloody making is distress without understanding—an accurate account of what the witness to cataclysmic moments of history feels, no doubt. But not the basis for an analytic understanding. History happens. There are of course agents making it happen—we see some of them in action—but for most of us it appears as that natural cataclysm Flaubert referred to in his conclusion to the story of the June Days, and in reaction to the Franco-Prussian War.

There is some family resemblance in novels on contemporary politics and history written by three other major writers whom we don't usually think of as historical novelists: Flaubert's contemporary and devoted friend Ivan Turgenev, and his disciples, in a more or less attenuated sense, Henry James and Joseph Conrad. Turgenev's *Virgin Soil*, published in French translation in 1877, immediately following its Russian edition, was to Flaubert "a marvel." It is more overtly—and with a very different form of narrative address—a generational study of Russia, focused on the attempts of déclassé upper-class radicals to "go to the people" and raise their revolutionary consciousness. It is very unlike anything Flaubert wrote. His praise of it is doubtless sincere—he admired Turgenev above all other contemporaries—but the novel probably offered him no lessons in a novel of politics, since its narrative presentation is so different. Yet it may have confirmed in him the sense that the contemporary novel could not eschew politics, and that even the work-in-progress, *Bouvard and Pécuchet*, had to make room for the political.

Henry James's *The Princess Casamassima*, published only in 1886, after Flaubert's death, marks a curious attempt by the novelist we think of as mainly preoccupied with the fine consciousness of the leisure class to deal with the shadowy world of London anarchists and one of their murderous plots. It even features an exiled Communard living among the plotters. It's very consciously James's attempt to see beneath the "vast, smug surface" of society, into what he sees as a subterranean world that conceivably puts the very existence of society into question. The book strikes me as a noble failure, for reasons that have some affinity to those that made *Sentimental Education* unappealing to Flaubert's contemporaries: James never finds a viable perspective to give his anarchists a living presence. Hyacinth Robinson's divided consciousness is as poor a register as Frédéric's for giving a sense of historical totality.

Then there is Conrad's *The Secret Agent*, published in 1907, again about anarchists, now plotting to blow up Greenwich Observatory. This very strange and dark novel displays such a radical lack of sympathy with virtually all its characters, with the exception of the mentally deficient and exploited Stevie, that it is sometimes hard to understand its motive at all. But it demonstrates once again the felt need, on the part of novelists of the late nineteenth to early twentieth centuries, even those of well-established reputation, to immerse the novel in politics. Or perhaps more accurately: to novelize the political, to write fictions in which contemporary political realities are inescapable contexts of life. The fate of modern society and humanity has by this point in history become so clearly dependent on the political that the ambitious novelist needs to deal with it. Human destinies cannot avoid the political. That surely is a lesson that the novel learns over the course of the nineteenth century and into the twentieth. However much you may think yourself an analyst of the soul, like that excellent soul Frédéric claims to possess at the start of *Sentimental Education*, that will not protect you from the incidence of political events. They will take their toll whatever your declared relation to them.

Flaubert in this and much of his subsequent work (including the sketch of *Sous Napoléon III*) claims the novelist's right to historiography. If the nineteenth century elevates history as the necessary discipline, that which presides over most explanation in the sciences of man, it also endorses on a massive scale the use of historical fiction to give a picture of the human history underlying political event, the kind of history not usually recorded in official chronicles of deeds. The result is what one might call the novelization of history, a movement that is still with us today. By that I don't mean the fictionalization of history, but rather the effort to see history through the lens and with the techniques of the novelist of social behavior. The claim is, as in d'Arthez's lesson to Lucien, that the novel can improve upon the work of the historian, come upon it with a richer understanding of the fabric of social existence, private life, and emotional meaning, dramatize what remains dry fact in many histories.

Here we come up against the unexpected fact that Flaubert's representation of 1848 in *Sentimental Education* isn't his last word on the event. He returned to it in the unfinished, posthumously published *Bouvard and Pécuchet*, where it resounds as the only real happening in the novel. The misadventures of the two copyists in farming and horticulture and garden design and archaeology and museology, etc., have given way to reading history and historical novels—with great admiration for Scott and the elder Dumas—when the sixth chapter of their narrative begins:

> The morning of February 25, 1848, the residents of Chavignolles learned, from a man coming from Falaise, that Paris was covered with barricades,—and the next day the proclamation of the Republic was posted at the town hall.
>
> This great event stupefied the bourgeois.

It's as if an unalterable cyclical form of life, one resistant to all Bouvard and Pécuchet's efforts at improvement, suddenly awoke to the Event. Everything is set on its head in this small Norman town. The local priest submits to the tide of history and presides at the planting of a Tree of Liberty. People start reading the newspapers for the first time. The two copyists join the National Guard. They think (like Frédéric) of presenting themselves as candidates for election to the Assembly. Then the unemployed workers begin demanding work, and bread, and the bourgeois begin to panic. Then comes word of the June Days in Paris, and reaction sets in. Bouvard and Pécuchet remain faithful to the fast disappearing republican dream. They lock horns with the *notaire* Marescot in a dispute about the proletarian Gorgu, whom Marescot considers a dangerous demagogue:

"But really," said Bouvard, "for just a few words! . . ."

"Excuse me, dear sir, but when words lead to crimes!"

"Still," replied Pécuchet, "where do you draw the line between innocent and culpable statements? What's forbidden at the present moment will later be applauded." And he took issue with the ferocious manner in which the insurgents were being treated.

Marescot naturally alleged the defense of society, public safety, the supremacy of the law.

"Excuse me," said Pécuchet, "the rights of the individual are as valid as the rights of all. And if someone turns the axiom back against you, all you have to offer in response is force."

Marescot, instead of replying, raised his eyebrows in disdain.

Bouvard and Pécuchet conclude that now the conservatives have come to talk like Robespierre.

The power of the reactionaries distresses them, the rising power of the clergy as well. They witness a sad confrontation between the local schoolmaster, Petit, a socialist who worships the Jacobins of the French Revolution, and the priest, the abbé Jeufroy, who comes to inform Petit that he must make room for sacred history and the catechism within the school day, because the very recent law of March 15, 1850 (the so-called *loi Falloux*), has given the clergy jurisdiction over primary education: a major victory for the Right in an ongoing struggle that would end only in 1881–1882, when French education was made free, universal, and secular. Petit had better obey, and had better start attending Mass, if he wants to keep his post.

This contest, played out everywhere in France, between free-thinking schoolmaster and politically dominant priest, with the clear victory of the latter, stands as Flaubert's symbolic understanding of the regress of history following the promise of 1848. Back to "sacred history." Soon Bouvard and Pécuchet realize that the republic itself is about to disappear.

Three million voters were excluded from universal suffrage. The bond required of newspapers was raised, censorship reestablished. People

railed against serial novels. Classical philosophy was considered dangerous. Bourgeois preached the dogma of their material interests and the
people seemed content.

Those in the countryside returned to their former masters.

The development of the reaction following the establishment of the republic and then the June Days comes to us in far greater detail in this novel
than in *Sentimental Education*, which insisted more on the utopian dreams
following the February revolution, often with satiric emphasis. Here, we
are more nearly in a tragedy of lost aspirations and possibilities. When the
republic is in fact extinguished in the coup d'état of December 2, 1851, the
reaction of Flaubert's protagonists discountenances the bourgeoise Madame Bordin who comes to them with this latest news:

> Madame Bordin entered.
>
> It was December 3, 1851. She was bringing the newspaper.
>
> They read quickly, side by side, the call to the people, the dissolution
> of the Assembly, the arrest of the deputies.
>
> Pécuchet went pale. Bouvard was staring at the widow: "What! You
> have nothing to say?"
>
> "What do you want me to do about it?" They neglected to offer her a
> seat. "I came here thinking the news would give you pleasure! Oh, you're
> not very nice today."
>
> And she left, shocked at their rudeness.

Her shock registers Bouvard and Pécuchet's gradual but perceptible movement from unthinking supporters of the bourgeoisie to something you
might call social democrats.

In their reaction to the coup d'état, Flaubert's two nerdy characters
have somehow ceased to be merely the butt of the joke. Their ineptitude
remains in place throughout and will of course lead them back in the
end to a decision to resume the practice of copying. But they have taken
on a certain autonomy and dignity over the course of the novel, and in
reaction to the events of 1848 and its sequels they become comparable

to characters in a traditional historical novel, politically aware and committed commentators on the action carried out on the national stage. It is hard to see them at this point simply as spokesmen for a universal stupidity, because their reactions to 1848 differ in intelligence and human sympathy from those of Marescot, Madame Bordin, and the other bourgeois of Chavignolles. Their defense of the republic, of freedom of speech, of human dignity may not in themselves rise above the cliché, but they clearly have a rightness and generosity to them when set against the petty, vindictive, and repressive reactions of their fellows. So that it appears that with the irruption of 1848 into the novel, Flaubert uses his two nerds in a new way, as informed and likeable commentators on events. Eventually they acquire the Flaubertian trait of revulsion from stupidity: "Then, a piteous faculty developed in their minds, that of perceiving stupidity and no longer being able to tolerate it."

What to make of this? If it may appear a violation of the premises on which he created Bouvard and Pécuchet, that violation has been in the making for some pages in the novel: they have taken on greater humanity, as if convincing their creator of a certain dignity of the ordinary (perhaps in resonance with Félicité of "A Simple Heart"). Perhaps more interesting in our context is the evolution they record in Flaubert's own political thought. It is of course true that in *Sentimental Education*, as here, the reactionaries are the object of Flaubert's most vehement critique. Dambreuse and his milieu, dining off their bream with pineapple after the June Days, are contemptible, and there is a parallel luncheon offered at the same moment of reaction by the Comte de Faverges in *Bouvard and Pécuchet*. But there is a new accent, in the later novel, in the novelist's apparent sympathy with the revolutionaries of 1848 and his revulsion at the reaction that brings the power of the priesthood over the schoolmaster wishing to teach secular history. The satirical treatment of their ideas and excesses is largely absent. Instead, there seems to be an approval of the copyists' defense of the republic and of freedom.

This replay of the Revolution of 1848 and its liquidation by Bonaparte offers confirming evidence of Flaubert's political evolution, his quiet conversion to republicanism in the wake of the Terrible Year. We may also find here the influence of George Sand and her continuing adherence to the principles of 1848. Flaubert now treats these with a new respect. We are of course dealing with a novel, with authorial attitudes that are refracted through his characters and his created action. But where the historical event is concerned, authorial attitude seems to come through. Flaubert did not need to replay 1848 in *Bouvard and Pécuchet*, which until Chapter 6 seemed to be "about" entirely different things. I think he wanted to test his characters (and maybe himself) once against the great historical event of his lifetime, no doubt because of its repetition in 1871. He wanted this strange novel to take on the test of historical crisis. It is one more sign of his deep allegiance to a historiographical mission for the novel.

The number of books of French history that Flaubert read in the course of writing *Bouvard and Pécuchet* was, as one would expect, astounding. There is no reason to believe it included the first works in what would eventually be a vast historiography of the Commune, other than his friend Maxime Du Camp's jaundiced firsthand account. The first eyewitness accounts by participants in the Commune began to appear outside of France in the mid-1870s: Prosper-Olivier Lissagaray's important *Histoire de la Commune de 1871* (*History of the Commune of 1871*) was published in 1876 in Brussels. But the great outpouring of memoirs and histories began only in the 1880s, following the vote for amnesty for the remaining Communards and their return from exile, and following Flaubert's death. The principal novel to come from a participant, *L'Insurgé* (*The Insurgent*), by Jules Vallès, appeared in 1886. So we cannot affirm that the modified portrait of 1848 that emerges in *Bouvard and Pécuchet* owes anything to accounts sympathetic to the Commune, and sympathy for the Commune was never something Flaubert expressed. Nonetheless, the revision provided in the later novel records a softening of attitude, a new sympathy for individual liberties and the plight of the defeated.

Flaubert in his last year of life—he died on May 8, 1880—was much preoccupied with correcting proof on new editions of both *Salammbô* and *Sentimental Education*: the former was reissued in October 1879, the latter in November. One senses his attempt to come to terms with the incomprehension that greeted *Sentimental Education* in its first publication, which he locates, in that letter to Edma Roger des Genettes of October 8, 1879, in a lack of "falsity of perspective," which may be a way to account for lack of popular success while declaring fidelity to a higher, more uncompromising sense of the writer's task. He more than once stresses that the reaction to the novel was "unjust." He wants to see his novel understood in a new historical context, post Terrible Year.

It is interesting, during these weeks preceding the new edition of the novel, to see how he responded to Du Camp's sending him volume 4 of *Les Convulsions de Paris*, Du Camp's extended personal and vitriolic account of the time when the Commune ruled in Paris. Flaubert advised Du Camp to let his narrative speak for itself, and to delete the incessant epithets he applied to the Communards: "idiots, madmen, criminals." He wrote, in November 1879, "The aim of History seems to me more elevated than that of railing against crimes!" In particular, he would like to erase a page where Du Camp talks about "the dangerous sides of Darwin's theory." That is impermissible: you cannot renounce Science in the name of Morality: "It is either one way or the other: either Evolution or Miracles. You have to choose." This need to choose points to the problem of French politics: even the socialists are caught up in "theological" thinking, rejecting "political economy"—which Flaubert sees as deriving from Malthus—as the basis of a needed scientific sociology. Du Camp's railing against the Commune becomes the occasion for a lecture on the imperative to put the study of society and politics on that scientific basis. Flaubert has not revised his low opinion of the Commune, but he has gained a perspective on its place in history that would be more illuminating than Du Camp's.

Zola published a serious article on the new edition of *Sentimental Education* on December 9, explaining that it was a novel that avoided the dramatic and novelistic and "that never lied." Flaubert responded warmly: "How you avenge me! My secret opinion is that you are right: it is an *honest* book." He also soon after read Zola's *Nana*, which he found extraordinary. Along with letters asking for information needed for *Bouvard and Pécuchet*, a book that was devouring him just as his two scriveners devoured books, there were a number of responses to books that were sent to him. He recognized in Maupassant's story "Boule de suif" the work of a major new talent. And, since Turgenev sent it to him, the French translation of Tolstoy's *War and Peace*, in three volumes: he loved the first two volumes, but found the last one too full of Russian philosophizing. Turgenev then made a long trip back to Russia (but not before sending Flaubert a gift of salmon and caviar), so he was missing from the ranks when Flaubert assembled his friends in Croisset for Easter dinner 1880: Goncourt, Zola, Maupassant, Daudet, Charpentier. The last reunion.

—·—

WE SEE FLAUBERT IN the last years and months of his life as the servant of art in Croisset—no writing seems to have been quite as daunting and frustrating as *Bouvard and Pécuchet*—but at the same time as someone fully engaged with the literature, the culture, and even the politics of his time. He was disappointed that his contemporaries didn't understand the historical lessons implicit in *Sentimental Education*. But that did not mean giving up on the historical enterprise. What was needed, as he said in that letter to Du Camp revisiting the story of the Commune, was a scientific basis for the study of society. A history that would be grounded in sociology, a science of society, of how men and moment behave together—that was knowledge worth having. And the novel was the form to show the way toward it.

Epilogue

I T's been my aim to see Flaubert's most ambitious novel, *Sentimental Education*, for what it is: an important foray into the novelistic writing of history as it is experienced by an individual and a generation—the kind of history that matters to us who live in it without controlling it. Flaubert's experiment was largely misunderstood, to his great perplexity and chagrin, because readers expected something else from the novel, especially from a historical novel: some authorial or narratorial overview that would allow them to come away with a meaning of the story. The historical novel traditionally existed to construe a meaning from a protagonist's experience of the forces exerted upon him or her by events. Even if the protagonists are among the humble of the earth, such as Renzo and Lucia in Manzoni's *The Betrothed*, what happens to them is clearly connected to and a result of doings among those who have power. That holds true even when the course of events escapes the powerful as well. Even accident is recovered for meaning. The novelist undertakes his narrative with a sense of an ending that, happy or unhappy, will illuminate the meaning of experience within history.

Flaubert's break from this tradition in his radically non-normative participant view of event has raised questions that take us on the one hand to the history of his time, and on the other to matters of reading and interpretation. He himself brings the two together in the comment that set me to thinking about the subject of this book. When in the ruins of Paris, in June 1871, he commented to Maxime Du Camp that if only his contemporaries had understood *Sentimental Education*, "this never could have happened," he links his contemporaries' inability to read and understand his novel to the cataclysmic events that ended in the Bloody Week. It is an implicit claim that knowing how to read his account of the prior upheaval, 1848, would have led one to understand how to prevent the next one. This insight almost turns Flaubert into a biblical prophet, he whose words will reveal their truth in the fullness of time—if only his contemporaries had eyes to see and ears to hear. Since they have not read and understood, they undergo a fate that can only be explained as a product of their stupidity.

This is to say that Flaubert's major, obsessive preoccupations all come to bear on this moment of missed meaning, as one might call it. When he laments that he published *Sentimental Education* too soon—that it would have found its natural conclusion in the undoing of the Second Empire, with the defeat at Sedan and the capture of the emperor—he again puts us face to face with his own conception of how that novel was profoundly shaped by its historical background, how in fact background is the wrong word, since what appears to be ground in the characters' lives must eventually be brought to the fore, to be the figure that matters more than the characters themselves. The notion that the Second Empire needed another novel that would pick up following the coup d'état of December 2, 1851, that stands as climax of *Sentimental Education*, in what was to be explicitly *Sous Napoléon III*, demonstrates again that it is only within historical and political time that the individual can make sense of life.

In the ruins of Paris, Flaubert discovers a kind of crisis of meaning occasioned by a historical cataclysm. It doesn't, for him, discredit what he has presented in his novel. Rather, it puts into question the good faith of his contemporaries and their ability to read. The crisis of meaning is doubled by a crisis of culture, or, as Flaubert says in his more enraged moments, a crisis of civilization. This is why the Terrible Year, including war, siege, radical takeover of Paris, and bloody class warfare, take on an importance not only in themselves but also as an object of thought for Flaubert in dialogue with Sand and other friends. How do you understand a proud nation, and a city that is the capital of Europe, coming to such a catastrophe? There are the political explanations, to be sure, and Flaubert never varies in his assignment of blame to "Badinguet's men," Napoleon III and his henchmen who killed off the Second Republic and instituted a glittering but graft-filled, totalitarian, and exploitative regime. Flaubert doesn't offer a particularized political analysis of the Second Empire's crimes and failures. He instead makes sweeping gestures that attempt to put this political moment in its place in a large evolution of history that is leading away from everything he prizes. So that the political generally ends up being the intellectual: every diagnosis eventually leads you to the abject failure of intelligence that has undone his compatriots. If *Sous Napoléon III* was to sum up on an epoch of false grandeur, perhaps *Bouvard and Pécuchet* gives the larger context, especially in the *Dictionary of Received Ideas*. Stupidity is the context that trumps all others.

But that is too all-inclusive to serve as an analytic instrument for understanding Flaubert's complex reactions during war, siege, and Commune. Some forty-four years later, the outbreak of World War I would come as a seismic shock to thinkers and writers who had believed that European civilization had settled into a narrative of progress. Henry James expressed it as eloquently as anyone: "The plunge of civilization into this abyss of blood and darkness by the wanton feat of those two infamous autocrats is a thing that so gives away the whole long age during which we have supposed the world to be, with whatever abatement, gradually bettering, that to have to take it now for what the treacherous years were all the while really making for and *meaning* is too tragic for any words."

To Flaubert, the outbreak of the Franco-Prussian War had the same effect: this was a betrayal of civilization, of everything he believed in and stood for. When the French armies collapsed, he felt shame and bitterness. When the Prussians started shelling Paris, he could not believe that even enemies could do such a thing in the modern world. The experience of enemy occupation was indescribable, an undoing of his whole world. Then the coming to power of the Commune laid bare class animus and a struggle among Frenchmen for which he was not quite prepared despite his studies of 1848, and the bloody suppression of the Communards revealed the barbarity of those who were supposed to be defending civilization against the barbarians. It was almost too much to fathom. Amid the stench of corpses and extinguished fires in Paris in June 1871, he could only lay a curse on all his countrymen for having given up on intelligence, on reading in a profound sense. Though Flaubert and the Commune stood at opposite ends of any kind of spectrum, they met in the ruins of Paris.

My own interest in thinking about this unexpected meeting of Flaubert and the Commune derives no doubt in part from personal experience. I spent the winter of 1967–1968 in Paris, as a young teacher working to complete his first book, and so was witness to the events of May 1968. The ghost of the seizure of power by the people of Paris in the Commune of 1871 lay across the Left Bank of Paris that cold spring. I was on my way to the Sorbonne library when I emerged from a Métro station to find myself between two battle lines: on the one hand, the police—not the usual Paris gendarmes, but the tough national police, the Corps Républicain de Sécurité, with shields and helmets—and on the other students armed with ashcan lids and cobblestones. I retreated back into the Métro that day, to carry my manuscript to safety. But I returned to the Latin Quarter every day in the following weeks, not quite as a participant—foreigners arrested were immediately deported from France—but as an observer very much caught up in the unfolding events, and in a spectacle of nearly erotic attraction.

Fascinating and enigmatic to an outsider was the way in which young French men and women apparently knew how you went about making a revolution. There were first of all the barricades. They were mainly built of cobblestones pried from the streets and carefully, laboriously, built into a defensive wall, rising at least chest high, and sometimes many stones thick. They could be enhanced by various reinforcing items, especially the semicircular grates that protect the roots of trees planted along Parisian sidewalks, occasionally an iron bedstead, later on some burned-out cars. The use of the barricade is not only to keep the enemy out, but also to create within its confines a liberated space, your space, in which you can move freely—turf that you have wrested for yourself from the urban complex. On this turf, the students governed.

And the ways in which to govern also seemed to come from deep within some consciousness of revolutionary activity. Political organization was largely in the form of the *comité d'action*, the small group of self-appointed volunteers who took charge of some sector of the work to be done. Even at the time, it was clear to me that this was not some Marxist model of state takeover. It had much more to do with native French models of socialism, and especially, I think, with the classical anarchism of Pierre-Joseph Proudhon. The idea was that power should be exercised by those directly interested in its exercise. It was not to be alienated in distant representative bodies that lost sight of the people on whose behalf they were in power. Jean-Jacques Rousseau claimed that representative democracy was no better than tyranny—and the French students in 1968 certainly could make a plausible case that President Charles de Gaulle and his National Assembly bore no relation to their needs and interests. Nor did the large national labor unions. Act locally, the idea seemed to be, and that can eventually have global consequences, since all action to return power to the people must start with local acts in the usurpation of power—or, they would have said, the reclamation of power.

Then there were the posters, the *affiches*, that came over the weeks to occupy every available piece of wall. A book was published from them post-May, *Les Murs ont la parole*: "The walls speak," though that doesn't quite capture it, since *avoir la parole*, to have the word, is equivalent to our "you have the floor." The walls were the place of political speech and indeed of legislation for the liberated space of the Sorbonne and its neighborhood. Some of the posters were artistic—I still have one written by the novelist Michel Butor and designed by the painter Bernard Dufour—some informational, some directive, some poetic: "Sous les pavés c'est la plage," one said: "Under the cobblestones lies the beach," a somewhat surrealist reference to the fact that when you dig up cobble-stones to make your barricade, you find a layer of sand (in which the cob-blestones are set) underneath, which gives you the notion that beneath the grim realities of the urban everyday lies an escape to the seashore, vacation, life as pleasure. "Il est interdit d'interdire," said another: "It is forbidden to forbid," a kind of oxymoron that plays on the French state's predilection for signs everywhere—in subways, buses, public gardens, for instance—interdicting various activities. If the interdict falls on in-terdiction itself, the double negative is seen as liberation.

And finally the longer texts, mimeographed and distributed, set the social program that was to govern the new world set free from the sur-plus repression (Herbert Marcuse's term) of late capitalist society. One particularly eloquent document drafted on the campus at Nanterre (given me by one of its authors, the notable art historian Louis Marin), read, in part:

> The crisis begun in May, 1968, is not a "crisis": through it, we enter into a new period of history. What has been aimed at and shaken, through critique and through struggle, is not only the political regime, but the social system; and not only capitalist private property, but the entire or-ganization of life, all the "values" that modern societies, whether of the West or the East, use or fabricate, impose or insinuate, to disarm desire. You have understood nothing about our movement if you do not see this: what swept across France—to the point of creating a power vac-uum—was not the spirit of professional demands, nor the wish for a political change, but the desire for other relations among human beings.

There you have what you might call the tragic utopianism of May 1968. It was not simply, not even primarily, a call for a new political order, but a call for a new social and human regime—the liberation of desire, the institution of new relations among human beings. That goal was not achieved; it was thwarted, ridiculed, and declared outside the reign of politics as usual. But as an aspiration of what politics ought to think about—as a claim to the primacy of human fulfillment—it remains in my mind a haunting reminder of how poorly the political responds to human needs and capacities.

It was years later that my study of the Paris Commune of 1871 allowed me to see how specifically that insurgency was informing their gestures. That was the last great French uprising—the historian François Furet saw it as the end of the revolutionary tradition—which, though unknown to most in its details, and indeed repressed from consciousness in much official French history (though to be revived with renewed interest following May 1968, and with the centennial of 1971), was nonetheless alive enough as part of tradition, almost folklore, you might say. The Commune of 1871 constructed barricades. It operated through "commissions" in charge of everything from the conduct of war to the collection of trash. It communicated largely through *affiches*, informing, instructing, rallying the people of Paris. It developed blueprints for the radical transformation of society. Though it probably was not the ongoing popular *fête*, as some historians have wished to see it, it surely embodied a movement toward the liberation of "the people" to manage their own affairs. The professional rulers of France were gone—they fled the city to Versailles—and the locals had to invent everything. In particular, it was a model where the exercise of power was very much in the hands of those affected by that exercise. It was a constant experience of self-invention—in dire circumstances of civil war, siege, shortages of every kind, and imminent invasion. It was a grand, enigmatic, and short-lived social experiment. "A sphinx to the bourgeois mind," Karl Marx called it. Sphinx-like it stands still as a key and puzzling moment in history that had enormous consequences for its contemporaries, and well beyond—Lenin, for instance, wrote a book about the Commune.

I have tried in this book to see war, defeat, the Commune and civil strife in relation to the greatest writer of the time, Flaubert, largely in his dialogue with a great woman novelist and his cherished friend, George Sand. They were not participants but rather thinkers—"intellectuals" a few decades before that term had been invented—who saw that not only the fate of their country but also the fate of humanity was in play, and that their own work was implicated in politics in complicated ways. Their anguished commentary on developing events took in the fate of the nation and also the place of culture within national politics. They both understood that if events had to be experienced, even submitted to, they also needed telling. Writing had the capacity to change lives and inflect the course of history. If you could make it understood in the midst of stupidity.

One question asked implicitly by *Sentimental Education* is whether we are up to historical event: whether our intellectual and moral faculties are capable of making sense of it, and determining an effective response to it. The novel implies that Frédéric and his companions, no doubt his whole generation, failed at the bar of history. That Flaubert somehow saw himself as having at least retrospectively succeeded in drawing a lesson from 1848, had his contemporaries only been able to understand it, is surely a sign of intellectual arrogance. But he thought that the research, the planning, the composition that had gone into the novel in some sense justified his claim. Though he certainly understood at the same time that this was wishful thinking: it would be too much to expect that those who lived the moment in the blind fury of dissension and division would easily accept a written version that seemed to declare a pox upon all the houses. It's by no means clear that even a benevolent reading of *Sentimental Education* sees that it maps a future course of political action, unless it might be the abstention from all action. Nonetheless, the novel remains a remarkable attempt at understanding. And also a remarkable claim to what the novel can be. The novelization of history in which *Sentimental Education* participates demonstrates perhaps better than any other genre what is at stake for the individual amid the forces of history. And *Sentimental Education* more than most other novels gives us an experience of seeking and failing to understand the meaning of our lives in history.

The idea of this book came to me a number of years ago when I was leaving Paris after a short stay, on my way to Charles de Gaulle Airport. Dominating the city as it recedes in the rear-view mirror is the Basilique du Sacré-Coeur atop Montmartre. Reminding myself that it had been built in expiation of the Terrible Year, I began to think of everything else that clustered around that momentous and tragic historical moment. Then I recalled Flaubert's comment to Du Camp as they viewed the ruins.

Here, surely, was a nexus of event, its recall, the attempt to give it meaning that was worth exploring further. As I did so, the greatness of Flaubert's prophetic novel became ever clearer to me. It is less popular than *Madame Bovary*, and no doubt will never claim the sort of affection on the part of readers that the earlier novel fosters. Yet it is more ambitious, possibly more important, and carries even more of the sad, still music of humanity. Its picture of humanity largely baffled and defeated by the unfolding of historical event still solicits our attention.

Acknowledgments

A s I noted in my Epilogue, the idea of this book came to me as I was leaving Paris one day in the early summer of 2011 and found myself staring at the distant image of the Basilique du Sacré-Coeur on the Butte Montmartre. I was very fortunate to be a member of the School of Historical Studies at the Institute for Advance Study (IAS) in Princeton that fall. There, with the extraordinary support and good company that IAS provides, I set aside the project I had applied to work on to begin this book instead. My research has also been supported by the Center for Human Values at Princeton University, and by the John W. Kluge Center of the Library of Congress, where I spent a very pleasant and helpful semester completing the project. My thanks in particular to Jane McAuliffe, Mary Lou Reker, Dan Turello, and Joanne Kitching of the center and the library. I also wish to thank the librarians of the Bibliothèque Historique de la Ville de Paris, which houses collections crucial to my research. I owe many debts of gratitude as well to other individuals, colleagues, and friends. Let me single out from among them for particular thanks Yair Minsker and Nicola Suthor for their helpful reactions to the presentation of my work at IAS, and Denis Hollier, Maurice Samuels, Raymond Anthony Jonas, Paolo Tortonese, Philippe Hamon, Philip Nord, Richard Sennett, John Logan, Rachel Bowlby, Steve Wasserman, Martine Reid, Robert Jay Lifton, D. A. Miller, John Merriman, and Maureen Chun for conversation, lecture invitations, bibliographical tips, and general friendship. Anna and Clara Brooks have lived with this book for some time without complaint.

It has made a great difference to this project, and to me, to have found so sympathetic and expert an editor as Lara Heimert, ably assisted by Leah Stecher, Shena Redmond, and Katherine Streckfus.

Notes

INTRODUCTION

xxi **"really Flaubert owed . . . ":** Edmund Wilson, "Flaubert's Politics," in *The Triple Thinkers*, rev. ed. (New York: Harcourt Brace, 1948 [1938]), 100.

xxi **turn into a republican:** See Michel Winock, *Flaubert* (Paris: Gallimard, 2013).

xxiii **participant through his work:** The view of Flaubert as having opted out of the history of his time—in part through the use he made of what was possibly an epileptic attack—is promoted at length in Jean-Paul Sartre's *L'Idiot de la famille*, 3 vols. (Paris: Gallimard, 1971–1972); English trans. Carol Cosman, *The Family Idiot* (Chicago: University of Chicago Press, 1981). Sartre's book on Flaubert continues an argument launched in *Qu'est-ce que la littérature?* in *Situations II* (Paris: Gallimard, 1947); English trans. Bernard Frechtman, *What Is Literature?* (London: Methuen, 1950).

CHAPTER 1: FROM EMMA BOVARY TO THE TERRIBLE YEAR

1 **bad behavior and its consequences:** On the trial and its reading of the novel, see Dominck LaCapra, *Madame Bovary on Trial* (Ithaca, NY: Cornell University Press, 1982). See also Elisabeth Ladenson, *Dirt for Art's Sake*

(Ithaca: Cornell University Press, 2007) and Marco Wan, *Masculinity and the Trials of Modern Fiction* (New York: Routledge, 2016).

2   **in his early forties:** For biographical information on Flaubert, I have turned often to the two most recent: Frederick Brown, *Gustave Flaubert* (New York: Little, Brown, 2006), and Michel Winock, *Flaubert* (Paris: Gallimard, 2013). Very helpful for any biographical research on Flaubert is Jean-Benoît Guinot, *Dictionnaire Flaubert* (Paris: CNRS Editions, 2010).

4   **almost until his death:** On Flaubert and Juliet Herbert, see Hermia Oliver, *Flaubert and an English Governess: The Quest for Juliet Herbert* (Oxford: Clarendon, 1980).

4   **"the moral history of the men . . . ":** Gustave Flaubert (GF hereafter) to Mlle Leroyer de Chantepie, October 6, 1864. For Flaubert's correspondence, I have used the great Pléiade edition in five volumes, edited by Jean Bruneau and, for vol. 5, Yvan Leclerc (Paris: Bibliothèque de la Pléiade, 1973–2007). I have consulted also the *Correspondance Gustave Flaubert–George Sand* (Paris: La Part Commune, 2011) and the two-volume selection in English translation by Francis Steegmuller, *The Letters of Gustave Flaubert* (Cambridge, MA: Harvard University Press, 1980–1982). Translations from the correspondence are my own.

5   **suburbs along the Seine:** The work on Paris of the Second Empire is vast. In my own thinking, a key reference has for many years been T. J. Clark, *The Painting of Modern Life* (New York: Knopf, 1985).

6   **"big, brilliant pearls":** Gustave Flaubert, *Vie et travaux du R. P. Cruchard*, ed. Bernard Molant, Matthieu Desports, and Yvan Leclerc (Rouen and Le Havre: Publications des Universités de Rouen et du Havre, 2005), 55.

7   **"ferocious liberal":** GF to Mlle Leroyer de Chantepie, March 30, 1857.

8   **"I insist that it be ultra-chic":** GF to Jules Duplan, November 12 [?], 1864.

8   **recite them from memory:** Maxime Du Camp, *Souvenirs littéraires*, 2 vols. (Geneva: Slatkine, 1993 [1906]), 2:269.

9   **tantalizingly political Flaubert:** The fragmentary sketches for the novel may be found in Gustave Flaubert, *Carnets de Travail*, ed. Pierre-Marc de Biasi (Paris: Balland, 1988), and are discussed at greater length in my Chapter 7.

9   **"pretend swine":** Edmond de Goncourt, *Journal*, ed. Robert Ricatte (Paris: Fasquelle, 1956), 2:1136.

10   **wrote scripts and made costumes:** On Sand's biography, see the succinct account by Martine Reid, *George Sand* (Paris: Gallimard, 2013).

10   **declared himself charmed:** GF to George Sand (GS hereafter), December 27, 1866; GS to GF, January 15, 1867.

11   **nowhere visible:** GF to Louise Colet, December 9, 1852.

12   **visual and specific:** On Flaubert's obsession with detail in *Madame Bovary*, see Naomi Schor, *Reading in Detail* (New York: Methuen, 1987), and Peter Brooks, *Body Work: Objects of Desire in Modern Narrative* (Cambridge, MA: Harvard University Press, 1993).

12   **interrupt them:** GF to Paul de Saint-Victor [?], September 12, 1867 [?].

13   **"I need details about the homes . . . ":** GF to Jules Duplan, August 27, 1868.

13   **when the needed information arrived:** GF to Jules Duplan, September 19, 1868.

14   **directly into the novel:** Maxime Du Camp to GF, June 20, 1868; September 22, 1868; 1st fortnight of October 1868.

14   **not argue or teach but expose:** GF to Louise Colet, April 6, 1853.

14   **"I *see* all the furniture . . . ":** GF to Hippolyte Taine, November 20 [?], 1866. Unless otherwise noted, all emphasis in quotations are reproduced from the original.

16   **"I have just swallowed . . . ":** GF to Edma Roger des Genettes, summer 1864.

16   **"All the Christianity I find . . . ":** GF to GS, July 5, 1868.

16   **"since they seem to me more criminal":** GF to GS, August 10, 1868.

17   **"Can one find a more triumphant . . . ":** GF to GS, December 18–19, 1867.

17   **"Finally! Someone who thinks . . . ":** GS to GF, December 21, 1867. Flaubert's epithet for Thiers is *étroniforme*; Sand's is *merdoïde*.

18   **"One has to choose . . . ":** GS to GF, January 1, 1869; GF to GS, January 1, 1869.

19   **"the *unconscious* poetics":** GF to GS, February 2, 1869.

19   **"Another gone . . . ":** GF to Maxime Du Camp, October 13, 1869.

20   **dictates of the grammarians:** Du Camp, *Souvenirs littéraires*, 2:339.

21   **"It's not boredom . . . ":** Barbey d'Aurevilly in *Le Constitutionnel*, November 29, 1869; Sarcey in *Le Gaulois*, December 3, 1869.

21   **"They think that 'you shouldn't be allowed. . . . '":** GF to GS, December 3, 1869.

21   **"Natural and Social History":** See Emile Zola, "Causerie," in *Oeuvres completes*, ed. Henri Mitterand (Paris: Cercle du Libre Précieux, 1968), 10:916–920.

21   **"I don't care in the least":** GF to GS, December 3, 1869.

21   **"None of this destroys . . . ":** GF to GS, December 7, 1869.

22   **"What a good woman . . . ":** GF to GS, December 10, 1869.

22   **"Don't say anything . . . ":** *La Liberté*, December 21, 1869; reprinted in Raymonde Debray-Genette, ed., *Flaubert* (Paris: Firmin-Didot, 1970), 41.

22   **"You seem astonished . . . ":** GS to GF, December 10–11, 1869.

23   **"Flaubert enjoys himself . . . ":** George Sand, *Agendas*, ed. Anne Chevereau (Paris: Jean Touzot, 1992), 4:234.

23   **"What fine and loveable people . . . ":** GF to GS, December 30, 1869.

23   **"Those were the best moments . . . ":** GF to GS, January 3, 1870.

CHAPTER 2: THE TERRIBLE YEAR

26   **standard fare:** These figures are given by David A. Shafer, *The Paris Commune* (London: Palgrave/Macmillan, 2005), 49.

29   **"Let us love one another . . . ":** GS to GF, June 27, 1870.

29   **" I am nauseated . . . ":** GF to GS, July 22, 1870.

29   **"I find this war infamous . . . ":** GS to GF, July 26, 1870.

29   **"Boast about Progress . . . ":** GF to GS, August 3, 1870.

30   **"Will this horrible experience . . . ":** GS to GF, August 7, 1870.

30   **"This human butchery . . . ":** GS to GF, August 15, 1870.

30   **he would go fight:** GF to GS, August 17, 1870.

30   **"That's what Universal Suffrage . . . ":** Ibid.

31   **"Greetings to you . . . ":** *Le Temps*, September 5, 1870.

31   **"You distress me . . . ":** GF to GS, September 10, 1870.

32   **wonderfully incongruous:** See *Album Flaubert* (Paris: Biblothèque de la Pléiade, 1972), 160.

32   **"Today I begin night patrols . . . ":** GF to Caroline Commanville, September 27, 1870.

32   **"The blood of my ancestors . . . ":** GF to GS, September 28, 1870.

33   **German Idealism and Goethe:** In a later letter to Sand, he asks: "What is the use of knowledge [*la Science*] when this people, full of scholars [*savants*] commits abominations worthy of the Huns!" (GF to GS, November 27, 1870). Following the war, many would ask if Prussian knowledge and scholarship were not in fact the source of their victory, and took this as a lesson for the reform of French education.

33   **"What saddens me . . . ":** GF to Maxime Du Camp, September 29, 1870.

33   **"Whatever happens, the world . . . ":** GF to Caroline Commanville, October 5, 1870.

33   **negotiations with Prussia:** Marshal Bazaine was court-martialed for treason following the war, in 1873, condemned, and sentenced to death; his sentence was then commuted to twenty years of imprisonment by his

colleague Marshal Mac-Mahon, now president of the republic. Bazaine escaped from his island prison by boat and spent his last years in exile in Spain.

34 **"There's never been, in the history of France . . . "**: GF to Caroline Commanville, October 13, 1870.

34 **"And we are without orders . . . "**: GF to GS, October 11, 1870.

34 **"Let's not despair . . . "**: GS to GF, October 14, 1870.

34 **"egotistical, and nasty . . . "**: GF to Caroline Commanville, December 18, 1870.

34 **"The present is abominable . . . "**: GF to Ernest Feydeau, October 17, 1870.

35 **"we have no authority . . . "**: GF to Caroline Commanville, October 24, 1870.

35 **"The ferocity of men . . . "**: GF to GS, November 27, 1870.

35 **"Paganisme, christianisme, muflisme"**: GF to Marie Régnier, March 11, 1871; GF to GS, March 11, 1871.

35 **"The conventional phrases . . . "**: GF to GS, November 27, 1870.

36 **"*I had no idea* . . . "**: GF to Caroline Commanville, January 23, 1871.

36 **"I live in sadness . . . "**: GF to Caroline Commanville, January 28, 1871.

37 **"odious music"**: GF to Princess Mathilde, March 4, 1871.

37 **"an indescribable state"**: GF to Caroline Commanville, February 1, 1871.

37 **"I never thought of myself . . . "**: GF to GS, March 11, 1871.

38 **"liberty full and entire . . . "**: GS to GF, March 17, 1871.

39 **impoverished seamstresses:** John Merriman, *Massacre* (New York: Basic Books, 2014), 20. Among the many books on the Commune, those that have been most valuable to me include, as well as *Massacre*: Robert Tombs, *The Paris Commune, 1871* (London: Longman, 1999); William Serman, *La Commune de Paris* (Paris: Fayard, 1986); David A. Shafer, *The Paris Commune* (London: Palgrave Macmillan, 2005); and Jacques Rougerie, *La Commune de 1871* (Paris: Presses Universitaires de France, 2009). See the largely documentary history of the Commune provided in Jacques Rougerie, *Paris libre 1871* (Paris: Editions du Seuil, 1971). See also Bernard Noël, *Dictionnaire de la Commune* (Paris: Mémoire du Livre, 2000), and the notable special issue of *La Revue Blanche* devoted to the Commune in 1898: *Enquête sur la Commune*, 3rd ed., with fifteen portraits by Félix Vallotton (Paris: Editions de la Revue Blanche, 1898).

40 **"sphinx so tantalising . . . "**: Karl Marx, *The Civil War in France*, in *Later Political Writings* (Cambridge: Cambridge University Press, 1996), 181.

40 **"the Washington of France":** See the succinct account of Commune political ideology by Jacques Rougerie, *La Commune de 1871*, 76–85.

41   **authority was far from centralized:** The best account of the internal
      workings of the Commune remains that of its earliest historian (and a
      participant), Prosper-Olivier Lissagaray, in *Histoire de la Commune* (Paris:
      Edition de Delphes, 1965 [1876]). For another entirely different contem-
      porary account, from a perspective critical of the Commune and a fine ob-
      server, see A.-M. Blanchecotte, *Tablettes d'une femme pendant la Commune*,
      ed. Christine Planté (Tisson, Charente: Du Lérot, 1996 [1872]).

41   **"The great social measure . . . ":** Marx, *Civil War in France*, 192.

42   **"Its true secret was this . . . ":** Ibid., 187.

42   **"The civilization and justice . . . ":** Ibid., 200.

42   **"a strong clerical . . . ":** GF to Edma Roger des Genettes, March 30, 1871.

42   **"The French Revolution . . . ":** GF to GS, March 31, 1871.

43   **unique opportunity:** GF to Edma Roger des Genettes, April 27, 1871.

43   **prisoner-of-war camps:** See especially Merriman, *Massacre*, 43.

43   **"You know what's worst . . . ":** GF to GS, April 24, 1871.

44   **"For me, the ignoble experiment . . . ":** GS to GF, April 28, 1871.

45   **"One feels sorry for a baby bird . . . ":** Ibid.

46   **"'Thank God the Prussians are there!' . . . ":** GF to GS, April 30, 1871.

47   **Eugene Pottier:** Eugene Pottier escaped to England, and then to the United
      States, where he subsisted by teaching French.

48   **"When I think of the gigantic stupidity . . . ":** GF to Princess Mathilde,
      May 22, 1871.

49   **"the coming Reaction":** GF to Charles Lapierre, May 27, 1871.

49   **rain shot on those below:** See Robert Tombs, "La lutte finale des barri-
      cades: Spontanéité révolutionnaire et organisation militaire en mai 1871," in
      La Barricade, ed. Alain Corbin and Jean-Marie Mayeur (Paris: Publications
      de la Sorbonne, 1997), 357–365.

50   **"A blinding light rises . . . ":** Lissagaray, *Histoire de la Commune*, 278.

50   **"The burning of Paris makes a day . . . ":** Edmond de Goncourt, *Journal*, ed.
      Robert Ricatte (Paris: Fasquelle, 1956), 2:810.

50   **"What have we done . . . ":** Emile Zola, *La Débâcle* (Paris: Gallimard/Folio,
      1984), 552.

50   **"But this bloodbath was necessary . . . ":** Ibid., 576.

51   **"the ultimate exorcism . . . ":** François Furet, *Revolutionary France* (Oxford:
      Oxford University Press, 1992), 506.

51   **Monsignor Georges Darboy:** Communard offers to exchange Darboy and
      other hostages against the return of the senior revolutionary leader Auguste
      Blanqui—who was arrested and imprisoned by Thiers on the eve of the

Commune—were rebuffed. It is conceivable that Thiers welcomed the martyrdom of Darboy as useful to repressive measures.

51 **"I managed to cross . . . ":** In Henri Mitterand, ed., *Emile Zola journaliste* (Paris: Armand Colin, 1962), 147. The complete text of Zola's articles makes clear that his sympathy for the defeated and slaughtered Communards comes in the context of complete hostility to the Commune. See *Lettres de Paris*, 1871, in Zola, *Oeuvres complètes* (Paris: Nouveau Monde Editions, 2003), 475–594.

52 **"All this part of the cemetery . . . ":** Mitterand, ed., *Emile Zola journaliste*, 147.

52 **"native populations":** William Serman points out that the principal Versaillais generals were veterans of the French colonial campaigns in Mexico and Algeria. *La Commune de Paris*, 463. The point was made earlier by Communard Benoît Malon in his book *La Troisième défaite du proletariat français* (Neuchâtel: G. Guillaume, 1871), 485–486.

52 **"It is good . . . ":** Goncourt, *Journal*, 2:819.

53 **"as we were looking . . . ":** Maxime Du Camp, *Souvenirs littéraires*, 2 vols. (Geneva: Slatkine, 1993 [1906]), 2:341–342.

53 **"The air of Paris . . . ":** GF to Caroline Commanville, June 8, 1871.

53 **"This ruin is a marvel . . . ":** Goncourt, *Journal*, 2:817.

53 **"Fire is a worker of genius":** Ludovic Hans and J.-J. Blanc, *Guide à travers les ruines (Paris et ses environs)* (Paris: A. Lemerre, 1871).

54 **"The spectacle yesterday . . . ":** GF to Agénor Bardoux, June 9, 1871.

54 **"I am *overcome*, less by the ruins . . . ":** GF to Marie Régnier, June 11, 1871.

54 **"I am overcome or rather nauseated! . . . ":** GF to GS, June 11, 1871.

55 **"The bourgeoisie of the whole world . . . ":** Marx, *Civil War in France*, 202.

55 **"I am as troubled . . . ":** GS to GF, June 14, 1871.

55 **"The madness, the stupidity . . . ":** GS to Ernest Feydeau, June 29, 1871.

56 **"It will be stupid . . . ":** GS to GF, July 23, 1871.

56 **"Its lack of elevation . . . ":** GF to GS, July 25, 1871. See also GF to Edma Roger des Genettes, October 6, 1871: "This is the first time that we see a government without metaphysics, without a program, without a flag, without principles, that is to say, without nonsense! . . . So many crimes have been committed by the ideal in politics that we need for a long time to stick to 'managing affairs.'"

57 **"brings a weight . . . ":** *Le Sémaphore*, November 15, 1872, in *Zola journaliste*, 152.

57   "Ah! How tired I am . . . ": GF to GS, September 6, 1871.

57   "our poor dear country": GS to GF, September 8, 1871.

57   "free and obligatory . . . ": GF to GS, September 8, 1871.

58   "You are so good . . . ": GS to GF, November 16, 1871.

58   "That will be true eternally . . . ": GF to GS, October 7, 1871.

58   "You are a troubadour . . . ": GS to GF, October 10, 1871.

59   "bloody idiots": GF to GS, October 12, 1871.

60   "I feel sorry for humanity . . . ": GS to GF, October 25, 1871.

61   "formidable and universal": GF to GS, November 14, 1871.

61   stroke of midnight: GS to GF, January 4, 1872.

62   "At your age . . . ": GS to GF, January 25, 1872.

62   "It is impossible that people . . . ": Ibid.

62   "I provided figures . . . ": GF to GS, January 28, 1872.

62   "I beg you . . . ": GS to GF, January 28, 1872.

63   "charming . . . not at all the great man . . . ": GF to GS, February 26, 1872.

63   "But I don't feel the need . . . ": GF to Edma Roger des Genettes, May 15, 1872.

64   more and more charming: GF to Caroline Commanville, March 5, 1872.

64   "in exquisite terms": GF to GS, March 11, 1872.

64   may have a new lover: GF to Léonie Brainne, March 31, 1872.

65   "Dear good master . . . ": GF to GS, April 6, 1872.

65   "What a bitter conquest . . . ": GS to GF, April 9, 1872.

65   loved without reservation: GF to GS, April 16, 1872.

65   happily give him: GS to GF, April 16, 1872.

65   "powerful bath": Ivan Turgenev to GF, June 26, 1872.

66   not at all changed: GF to Caroline Commanville, June 13, 1872.

66   "being alone is hateful": GS to GF, October 26, 1872.

66   "modern carrion": GF to GS, October 28, 1872.

66   "nonetheless they smell . . . ": Ivan Turgenev to GF, November 8, 1872.

67   "Public stupidity submerges . . . ": GF to Ivan Turgenev, November 13, 1872.

67   "a Red! Not out of sympathy . . . ": GF to Baronne Lepic [?], November 20, 1872.

68   demanding greater faith: GS to GF, December 8, 1872.

69   live together?: GF to GS, April 24, 1873.

70   "Honor will be saved . . . ": GF to Léonie Brainne, October 2, 1875.

70   "I think you will find the moral thrust . . . ": GF to GS, May 29, 1876.

CHAPTER 3: A TOUR OF THE RUINS

72 **parked beside the ruins:** Théophile Gautier, *Tableaux de siège* (Paris: Charpentier, 1894 [1871]), 338.

75 **"a monument to barbarism . . .":** Decree of the Commune, April 12, 1871, cited in A.-M. Blanchecotte, *Tablettes d'une femme pendant la Commune*, ed. Christine Planté (Tisson, Charente: Du Lérot, 1996 [1872]), 127. My interest in the ruins of the Commune was first sparked by Daryl Patrick Lee, *Uncanny City: Paris in Ruins* (unpublished dissertation, Yale University, 1999). See also his contribution to Sylvie Gonzalez, ed., *Bruno Braquehais: Un Photographe sous la Commune*, Exposition du 9 mars au 19 juin 2000 (St. Denis: Musée d'Art et d'Histoire). On the Commune photographs, see also *La Commune photographiée*, catalog of an exhibition at the Musée d'Orsay (Paris: RMN, 2000); Jean Baronnet and Xavier Canonne et al., *Le Temps des cerises: La Commune en photographies* (Brasschaat, Belgium: Editions Pandora, 2011); and Bernard Noël and Jean-Claude Gautrand, eds., *La Commune* (Paris: Nathan/Photo Poche, 2000).

75 **experiencing the world:** The culture of the Commune has been studied in an interesting book by Kristin Ross, *Communal Luxury* (London: Verso, 2015). One of the tragedies of the Commune is how little understood it was, or even could have been, considering the way its goals and culture were willfully distorted by the government and official news organs, during and after.

76 **author of the album:** Jules Andrieu, *Les Désastres de la guerre*, set of photographs (Paris, 1871).

76 **"a day whose memory . . .":** Preface by Alfred d'Aunay to Alphonse Liébert, *Les Ruines de Paris, et de ses environs, 1870–71. Cent Photographies, par A. Liébert. Texte par Alfred d'Aunay*, 2 vols. (Paris: Editées par la Photographie américaine A. Liébert, 81, rue St. Antoine, 1872). There is another volume that contains the same one hundred Liébert photographs reduced to postcard format, mounted in an album without d'Aunay's preface: *Les Ruines de Paris et de ses environs, 1870–1871: Siège et Commune* (Paris: A. Huet et Vollat, n.d.). Perhaps this preceded the luxurious format volume.

77 **"convulsed by horror . . .":** Karl Marx, *The Civil War in France*, in *Later Political Writings* (Cambridge: Cambridge University Press, 1996), 202.

77 **"The *ruins of Paris!* . . .":** Blanchecotte, *Tablettes*, 259.

77 **results of French fratricide:** See, especially, Eric Fournier, *Paris en ruines: Du Paris haussmannien au Paris communard* (Paris: Editions Imago, 2007), 224–227.

78   **emptinesses that accuse:** Georges Bell, *Paris incendié* (Paris: E. Martinet, 1872).

78   **"only photography . . . ":** Anon., *A travers les ruines de Paris* (Paris: A. Josse, 1871), 6. ("La photographie seule, avec son réalisme brutal et son impitoyable precision, peut rendre l'aspect de ces choses indescriptibles qui furent des maisons, des palais, des villes.")

78   **"This sight had the sun . . . ":** Alphonse Liébert, *Les Ruines de Paris, et de ses environs, 1870–71.* ("Mais la vision a eu le soleil pour témoin, et le soleil a fixé sur le Bristol ce souvenir lugubre.")

78   **"the more one looks . . . ":** Bell, *Paris incendié*, 23.

79   **plain of Satory:** On the publication of Appert's photomontages, see *La Commune photographiée*, 42–45.

81   **literalizing sites of memory:** See the website of the Comité National pour la Reconstruction des Tuileries, www.tuileries.org.

81   **"splendid horrors":** Blanchecotte, *Tablettes*, 259.

81   **"the street of another Pompeii . . . ":** *A travers les ruines de Paris*, 21. On the use of Pompeii as figure in nineteenth-century French historiography, see Goran Blix, *From Paris to Pompeii: French Romanticism and the Cultural Politics of Archaeology* (Philadelphia: University of Pennsylvania Press, 2009).

82   **"Above all we were struck . . . ":** Gautier, *Tableaux de siège*, 327.

82   **"The ruin is magnificent . . . ":** Edmond de Goncourt, *Journal*, ed. Robert Ricatte (Paris: Fasquelle, 1956), 2:817.

82   **"The Ministry of Finance . . . ":** Ludovic Hans and J.-J. Blanc, *Guide à travers les ruines (Paris et ses environs)*, (Paris: A. Lemerre, 1871), 8.

82   **"It makes one dream . . . ":** Gautier, *Tableaux de siège*, 315–316.

83   **"Victory on her chariot . . . ":** See Lee, *Uncanny City*, 198.

84   **fictional narrative:** For example, a contemporary English eyewitness account of the Commune gives a portrait of the *pétroleuse* that strikes one as literary and generic rather than something seen: "She walks with a rapid step, near the shadow of the wall; she is poorly dressed; her age is between forty and fifty; her forehead is bound with a red checkered handkerchief, from which hang meshes of uncombed hair. The face is red and the eyes blurred," and so on. John Leighton, *Paris Under the Commune* (London: Bradbury and Evans; New York: Scribner, Welford, 1871), 35.

85   **"Perhaps we have an invincible resistance . . . ":** Roland Barthes, *Camera Lucida [La Chambre claire]*, trans. Richard Howard (New York: Hill and Wang, 1981), 87–88.

CHAPTER 4: A GENERATION ON TRIAL

87   **"*L'Education sentimentale* is a book that for many years . . . ":** Franz Kafka
      to Felice Bauer, November 15, 1912.

89   **"On September 15, 1840 . . . ":** Gustave Flaubert, *L'Education sentimen-*
      tale, ed. Stéphanie Dord-Crouslé (Paris: Garnier Flammarion, 2003), 49.
      The best available English translation is *Sentimental Education,* trans. Robert
      Baldick, revised by Geoffrey Wall (London: Penguin Books, 2004), 5. The
      translations are my own, but in the notes below I will give page numbers for
      both the French and English versions. The Baldick-Wall is very readable—
      perhaps too readable. It does not keep faith with the resolutely spare and
      exact quality of Flaubert's prose, and constantly recasts the structure and
      movement of his sentences.

89   **"People were arriving . . . ":** Flaubert, *L'Education sentimentale,* 49/5.

90   **"He found that the happiness . . . ":** Ibid., 50/6.

90   **"seemed to slow the progress . . . ":** Ibid., 52/7.

91   **"moving sidewalk":** Marcel Proust, "A propos du 'style' de Flaubert," in
      Chroniques, reprinted in Raymonde Debray-Genette, ed. *Flaubert* (Paris:
      Firmin-Didot, 1970), 47.

91   **"to represent, by means . . . ":** Alessandro Manzoni, *Del Romanzo storico,*
      in *Opera completa* (Napoli, 1860), 518. My translation. In English: *On the*
      Historical Novel (Del Romanzo Storico), trans. Sandra Bermann (Lincoln:
      University of Nebraska Press, 1984), 76.

91   **at least fifty years prior:** See Richard Lee, "Defining the Genre," Histor-
      ical Novel Society, https://historicalnovelsociety.org/guides/defining-the
      -genre.

92   **"Remember Rastignac . . . ":** Flaubert, *L'Education sentimentale,* 68/21.

93   **"one of those shivers . . . ":** Ibid., 109–110/56–57.

93   **"When he had closed the door . . . ":** Ibid., 110/57.

95   **"Why, why *him?*":** Henry James, "Gustave Flaubert" (1902), in *Literary*
      Criticism, vol. 2, *French Writers, Other European Writers, The Prefaces to*
      the New York Edition (New York: Library of America, 1984), 326–327.
      Among many studies of *L'Education sentimentale,* let me single out as es-
      pecially helpful the pages in Jacques Neefs and Claude Mouchard, *Flaubert*
      (Paris: Balland, 1986). See also Victor Brombert, *The Novels of Flaubert: A*
      Study of Themes and Techniques (Princeton, NJ: Princeton University Press,
      1966); the essays collected in Raymonde Debray-Genette, ed., *Flaubert*
      (Paris: Firmin-Didot, 1970), including those by Sand, Zola, Proust, and

also Gérard Genette, "Silences de Flaubert"; Jonathan Culler, *Flaubert: The Uses of Uncertainty*, rev. ed. (Ithaca, NY: Cornell University Press, 1985 [1974]).

95   **"I'll roll down the Champs-Elysées . . . ":** Honoré de Balzac, *Illusions perdues* (Paris: Gallimard/Folio, 2013), 202.

95   **but to nothing more:** See my longer comparative discussion of these two passages in my chapter "Retrospective Lust, or Flaubert's Perversities," in *Reading for the Plot* (New York: Knopf, 1984; reprint, Cambridge, MA: Harvard University Press, 1992).

95   **"Behind the Tuileries . . . ":** Flaubert, *L'Education sentimentale*, 76/28.

96   **"He now possessed it . . . ":** Ibid., 298/225.

97   **"The Polonaise, who abandoned herself . . . ":** Ibid., 194–195/132–133.

98   **"What's the use? . . . ":** Ibid., 199/137.

99   **"He seemed to be harnessed . . . ":** Ibid., 203/140.

99   **"trembling voice":** Ibid., 282/212.

99   **"les pyroscopes . . . ":** Ibid., 284/213.

100   **"a noise like the crackling . . . ":** Ibid., 384/305.

101   **"It's from too much happiness . . . ":** Ibid., 384/306.

102   **"free fifty prisoners . . . ":** Ibid., 388/310.

102   **"Suddenly the *Marseillaise* . . . ":** Ibid., 391–392/312–313.

103   **"An obscene curiosity . . . ":** Ibid., 393/314.

103   **"In the antechamber . . . ":** Ibid.

104   **"We'll be happy now!":** Ibid., 395/316.

104   **"the Republic, or Progress . . . ":** Ibid., 404/323–324.

104   **"Frédéric, man of all weaknesses . . . ":** Ibid., 404/323.

104   **expert historian:** See Maurice Agulhon, *1848 ou l'apprentissage de la république* (Paris: Editions du Seuil, 1973), 48.

104   **"They visited them all . . . ":** Flaubert, *L'Education sentimentale*, 406–407/325–326.

105   **"a lightning flash . . . ":** Ibid., 407/326.

106   **"they terrified the bourgeois . . . ":** Ibid., 401/320.

106   **"Now, Property rose . . . ":** Ibid.

108   **"The men that one glimpsed . . . ":** Ibid., 428/345.

108   **"immobile luxury . . . ":** Ibid., 432/349.

108   **"a retrospective and inexpressible lust":** Ibid., 431/347.

109   **"Each discovers in the other . . . ":** Ibid., 442/357.

109   **"There were rough oaks . . . ":** Ibid., 435/351.

109   **"ended by filling the whole landscape . . . ":** Ibid., 436/352.

110   **"On the ruined barricades . . . ":** Ibid., 446/361.

111   **"despite victory, equality . . ."**: Ibid., 449/364.

112   **"Under the green leaves . . ."**: Ibid., 454/368.

112   **"It was over, that life . . ."**: Ibid., 495/408.

113   **"The divvying up . . ."**: Ibid., 535/445.

113   **"Frédéric, his jaw dropping . . ."**: Ibid., 541/450.

114   **admirable thing in the novel:** Proust, "A propos du 'style' de Flaubert," in Debray-Genette, *Flaubert*, 54–55.

114   **"He traveled . . ."**: Flaubert, *L'Education sentimentale*, 542/451.

114   **"It doesn't matter . . ."**: Ibid., 544/453.

115   **"And, exhuming their youth . . ."**: Ibid., 550/458.

116   **"Only in the novel . . ."**: Georg Lukács, *Theory of the Novel*, trans. Anna Bostock (Cambridge, MA: MIT Press, 1973), 122.

116   **"the only novel that attains . . ."**: Ibid., 125–127.

116   **"So many crimes . . ."**: GF to Edma Roger des Genettes, October 6, 1871.

117   **"retrospective prophecy":** Carlo Ginzburg, "Spie: Radici di un paradigma indizario," in *Miti Emblemi Spie* (Turin: Einaudi, 1986), 117; English trans. John and Anne Tedeschi, "Clues," in *Clues, Myths, and the Historical Method* (Baltimore: Johns Hopkins University Press, 1989), 117. The term "retrospective prophecies" is my own translation from Ginzburg's Italian original: *"profezie retrospettive,"* which the official translation rephrases as "the ability to forecast retrospectively," which I think weakens the sense.

118   **"Frédéric is us!":** Michel Winock, *Flaubert* (Paris: Gallimard, 2013), 287–303.

120   **"seems always to see humanity . . ."**: Edmund Wilson, "Flaubert's Politics," in *The Triple Thinkers*, rev. ed. (New York: Harcourt Brace, 1948 [1938]), 100.

120   **"so that, without pleasing anyone . . ."**: Flaubert, *L'Education sentimentale*, 282/211.

121   **"We are amazed to find . . ."**: Wilson, "Flaubert's Politics," 113–114.

CHAPTER 5: HEARTS AND MINDS

123   **"The immense disgust . . ."**: GF to GS, July 25, 1871.

123   **"I will try to *vomit my bile* . . ."**: GF to Ernest Feydeau, December 29, 1872.

124   **future remedies:** For an example of extreme reaction to the Terrible Year, see Ernest Renan, *La Reformé intellectuelle et morale* (Paris: Perrin, 2011 [1871]). Though Flaubert in 1871 approved of some of what Renan wrote in this nationalist, corporatist, militarist, and antiegalitarian tract, his own

position evolved toward something far more nuanced and more fully committed to freedom.

126   **irreconcilables of modern France:** On the significance of the Battle of Loigny and its sequels, see Raymond Anthony Jonas, *France and the Cult of the Sacred Heart* (Berkeley: University of California Press, 2000), 164–171. Jonas's excellent book has shaped much of my thinking in this chapter. See also Jacques Benoist, *Le Sacré-Coeur de Montmartre de 1870 à nos jours* (Paris: Editions ouvrières, 1992).

126   **"This temple . . . will stand . . .":** Cited in David Harvey, "Monument and Myth: The Building of the Basilica of the Sacred Heart," in *The Urban Experience* (Baltimore: Johns Hopkins University Press, 1989), 218.

127   **"It is here, it is here . . .":** Cited by Harvey, "Monument and Myth," 202.

127   **divine love for humanity:** Jonas, *France and the Cult of the Sacred Heart*, 3.

128   **"to protect us against the lightning . . .":** Cited by Jonas, in ibid., 201.

129   **loss of jobs for the workers:** Harvey, "Monument and Myth," 226–227.

130   **"to efface by this work . . .":** Ibid., 219.

130   **"redeem once again . . .":** Jonas, *France and the Cult of the Sacred Heart*, 200.

131   **"at war with the spirit . . .":** Harvey, "Monument and Myth," 220.

132   **"the symbol and the rallying sign . . .":** René Rémond, "La Fille ainée de l'Eglise," in Pierre Nora, ed., *Les Lieux de mémoire III, Les France* (Paris: Gallimard, 1992), 574.

133   **"Always remember . . .":** Jules Michelet, *Jeanne d'Arc*, cited in Michel Winock, *Jeanne d'Arc*, in *Lieux de mémoire III, Les France* (Paris: Gallimard, 1992), 702.

133   **used the symbolic in their conflict:** Winock, *Jeanne d'Arc*, in *Lieux de mémoire*, 675–733.

134   **"hideous":** GF to Edma Roger des Genettes, November 8, 1879.

134   **"a return to its traditions . . .":** Henri, Comte de Chambord, *Textes politiques: Lettres et manifestes choisis et annotés par Serge Desplanches* (Paris: Communication & Tradition, 1995), 56.

135   **"I believe that we will have the Henri V":** GS to GF, October 3, 1873.

135   **mentality of men:** GF to Edma Roger des Genettes, October 30, 1873.

135   **"A Christian nation cannot with impunity . . .":** Chambord, *Textes politiques*, 58.

136   **"a pretext invented . . .":** Ibid., 64.

136   **"Does anyone think . . .":** GF to Caroline Commanville, November 4, 1873.

137   **"hosannah!":** GF to Princess Mathilde, November 12, 1873.

138   **"Have you read 93 . . .":** GF to GS, February 28, 1874.

139   **"Venez, citoyenne":** Victor Hugo, *Quatrevingt-treize* (Paris: Classiques

Garnier, 1963), 21. There is currently no good English translation in print. On Hugo's novel, see Victor Brombert, *Victor Hugo and the Visionary Novel* (Cambridge, MA: Harvard University Press, 1984), and Kathryn M. Grossman, *The Later Novels of Victor Hugo* (Oxford: Oxford University Press, 2012).

141 **"We don't overthrow . . . ":** Hugo, *Quatrevingt-treize*, 289.

141 **"The scaffold is the only edifice . . . ":** Victor Hugo, *Bug-Jargal et Le Dernier Jour d'un condamné* (Paris: Livre de Poche, 1970 [1829]), 373 (preface to 1832 ed.); English trans. Geoff Woollen, *The Last Day of a Condemned Man and Other Prison Writings* (Oxford: Oxford World Classics, 1992).

141 **"In the past the social edifice . . . ":** Hugo, *Bug-Jargal et Le Dernier Jour d'un condamné*, 397.

142 **"Books make crimes":** Hugo, *Quatrevingt-treize*, 452.

143 **"Above the scales . . . ":** Ibid., 472.

143 **"On one hand, inextricable gothic complexity . . . ":** Ibid., 484.

143 **"I am your daughter":** Ibid., 485.

143 **absolves the present moment:** Ibid., 478.

144 **"And these two souls . . . ":** Ibid., 491 ("Et ces deux âmes, soeurs tragiques, s'envolèrent ensemble, l'ombre de l'une mêlée à la lumière de l'autre").

CHAPTER 6: "A SIMPLE HEART"

147 **acts of censorship:** GF to Edma Roger des Genettes, September 17, 1877.

147 **"After five minutes thinking . . . ":** GF to Léonie Brainne, August 23, 1877.

148 **"Merde pour Mac-Mahon":** GF to Guy de Maupassant, October 31, 1877.

148 **"Merde pour l'Ordre moral":** GF to Emile Zola, October 9, 1877.

148 **"Bayard of modern times":** GF to Zola, October 5, 1877.

148 **"I didn't like this king . . . ":** GF to Edma Roger des Genettes, September 17, 1877. "Monsieur Prudhomme" refers to the incarnation of the self-satisfied bourgeois as created in the caricatures of Henry Monnier.

148 **"a very good book":** GF to Maupassant, October 31, 1877.

148 **"We had a private meeting . . . ":** GF to Edmond Laporte, January 19, 1878.

150 **"You will understand me . . . ":** GS to GF, October 25, 1871.

150 **"To withdraw your soul . . . ":** GS to GF, January 12, 1876.

151 **"There is no point in preaching . . . ":** GF to GS, February 6, 1876.

151 **"You will see . . . ":** GF to GS, May 29, 1876.

151 **"In order not to offend . . . ":** GF to Ivan Turgenev, June 25, 1876.

152 **"The *Story of a Simple Heart* is quite simply . . . ":** GF to Edma Roger des Genettes, June 19, 1876.

152   **Félicité is beyond irony:** Much has been written about "A Simple Heart."
      See, in particular, Shoshana Felman, "Illusion réaliste et répétition roman-
      esque," in *La Critique générative* (Paris: Cahiers Change, 1973), 286–297;
      Julian Barnes, *Flaubert's Parrot* (London: Jonathan Cape, 1984); and the
      discussions in Victor Brombert, *The Novels of Flaubert* (Princeton, NJ:
      Princeton University Press, 1984), and Jonathan Culler, *Flaubert: The
      Uses of Uncertainty*, rev. ed. (Ithaca, NY: Cornell University Press, 1985
      [1974]).

152   **"For half a century . . . ":** Gustave Flaubert, "Un Coeur simple," in *Trois
      Contes*, ed. Pierre-Marc de Biasi (Paris: Garnier/Flammarion, 1986), 43;
      English trans. A. J. Krailsheimer, "A Simple Heart," in *Three Tales* (Oxford:
      Oxford World Classics, 1999), 3. Translations used here are my own. Page
      numbers are provided below for both the French and English editions.

153   **"At the age of twenty-five . . . ":** Ibid., 45/4.

153   **"Then years went by . . . ":** Ibid., 65/25–26.

154   **"She had had, like anyone else . . . ":** Ibid., 45/4.

154   **"in March, 1853, she was seized . . . ":** Ibid., 74/35.

154   **"love story":** Ibid., 46/6.

154   **"Sowing, harvesting, cider presses . . . ":** Ibid., 54–55/14–15.

154   **"They became associated . . . ":** Ibid., 73/34.

155   **stupidity, *bêtise*:** See Jonathan Culler's discussion of stupidity in Flaubert in
      Flaubert: The Uses of Uncertainty.

155   **"He reached for his atlas . . . ":** Flaubert, "Un Coeur simple," in *Trois Contes*,
      60/20.

156   **"Lord! how stupid . . . ":** Ibid., 70/30.

156   **"As if to distract her . . . ":** Ibid., 70/31.

157   **"The azure vapor . . . ":** Ibid., 78/40.

158   **"family reading":** GF to Léonie Brainne, August 23, 1877.

158   **"I had begun *Un Coeur simple* with her in mind . . . ":** GF to Maurice Sand,
      August 29, 1877.

158   **"I was overtaken by such tenderness . . . ":** GF to Caroline Commanville,
      October 26, 1871.

159   **"There is, first of all . . . ":** Gustave Flaubert, *Bouvard et Pécuchet*, ed.
      Stéphanie Dord-Crouslé (Paris: Garnier/Flammarion, 1999), 91–92; En-
      glish trans. Mark Polizzotti, *Bouvard and Pécuchet*, 2nd ed. (Normal, IL:
      Dalkey Archive Press, 2005), 39. I have consulted Polizzotti's excellent
      translation with profit.

160   **"*presto*, in the manner of Swift . . . ":** Ivan Turgenev to GF, July 12, 1874.

160   **"more or less witty . . . ":** GF to Ivan Turgenev, July 29, 1874.

161   **"One thus would find there . . . ":** GF to Louise Colet, December 16, 1852.

162   **"substantial preface":** GF to Louis Bouilhet, September 4, 1850.

162   The **"commonplace":** Jean-Paul Sartre, "Préface," in Nathalie Sarraute, *Portrait d'un inconnu* (Paris: Éditions de Minuit, 1948).

162   **"ideal type":** Michel Winock, *Flaubert* (Paris: Gallimard, 2013), 442.

163   **exploration of language itself:** "If you pushed far enough into language you found yourself in the embrace of thought." Henry James, review of *Correspondance de Flaubert, Quatrième Série* (1893), in *Literary Criticism*, vol. 2, *French Writers, Other European Writers, The Prefaces to the New York Edition* (New York: Library of America, 1984), 312.

163   **"She had trouble imagining his person . . . ":** Flaubert, "Un Coeur simple," in *Trois Contes*, 55/15.

163   **significance in the everyday:** See Charles Taylor, *Sources of the Self* (Cambridge, MA: Harvard University Press, 1989), 394.

164   **"BUDGET. Never balanced . . . ":** *Dictionnaire des idées reçues*, in Flaubert, *Bouvard et Pécuchet*, ed. Dord-Crouslé, and *Dictionary or Accepted Ideas*, in English trans. by Polizzotti, in *Bouvard and Pécuchet*, 2nd ed. (Normal, IL: Dalkey Archive Press, 2005). The original French:

> *Budget. Jamais en équilibre.*
>
> *Hôtels. Ne sont bons qu'en Suisse.*
>
> *Huîtres. On n'en mange plus! elles sont trop chères!*
>
> *Censure. Utile! on a beau dire.*
>
> *Braconniers. Tous forçats libérés.—Auteurs de tous les crimes commis dans les campagnes.—Doivent exciter une colère frénétique: «Pas de pitié, monsieur, pas de pitié!»*
>
> *Républicains. Les républicains ne sont pas tous des voleurs, mais les voleurs sont tous républicains.*
>
> *Célibataires. Tous égoïstes et débauchés.—On devrait les imposer.—Se préparent une triste vieillesse.*
>
> *Équitation. Bon exercice pour faire maigrir. Exemple: tous les soldats de cavalerie sont maigres.—Pour engraisser. Exemple: tous les officiers de cavalerie ont un gros ventre.*
>
> *Blondes. Plus chaudes que les brunes (voy. Brunes).*
>
> *Brunes. Sont plus chaudes que les blondes (voy. Blondes).*
>
> *Négresses. Plus chaudes que les blanches (voy. Brunes et Blondes).*
>
> *Rousses. (Voy. Blondes, Brunes et Négresses).*

166   **"When she reached the heights . . ."**: Gustave Flaubert, "Un Coeur simple,"
       in *Trois Contes*, 71–72/32–33.
166   **"This royal garment . . ."**: GF to Ivan Turgenev, July 27, 1877.
167   **Léonie Brainne:** GF to Léonie Brainne, December 10–11, 1878.

CHAPTER 7: THE HISTORICAL IMAGINATION

169   **"The *subject* of the novel . . ."**: GF to Edma Roger des Genettes, May 27,
       1878. Flaubert appears to have first mentioned *Sous Napoléon III* in a letter
       to the same correspondent on July 14, 1874.
170   **"The hero, a *democrat* . . ."**: Gustave Flaubert, *Carnets de Travail*, ed. Pierre-
       Marc de Biasi (Paris: Balland, 1988), 549.
170   **the word "catholic":** Anne Green, "*Sous Napoléon III:* New Thoughts on
       Flaubert's 'Second Empire Novel,'" *Dix-Neuf* 15, no. 1 (April 2011): 48–58.
171   **Prussians marched past:** Maxime Du Camp, *Souvenirs littéraires*, 2 vols.
       (Geneva: Slatkine, 1993 [1906]), 2:371. See on this topic Marie-Jeanne
       Durry, *Flaubert et ses projets inédits* (Paris: Nizet, 1950), 254–255. Du
       Camp's reports of conversations with Flaubert need always to be taken with
       a grain of salt: he was something of an inveterate liar, though one senses that
       his reports contain at least a grain of poetic truth.
171   **"It was all fake . . ."**: See, for instance, his notes on Eugène Janvier, notori-
       ously corrupt *préfet* during the Empire, in *Carnets de Travail*, 558–559.
171   ***"the falsity of perspective"***: GF to Edma Roger des Genettes, October 8, 1879.
173   **"You'll thus do a picturesque history . . ."**: Honoré de Balzac, *Illusions
       perdues* (Paris: Gallimard/Folio, 1988), 228. Balzac discusses Scott's im-
       portance and influence in his general introduction, or *Avant-Propos*, to *La
       Comédie humaine* in 1842.
173   **revival of history writing:** See Augustin Thierry, *Lettres sur l'histoire de
       France*, cited in Sophie-Anne Leterrier, *Le XIXe siècle historien* (Paris: Belin,
       1997), 103.
174   **ancient struggle of Gauls and Franks:** See Jean Walch, *Les Maîtres de l'his-
       toire, 1815–1850: Augustin Thierry, Mignet, Guizot, Thiers, Michelet, Quinet*
       (Geneva: Slatkine, 1986), 25. See also Lionel Gossman, *Between History and
       Literature* (Cambridge, MA: Harvard University Press, 1990).
174   **"There is almost no great idea . . ."**: Guizot, *Histoire de la civilisation en
       Europe*, 6–7, cited in Walch, *Les Maîtres de l'histoire*, 34.
175   **imposed by the Church:** See Walch, passim; see also Pim den Boer, *History
       as a Profession: The Study of History in France, 1818–1914*, trans. Arnold J.
       Pomerans (Princeton, NJ: Princeton University Press, 1998).

175 **"But for Scott the historical characterization . . . ":** Georg Lukács, *The His- torical Novel*, trans. Hannah and Stanley Mitchell (Cambridge, MA: MIT Press, 1971), 41.

176 **"to represent, by means of an invented action . . . ":** Alessandro Manzoni, *Del Romanzo storico*, in *Opera completa* (Napoli, 1860), 518. See the fine English translation and helpful commentary by Sandra Bermann, *On the Historical Novel* (Lincoln: University of Nebraska Press, 1984).

178 **"the capitalization of spirit":** See Georg Lukács, "Illusions perdues," in *Studies in European Realism*, trans. Edith Bone (London: Hillway, 1950).

179 **starting in 1833:** See Peter Brooks, *History Painting and Narrative: Dela- croix's Moments* (Oxford: Legenda, 1999).

179 **"time perspective":** Erich Auerbach, *Mimesis: The Representation of Real- ity in Western Literature*, trans. Willard R. Trask (Princeton, NJ: Princeton University Press, 1953), 462–463.

179 **"like a pistol-shot . . . ":** Stendhal, *Le Rouge et le noir*, ed. Anne-Marie Meininger (Paris: Gallimard/Folio, 2000), 503.

181 **"right to the novel":** Edmond de Goncourt and Jules de Goncourt, preface to *Germinie Lacerteux* (Paris: Garnier/Flammarion, 1990 [1865]), 55.

181 **very much including history:** See Pim den Boer, *History as a Profession*, 176. The Third Republic also saw the birth of literary history as a dominant academic discipline, as exemplified in the work of Gustave Lanson. See An- toine Compagnon, *La Troisième république des lettres, de Flaubert à Proust* (Paris: Éditions du Seuil, 1983).

182 **"penetrated especially . . . ":** Cited in Michel Winock, *Flaubert* (Paris: Gal- limard, 2013), 219.

183 **"Much too much bric-à-brac . . . ":** Baudelaire, letter to Auguste Poulet- Massis, December 13, 1862, cited in Jean-Benoît Guinot, *Dictionnaire Flau- bert* (Paris: CNRS Editions, 2010), 60.

183 **"In the midst of the servants . . . ":** Gustave Flaubert, *Salammbô* (Paris: Gallimard/Folio, 1970 [1862]), 115–116; English trans. A. J. Krailsheimer (London: Penguin, 1977).

184 **"Certain crises in the personal destinies . . . ":** Lukács, *The Historical Novel*, 41.

186 **"The rue Saint-Victor was completely dark . . . ":** Flaubert, *L'Education sentimentale*, 445/360.

187 **"a marvel":** GF to Ivan Turgenev, March 10–11, 1877.

188 **"vast, smug surface":** See Henry James, Preface to *The Princess Casamassima*, in *Literary Criticism*, vol. 2, *French Writers, Other European Writers, The Pref- aces to the New York Edition* (New York: Library of America, 1984), 1102.

189 **"The morning of February 25 . . . ":** Gustave Flaubert, *Bouvard et Pécuchet*, ed. Stéphanie Dord-Crouslé (Paris: Garnier/Flammarion, 1999), 212; English trans. Mark Polizzotti, *Bouvard and Pécuchet*, 2nd ed. (Normal, IL: Dalkey Archive Press, 2005), 134.

190 **"'But really' . . . ":** Ibid., 226/146.

190 **"Three million voters . . . ":** Ibid., 232/151.

191 **"Madame Bordin entered . . . ":** Ibid., 242/158.

192 **"Then, a piteous faculty . . . ":** Ibid., 298/205.

193 **astounding:** The reading list has been reconstructed by Stéphanie Dord-Crouslé at http://flaubert.univrouen.fr/ressources/bp_reconstitution _histoire.pdf.

194 **"unjust":** GF to Georges Charpentier, October 15, 1879.

194 **"The aim of History . . . ":** GF to Maxime Du Camp, November 13, 1879.

194 **"that never lied":** Emile Zola, "Revue dramatique et littéraire," *Le Voltaire*, December 9, 1879, in *Oeuvres completes*, ed. Henri Mitterand (Paris: Cercle du Libre Précieux, 1968), 12:606–609.

194 **"How you avenge me! . . . ":** GF to Emile Zola, December 10, 1879.

EPILOGUE

199 **"The plunge of civilization . . . ":** Henry James to Howard Sturgis, August 5, 1914.

201 **"The walls speak":** See *Les Murs ont la parole*, ed. Julien Besançon (Paris: Tchou, 1968).

202 **"The crisis begun in May . . . ":** See my translation of this document published in my essay "The Fourth World: Paris," *Partisan Review* 36, no. 1 (1969): 11.

Index

© Maureen Chun

PETER BROOKS, Sterling Professor Emeritus of Comparative Literature at Yale University, currently teaches in the Center for Human Values and the Department of Comparative Literature at Princeton University. He was the founding director of the Whitney Humanities Center at Yale. He has received fellowships from the Guggenheim Foundation and the National Endowment for the Humanities as well as the Andrew W. Mellon Foundation Distinguished Achievement Award. He is the author of several influential books, including *Henry James Goes to Paris, Reading for the Plot, The Melodramatic Imagination,* and *Troubling Confessions,* as well as two novels. He is a contributor to the *New York Review of Books* and the *Times Literary Supplement.*